MOTION AND REPRESENTATION

MOTION AND

REPRESENTATION

The Language of Human Movement

NICOLÁS SALAZAR SUTIL

THE MIT PRESS CAMBRIDGE, MASSACHUSETTS LONDON, ENGLAND

This book was set in Solex by the MIT Press. Printed and bound in the United States of America.

Library of Congress Cataloging-in-Publication Data is available.
ISBN: 978-0-262-02888-2

10   9   8   7   6   5   4   3   2   1

Para la Juanita, a través de mi madre

CONTENTS

ACKNOWLEDGMENTS

My gratitude is due to a number of people who have supported me in the making of this book. First, I would like to thank my collaborators at C8 for the creative work, especially Juley Hudson, Max Worgan, and Sebastián Melo. I would also like to thank colleagues at the University of Surrey with whom I have carried out a great deal of the research featured in this book. Special thanks are due to Rebecca Hoyle and the MILES team (Mathematics and Modeling in Life and Social Sciences) and to Rachel Fensham. My thanks are also due to the Institute of Advanced Studies and the School of Arts, both at the University of Surrey, for supporting me in the organization and funding of the event "Corporeal Computing," where many ideas and connections established in this book were developed.

I am exceedingly indebted to those artists and scientists who have granted me permission to publish images of their work, especially Paul Kaiser (and OpenEnded Group), Arthur Elsenaar, Martine Époque, and Denis Poulin (LarTech), as well as Brenton Cheng, Mitchell Robiner, Marilynn J. Taylor, and Barnett Lyon. I am also grateful to Norman Badler for inside information regarding the creation of the Bubbleman software, and to Tom Calvert for the creation and development of Life Forms. My thanks are also due to Brian Rotman, who has granted me permission to publish his diagrams and instructions for the piece *Ordinal 4*, and to Fernando Zalamea, who granted me permission to publish his chronophotographic diagram.

Furthermore, I would like to thank all the dancers, movers, and performers I have worked with, especially over the last three years, whose work has proved invaluable in refining my understanding of human movement: Angelina Jandolo, Sarah Rogers, Joop Oonk, Melina Scialom, Bernardette Lemon, Jack Lawless, Wei Ting, Ana Oliveiro, David Alonso, and Maria Jose Pantoja.

Of course, I would like to thank the MIT Press, especially Roger Conover, Justin Kehoe, and Matthew Abbate for their unswerving support and outstanding editorial work. Finally, I would like to add my eternal gratitude to my wife Carol, and to my two children, Lucian and Leo.

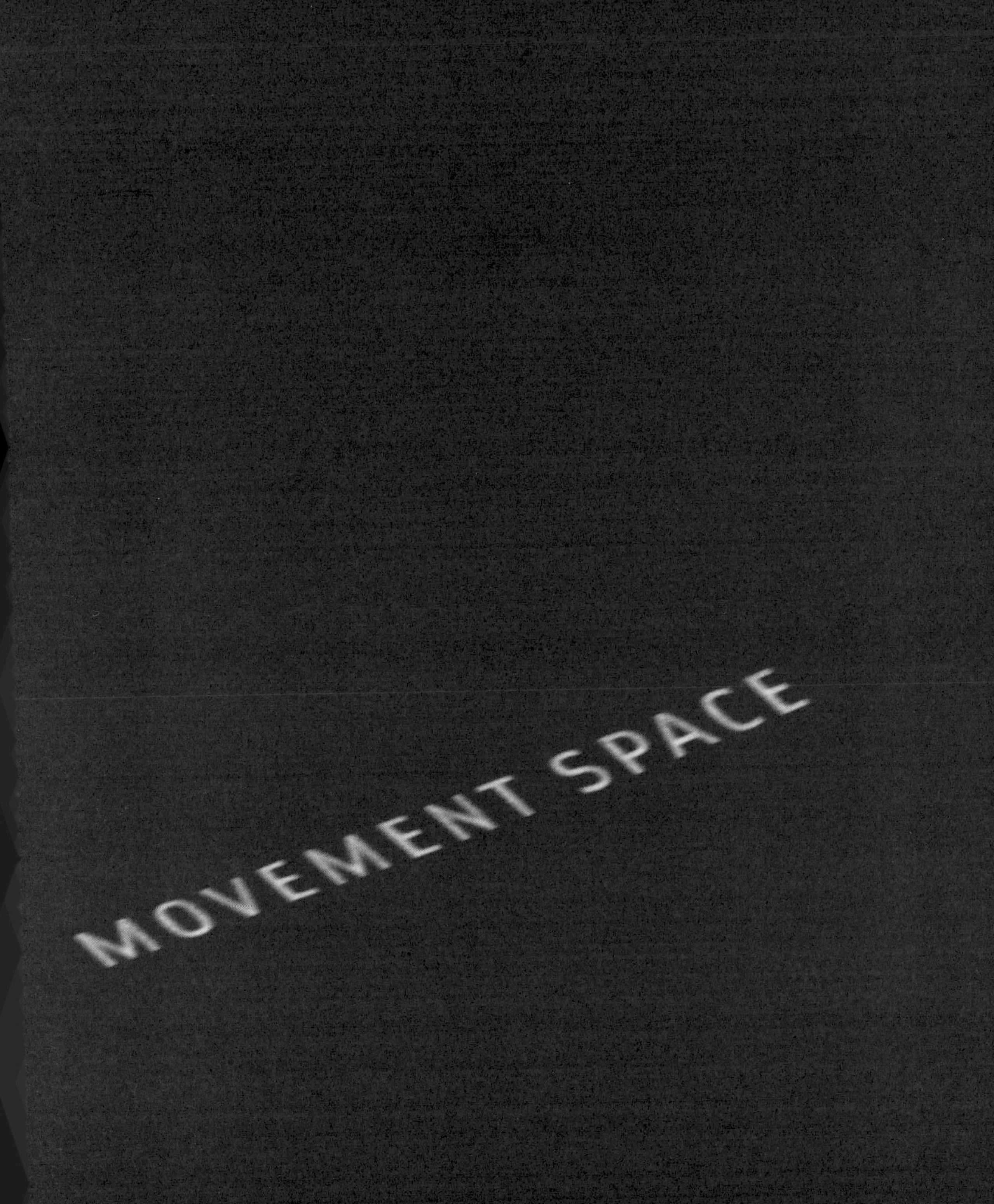
MOVEMENT SPACE

So, rather than drawing the pathway of this book as an objective or subjective move from beginning to end, from chapter 1 to chapter 12, I want to consider the unfolding of *Motion and Representation* in terms of a trajective determination that explains the essence of the path I have taken. In other words, this book is written so that at every stage of the way, my trajectory is caught inside this "being of movement" of which Virilio speaks. In doing so, I am provoking an understanding of movement that is paradoxical, because it is never moored in a single position, whether objective or subjective. As I understand it, total movement is neither pure representation nor pure physical/personal experience. Movement is always caught in between—similar to what Deleuze (1997) called, after Bergson, the "centers of indetermination." Thus, movement is caught between time and space, or proxemics and chronemics (part I); it is caught between innermotion and outermotion, or between a determination in mental and physical life (part II); it is caught between lived-in movement and represented movement; between movement performance and recorded notation (part III), and between different technological systems available for the material record of movement, affording a trajective split between local and global determinations (part IV).

To follow this book through ought to resemble not only the essence of the path but also what for Michel de Certeau (1984) is the essence of *walking the path*. Here is a framework that reinforces, according to de Certeau, the parallelism between linguistic and pedestrian enunciation, a kind of walk-talking, or walk-thinking—what Ingold and Vergunst call "walking or thinking in movement" (2008, 3). This book is thus laid out like a pedestrian theory, a walking theory. Examples of "walk-talking" alluded to in this book include Aristotle's idea of the walking syllogism, odography (the writing of footsteps), foot-tracking notation, and Samuel Beckett's walk-talkers. As de Certeau points out: "Here-there is necessarily implied by walking and is indicative of a present appropriation of space by an 'I.' [It is] also the function of introducing an other in relation to this 'I' and of thus establishing a conjunctive and disjunctive articulation" (1984, 99). Walking involves a step-by-step process, but also a continuous process of thinking. Two completely different processes, one discrete and one continuous, are thus integrated. This book is the product of many long walks and drives, and many streams of thought underlying these journeys. This is the trajective sense, and this is the essence of the book's trajectory. In this way, *Motion and Representation* will expose a trajective relationship between lived-in movement and the impression movement leaves in the domain of representation.

mix. One important aim of this book is to identify cross-traffic between mathematical/computational languages of movement and formal motor languages found within the movement arts. To provide some degree of coherence, I intend to focus on cross-pollination not so much between these disciplines as between different domains of inscription. For instance, I will pay attention to the way in which formalisms can migrate from mathematical to choreographic domains (i.e., Laban's choreutic shapes, Oskar Schlemmer's balletic mathematics, Forsythe's dance geometries), or from mathematical to formal graphic studies of movement (i.e., Marey's chronophotographic geometry). These examples point toward a mixing of the creative practice of movement and a common ground of kinetic creativity, or kinetopoiesis. To begin to integrate creative movement knowledge in a coherent way is perhaps the most significant contribution of this book.

But the drive for synthesis is not free of pitfalls, nor can it be addressed without critical intervention. Although current techniques and technologies of movement representation allow for plenty of fusion (and this applies to various disciplines, from mathematics to dance), an integrated understanding of the complexity of human movement across disciplines still remains elusive. Although knowledge has become increasingly mobile and dynamic, and thus increasingly liable to synthesis, technological mediation also leads to specialization and the isolation of disciplinary knowledge of movement, provoking less crossover and less commutability between highly specialized research programs. These include transportation, security, sports analysis, biomedicine, biomechanics, robotics, and kinetic arts, to mention but a few. Despite daunting levels of specialization within the contemporary science of human movement, it is still worth asking, How can movement, as wonderfully complex as it is, be integrated into a way of knowing or thinking that brings about a more holistic and integrated perspective?

Trajectory/trajectivity

Usually, the final section of an introduction is reserved for the outline of a trajectory, a summary of chapters. However, I will not provide that summary, for reasons that will soon become apparent. All there is to say on this subject is that this book has four parts and twelve chapters. Instead of a trajectory, I wish to consider what the *trajectivity* of this book might be. According to Paul Virilio (1997), it is possible to describe the essence of the path or journey. Despite myriad disciplinary studies and debates on movement and mobility, he points out, the question of the path is hardly ever addressed explicitly. One hears of "objectivity and subjectivity, certainly, but never trajectivity," Virilio writes, adding: "there is little understanding of the vectorial nature of the transhumant species that we are, of our chorography. Between the subjective and the objective it seems we have no room for the *trajective*, that being of movement from here to there, from one to the other, without which we will never achieve a profound understanding of ... the regimes of appearances related to the history of techniques and modalities of displacement" (1997, 24).

My second key frame concerns analysis. As I understand it, movement analysis cannot be re-moved from a concrete way of knowing movement, whether anatomical, mechanical, or computational. Previously, movement eidesis involved knowing movement in relation to abstract descriptions like Zeno's arrow in flight. As I pointed out, this example helps illustrate the philosophical notion that kinesis is but an illusion or semblance of true Being. Zeno's problems of movement can be addressed in more ways than one, however. Rather than being seen as an illustration of an abstract idea, the arrow in flight can be treated as a strictly mathematical problem involving the calculation of continuous variables from discrete ones, to be solved using mathematical differentiation. Thus, unlike eidesis, movement analysis concerns a concrete knowledge of movement applied to a particular problem. When I say that movement analysis is concrete, I do not necessarily mean that analytical works study physical movement, but that movement analysis relates to specific (i.e., concrete) problems existing within material or physical life. Zeno's problem is the best example I can think of regarding this passage from eidesis to analysis.

Aristotle wrote that knowledge of nature has to be grasped with clarity, and that this understanding can be achieved only with the aid of analysis. Aristotle thus could be credited for laying the foundations of a movement analysis framework that will support a number of other analytical frameworks referenced in this book. According to Aristotle's method, to conduct analysis involves advancing from generalities to particulars, so that things become known not via haphazard inspiration but via rational comprehension. Movement analysis provides thinking tools (or language machines) to break down and recompose an object of knowledge in methodical and systematic ways. According to Aristotle, analysis also provides a terminological understanding, in that by breaking down a process into its particulars one must also name its parts, and thus designate them accurately. Movement analysis generates terms (and terminations). By this definition, movement analysis is a toolkit to break down the complexity of movement into countable or nameable parts.

Through analysis, the study of movement can be objectified. Breaking movement down can lead to analyzing a phenomenon in terms of quantifiable parts. Analysis grants a third-person perspective, or an epistemology of movement in the third person. But, like any other form of knowledge that seeks to arrest its object of study, analysis relies on a plane of representation. One needs names, numbers, code, symbols, or some other means of description. To conceive movement in this way, one also needs tools to visualize and scope the natural appearance of living movement. And so, regardless of how objective the science of movement analysis might claim to be, it is ultimately liable to the arbitrary influences of technological mediation and representation.

Movement synthesis is the final key frame. To address it, I would like to consider how knowledge of movement is generated in a historical context characterized by technological connectivity and mobility. The more we move, and the more mobile we become, the more we are likely to provoke different and previously unconnected traditions of knowledge to meet, to clash, and possibly to collection of infinite points of stillness. Zeno concluded that because the arrow cannot be still while flying, the perception we have of its movement is an illusion. With this, he validated Parmenides' idea that movement does not exist; or rather, that it does not belong to the same plane of existence as true, unchanging and self-similar Being. Zeno also came up with his famous paradoxes to argue that movement negates reasoning, and that motion blurs rational thought. This philosophical idea of movement became central to subsequent dialectical inquiries into the nature of true Being.

Plato wrote in the *Sophist* that being, motion, and rest (or *ousia*, *kinesis*, and *stasis*) are the highest concepts in kind when it comes to understanding dialectics. On investigation, it soon becomes clear that the Greek philosophical tradition hinges on a basic dichotomy: How does movement stem from rest? How does the whole originate from its parts, and how can a continuous line be made up of discrete points? The idea of movement is entangled, at least within this tradition, with that of motionlessness. We can scarcely conceive of kinesis without invoking thoughts of stasis. Two positions arose: either movement exists, and the world of the phenomenal is "real," or else movement does not exist, in which case the world of the real refers to some extraphysical domain, which does not change or move. These two positions inform the metaphysical and mechanical perspectives on the philosophy of movement, which cut through centuries of study into the eidetic nature of motion. Many centuries later, Rudolf Laban made the same distinction in terms of the "dream-architectures" and "mechanical architectures" of movement. "It is obvious," he wrote, "that a dreamer and a man with a mind oriented towards mechanics will look upon movement differently" (1966, 5).

If the philosophical literature enshrines a split between motion and motionlessness, my aim is to reconnect these terms. The relationship I would like to explore does not involve kinesis and stasis, in the Greek philosophical sense, but movement and its representation. Hence the book's title. But instead of arguing for a dialectical division, my aim is to show how this relationship has been transformed, not least by media technology. Whereas representation was seen to be static in the geometrical rationality underlying Greek thought, today we can represent movement in motion, and we can conceptualize it in motion.

My argument follows from the lack of integration between the metaphysical and mechanical perspectives, as we move toward a more contemporary way of thinking movement. Beyond the rigid dialectics, contemporary thinking is informed by an unstable materiality of reflection and representation. We do not know movement through re-moved reflection only, nor through mechanized thinking; we also think and perform movement by shifting from one position to another, or by inserting ourselves in more distributed systems of knowledge production. Plato's communion of motion and motionlessness can be reprogrammed in the history of the digital era in the sense that knowledge of movement is no longer purely abstract or purely concrete; it is neither metaphysical nor mechanical, neither mind nor body, but always in between.

modalities of movement representation. I make no attempt to take sides or to debate the advantages and disadvantages of each medium. However, I will say that the mediation of movement is susceptible to changing conditions of material representation, which in the current digital era favor animation and motion capture over and above movement notation. Finally, this book is intended to provide a critical examination of these dominant media, which are liable to problems arising from the division and bureaucratization of knowledge and the corporative organization and commercialization of mediated movement. Thanks to commercial media technologies like motion capture and electronic motion, movement is increasingly being circulated within creative industries in a commodity form. This material transformation of the knowledge of movement according to technical and technological conditions encourages more mobile ways of knowing, and more dynamic ways of turning knowledge into commoditized data, particularly in the context of electronic communication (chapter 12). The more mobile and exchangeable the knowledge, the more valuable it becomes. My proposed framework is intended to show how an economy of movement can be seen to be shifting from knowledge *of* motion, to knowledge *in* motion.

Key frames

The core conceptual and theoretical structure of this book could be said to resemble a sequence of key frames. In the field of animation, key frames define how many and which bodily poses the viewer will see along a given animated sequence. The key frames that make up this investigation refer to three important ways of approaching integrated human movement: eidesis, analysis, and synthesis. The first key frame reveals the *idea* of movement, which in turn refers to a process of conceptualization. In the literature, one finds this notion often addressed in terms of *abstract movement*—or what I call "movement re-moved." The second frame (movement analysis) is concerned with the notion of *concrete movement*. Movement analysis involves knowledge of kinetic activity rooted in more situated and contingent phenomena, especially the study of anatomical and machine movement. Synthesis, on the other hand, involves a combination of the above, or a mixing of different movement systems (i.e., human-machine), especially via technological means.

And so on to my first frame: movement eidesis. A good example of what an idea of movement might involve is Zeno's paradox of the arrow in flight, which is where many histories of movement start. The optical image of the arrow's flight is of no relevance. The moving arrow is not knowable by sense perception, nor does it refer to a memory of past experience. What matters here is the concept. Nor are we dealing with movement in progress; instead, the flight refers to motion that has been recorded in written form (at least as it survives in Aristotle's polemic). This also implies that the shape of the flight is set, that it is no longer ongoing. The flight is in fact a line from point A to point B. This trajectory can be represented as a dotted line, since Zeno assumed that motion is a

Mediating movement

It is important to stress that the term "capture" does not refer only to the technological medium of motion capture (although this medium is discussed at length in chapter 11). While many efforts to represent movement rely on visual forms of capture (cinema and photography especially), the approach I have taken here hinges not on a *vision* of motion but on the structural *conception* of motion. The ubiquity of the visual record is partly responsible for our optically biased standpoint for conceptualizing movement. However, vision is quite a different sensory domain when compared to total movement. Seeing someone move is not the same as moving per se. Indeed, sight often buries movement under the veneer of image, or "movement-image," to borrow the term from Deleuze (1997). By contrast, corporeal movement can trouble sight, in that movement can blur optical vision. To allow the mind to cope with motion perception, vision typically enforces a saccadic or frame-by-frame strategy. Meanwhile, corporeal movement involves a category of sensations that can be felt independent of sight (e.g., proprioception, exteroception, interoception). And here lies the problem. My intention is to stay away, as far as possible, from vision-dependent discourse. This decision is informed by the fact that although we can appreciate motion through vision, in doing so we run the risk of projecting images onto discourse, rather than generating knowledge of human motion, or even knowledge *in* motion.

In a mediasphere dominated by the popularity of photography, cinematography, video, or television, this study is a plea for a different history, one that runs its course closer to Friedrich Kittler's history of the technology of inscription (1999). I will assume that for every language there must by necessity be a form of script; in other words, human movement must have preceded formal communication in the same way that spoken language preceded the technology of writing. By "writing," I mean the inscription of some form of kinetic signature. The term "script" applies to both the creative writing of movement (inventive kinetography) and the production of a standard record (movement notation). This script can be represented in various ways: symbolically, graphically, or computationally. It follows that there are at least three representational modalities of kinetic signature, which correspond to the three inscriptional media I intend to tackle in this book. Inscriptional technologies can record human movement in terms of a written record (notation), a visual record (animation), and a computational record (motion capture). Combinations of these can lead to mixed-media forms of inscription, which will be considered in the latter part of this book.

Since a major critical and theoretical body of work has yet to emerge that responds critically to the interactions between notation, animation, and motion capture, and since no such body of work has yet revealed an understanding of the almost inevitable transmedia relations between these technologies, this book is intended to contribute to a field that is largely uncharted within media and cultural studies. Although media tend to mix and cooperate in the contemporary digital era, I want to emphasize that notation, animation, and motion capture should be treated as three very different of which will be addressed here: geometry (and geometric topology), which defines the *spatial* determination of movement; arithmetic progression, which describes the *temporal* determination of movement; and coordinates, which defines the *locational* determination of movement.

The split between the abstract and the concrete could be put forward easily as a theory of movement, and not for the first time, but here I run the risk of building an argument that is likely to raise eyebrows. Leibniz conceived a "Theory of Concrete Motion" and a "Theory of Abstract Motion" to refer to the structure of matter, cosmology, and chemistry, on the one hand, and the mathematical laws of physical movement on the other (see Wilson 1989, 52). Merleau-Ponty (2010) spoke of concrete versus abstract movement in order to highlight a distinction between the intellectual and motor significance of movement suffered in certain pathological phenomena, adding: "we are brought to the recognition of something between movement as a third person process and thought as a presentation of movement ... whereas for the normal person every movement is, indissolubly, movement and consciousness of movement" (126–127). When I think of a digital condition of possibilities, a digital way of thinking movement, I imagine alternatives. For instance, I imagine myriad technologies that can detect gesture and bodily movement and can process these as physical signals in order to translate them into code, into abstract representation. What this not-so-material condition of digital culture seems to be grounded on is the enveloping of concrete and abstract, the hard and the soft, the mental and the physical. So rather than speaking of abstract/concrete movement, we ought to speak of the indissoluble category of the abstract-concrete. Thus, the language machines I envisage here are not abstract machines in the sense put forward by Deleuze and Guattari (2011)—they are not concrete machines in a phenomenological sense either; these machines I have in mind obey a logic of seesaws, of pendulums, of oscillation, in the sense that the digital artifact is by definition two things at once: it is number and material object, it is software and hardware, it is intelligence plus smart device or machinic robot, and so it is in this integration that total movement can now be conceptualized and theorized. What total movement affords in the present cultural context is the passage from physical to mental and back, from current to signal, from electricity off/on to bits 0/1—this direct passage means that the terms "abstraction" and "concretion" are no longer collector items for dialecticians. When we move, when we move digitally, that is (and we must not forget that our brains are also digital machines), we move in abstraction and concretion at the same time. We entangle ourselves in a two-way and coextensive process. We move in thought and body, in software and hardware, and therefore the language machines we can come up with must generate new possibilities of movement representation that no longer carve up thought and body into separate domains. We cannot accept systems that only represent the intellectual content of movement, say in the way symbolic movement notation does (see chapter 7). My focus is on those language machines that understand that the abstract is embodied, that the concrete is "re-moved, and thus that the two categories are feeding into one another because they contain elements of each other.

mental and motor aspects, I recognize that I am concerned with a generalization of movement—not with a specific disciplinary understanding. This is perhaps the single most important feature of this book, not least because very few cultural and media theories of human movement have provided this kind of transdisciplinary integration.

Language machines

American choreographer William Forsythe (Forsythe and Kaiser 1999) coined the phrase "language machine" to denote tools and devices that yield choreographic structures in space and over time, involving formally prescribed ways of moving the human body. But because movement is, as I said, a vast reservoir of potential communication that transcends language, the ways in which it can be formalized, the means by which it can be narrowed down to a language, are not only confined to the movement arts, to dance. In the same way that the formalization of positions and transpositions constitutes a basis in the creation of the language machine that is the choreographed body, there are language machines that formalize movement in more abstract ways within the orbit of mathematics and formal logic. What concerns me are underlying commonalities between families of language machines, and the possibility of a common origin in the deepest and also most abstract appearance of conceptualized movement, before we enter the plane of representation, which I believe is a vision shared by various movement disciplines. One example of this is the kind of protogeometrical vision that can underlie both the seemingly different structures found in formal dance (e.g., ballet or Forsythe technique) and mathematical geometry.

Throughout this book I will consider two facets of a language machine: the abstract and the concrete. The concrete aspect of a language machine refers to the actual embodiment or materialization of a motor language through physicalized or mechanized movement performance. Thus, a concrete language of movement is performed closer to some kinetic hardware: a body or mechanical/computational device. A number of specialized languages are consulted throughout this book. Some of these can be categorized within the movement arts (e.g., choreutics, balletic mathematics, ballet). Other concrete languages discussed here refer to everyday movement (e.g., human gait, industrial movement) or to somatic practice, as in the case of tai chi. Yet another category of concrete movement refers to technological systems of motion representation (e.g., motion capture and data transfer protocols). Finally, some of the concrete languages of movement discussed here refer to the languages of motion visualization (e.g., geometric animation and key frame animation). The abstract domain of a language machine, on the other hand, concerns the conception of movement in its purely formal expression, especially within the disciplines of logic and mathematics. This abstract determination can also be performed closer to a technologized mathematics—a computer language or software. Language machines are underpinned by many disciplines of abstraction, three almost the same. He concludes: "we may gather that [linguistic] language is simply an element within a much larger, more general category of function" (2002, 228). The etymology does not help, unfortunately, since the term "language" (from the Latin *lingua*, or tongue) is often confined to the articulation of sounds produced by the human vocal apparatus, and to the representation of these sounds in written letters and words. My intention is to bypass the linguistic understanding of a language in order to consider a general category, as proposed by Llinás, which includes both linguistic and motor languages. My intention is to focus on what I call "kinetic formalism," by which I mean an external and rule-bound representation of mentally constructed bodily movement.

Kinetic formalization is also the process by means of which key bodily poses and transitions are constructed, based on the combination of arbitrarily chosen primitive units of movement. From yoga to ballet, from key frame animation to pose recognition computation, the same basic premise applies as a general rule. Across many techniques of expression and composition, kinetic formalization is thus based on rules of segmentation and interconnection, or position and transposition, which provide a general framework to understand how motor languages are articulated. Sports, dance, gymnastics, live animation, and kinetic art are some examples where human movement is performed based on rules of position and transposition, and where one might expect to find evidence of a formal language of embodied movement. This book pays serious attention to the occurrence of kinetic formalisms within a creative framework—I will refer to this as "kinetopoiesis," i.e., the making of cultural and artistic objects via intentional and formally constructed movement.

Because human movement involves both a corporeal and a mental dimension, I will use the term "total movement" to refer to an integration of these two determinations. Having factored out unintentional movement (e.g., trembling, twitching, automatism), this book must focus on an intentional will to move, what Llinás calls "purposeful movement" (2002, 228). Whatever the motive may be—and I hope this book will go some way toward clarifying this issue—motion is the prolongation or secretion of an inner motivation. Motion is the outcome of premotor thoughts, and conversely, inner motives are triggered as a result of outer motion. The ambition of this book is to identify crossovers that call for a more integrative cultural theory of human movement based on the interaction between two arms of movement research. As Tim Cresswell has pointed out: "Writing on mobility remains either very specific (about computer patterns, migrations, or dance for instance), or maddeningly abstract—the kind of work that talks of points A and B." Cresswell adds: "Connections need to be made between the determinedly different approaches applied to the different facets of human mobility" (2006, 7). What applies according to Cresswell to the field of mobility also applies to movement studies. As such, it makes sense to focus on how the representation of movement can be contested, copied, and collaboratively shared between motor and mental determinations. The transdisciplinary framework I am proposing does not privilege either of the two approaches. In combining

Motion and representation

The more deeply one investigates human movement, the more apparent it becomes that this most mundane of activities constitutes a complex, intriguing, and extensive area of human experience. It also becomes apparent that human movement is not fortuitous, but that it is involved with the fulfillment of inner motive and intelligent activity. So to state my thesis: human movement is not only a natural phenomenon; it is not only subject to human anatomy and biology. Human movement is liable to changing material conditions of expression, which are liable to the determining forces of society and culture: of race, of age, of gender. More specifically, my concern is how human movement is conceptualized, and how it enters the orbit of cultural expression through different historical conditions of technical and technological representation. The main argument of this book therefore moves in two directions at once: technological intervention transforms the representation of movement; representation in turn transforms the way we move or what we understand by movement. Given its capacity to be represented externally, movement then encounters a kind of ecstasy, a means of coming out of itself (i.e., within the plane of representation) which allows it to return to its own interiority, albeit changed. Thus, movement evolves historically, or at the very least it is transformed by material histories of representation and mediated interpretation. But what exactly does this representation entail? And how does human movement conform to the rules of a movement language?

When it comes to defining "motor language," there are two things to bear in mind. First, pure movement and language should be considered two different conceptual categories. Thus, although human movement is a reservoir of human communication and transportation whose full scope escapes language and formal notation, what concerns me is precisely the narrowing of this scope. The creative tension between infinite movement and finite systems of representation is the subject of this book. Second, the use of the word "language" does not mean that my investigation is grounded in linguistics. Language should be understood from the outset as something other than speech, and something other than word-based communication. Nor am I concerned with theoretical approaches like structuralism, semiotics, or the philosophy of natural language. Colombian neuroscientist Rodolfo Llinás (2002) has argued that abstract thinking must have preceded language during evolution, and by the same token, "the premotor events leading to the expression of language are in every way the same as those premotor events that precede any movement that is executed for a purpose." Llinás adds that linguistic language and purposeful movement are so similar as to be

PART I

MOVEMENT SPACE

1

A stereotype of space

"Stereo" is synonymous with all things 3D. Stereoscopy is 3D vision, stereophony is 3D sound. Today's vernacular is full of terms bearing these common prefixes. Think, for instance, of 3D printing, 3D imaging, 3D TVs, 3D games, 3D film. By the same token, one could argue that corporeal movement is by definition "stereotypical." In the strictest sense, this means corporeal movement is typified by a three-parameter space. Barring the dimension of time, which I will address separately, bodily movement is performed in three orientational planes, known as horizontal, vertical, and sagittal. But there is a problem with this definition—it is far too stereotypical. It fulfills the hackneyed notion that human movement refers only to an action undertaken by the body in extensional space—i.e., to positional or locational changes performed by the corporeal body inside the space it occupies. My intention is to challenge this stereotype, by arguing that human movement is much more than that. Integrated human movement is not determined only by the corporeal body, nor is it determined by the occupation of stereotypical space. Nevertheless, even though this book is intended to reveal other dimensions of movement, the definition of human movement as a corporeal phenomenon performed in three-dimensional space is a good place to start.

This opening chapter will focus on two different conceptions of stereotypical movement space. One involves the understanding of how bodies move along surfaces. For instance, I will consider how the corporeal body moves along a floor or against a wall, or even how the body can be imagined to "touch" points located on virtual surfaces surrounding the corporeal body—for example, how da Vinci's famous image of the Vitruvian Man depicts a human model "touching" the edges of a square and circle. The other conception of movement space I will discuss has to do with the understanding of space as volume. The key parameter within this framework is the room or bulk of space contained within a perimeter. To help the reader to better understand these epistemologies of movement space, I will focus on two languages of corporeal movement: Rudolf Laban's language of choreutics, and Oskar Schlemmer's balletic mathematics. My claim is that while Laban was concerned primarily with movement along virtual surfaces, Schlemmer was concerned with volumes. This may seem trivial. In fact, this distinction will reveal that surface and volume are the basis for two very different conceptions of stereotypical space. Furthermore, these two epistemologies invite very different *cultures* of space.

Both Laban and Schlemmer developed an understanding of movement space through an application of solid geometry to movement art research. By "solid," I do not mean a material state, as opposed to a liquid or gas. Solids are three-dimensional geometric objects. Some better-known examples include pyramids, cylinders, cones, cubes, and spheres. Choreutics, as we will see presently, is an embodied language of movement developed by Laban based on the idea that the cor-

poreal body creates harmonic structures as it moves within a virtual solid, which are conventionally represented as regular polyhedra. Laban imagined that inserting the moving subject within a
3D mesh, and training the moving body to "touch" specific points on the surface of this 3D grid,
will produce a formal way of moving; indeed, it will produce a language of movement defined by
harmonic spatial relations. Schlemmer's balletic mathematics, on the other hand, approached the
question of formal movement design from a distinctly volumetric perspective. Schlemmer (1961)
was concerned with the way in which a surrounding geometric volume could transform the human
body—for instance, through a relationship between the human body and the architecture of a room
or building. As we will see shortly, Schlemmer's approach is fundamentally different from Laban's,
because Schlemmer wanted to *transform* the corporeal body and the way the corporeal body moves
in space.

It is important to point out that the principles of geometric and solid modeling provide a
foundation not only in formal systems of movement analysis in the performing arts, but also in computer-
aided design (CAD). In effect, the language of solid geometry is general and abstract enough to be
applied across a number of formal disciplines of digital spatial composition. Solid modeling is also
used in computer-generated imaging to represent digital objects with a high level of physical fidel-
ity. Generally speaking, solid modeling supports the creation, visualization, animation, annotation,
and analysis of digital models of physical objects. Digital modeling and rapid prototyping may have
little in common with the languages of choreutics and balletic mathematics, which I will discuss
in more detail in due course. However, the mathematical formalisms underpinning these different
approaches are the same.

It is not surprising that the same distinction cutting through the works of Laban and Schlemmer
should be found in the construction of computer-generated objects. Within a computer-generated
imaging framework, stereotypical space can also be approached as a distinction between surfaces
and volumes. This distinction is important particularly within the context of mesh computing, which
comprises a large subfield of computer graphics and computer-aided geometric design (CAGD). In
fact, meshes are one of the basic building blocks in 3D computer graphics, and thus are extensively
used in graphic design software tools including Maya and Autocad, or dance animation software like
LifeForms. The polygon mesh is a collection of vertices, edges, and faces that make up the "skin" or
outer layer of a computer-generated object. For instance, figure 1.1 shows polygon mesh processing
used to render interactive digital versions of a dancer derived from motion capture data developed
as part of the iWeave project (2012–2013) carried out at the University of Surrey.[1]

These images also help illustrate my argument. Within computer-generated mesh graphics, 3D
objects can be designed through either a polygon mesh (as in the case illustrated here) or a volume
mesh. In other words, one can create a digital object either by surface representation or by representing the interior volume of the object. Because the surface of a digitally generated skin already

implies a sense of volume, polygon mesh generation is the preferred option across a number of systems used in computer-aided design (CAD). But how can we represent *movement* within this stereotypical space? And how can movement and space become coextensive? Or as Laban puts it, how can "space [be] ... a hidden feature of movement and movement ... a visible aspect of space" (1966, 4)?

To answer these questions, I will first consider how a particular solid (the sphere) can be used to model a philosophical conception of movement space, thus focusing on the frame of eidesis. Subsequently, I will discuss how Laban could draw on the language of crystallography to develop a system of movement analysis based on his utilization of regular convex polyhedra; that is, solids that are made of differentiated points or vertices. Finally, I will argue that Schlemmer's approach to movement space can be said to be less anthropocentric than Laban's, in the sense that Schlemmer did not locate the human subject in the center of a virtual space, as was the classical ideal. Rather, by questioning whether space should be transformed in deference to the human figure or vice versa, Schlemmer's language of balletic mathematics champions the transformation of the human body into a structure that is depersonalized and even dehumanized by geometric space.

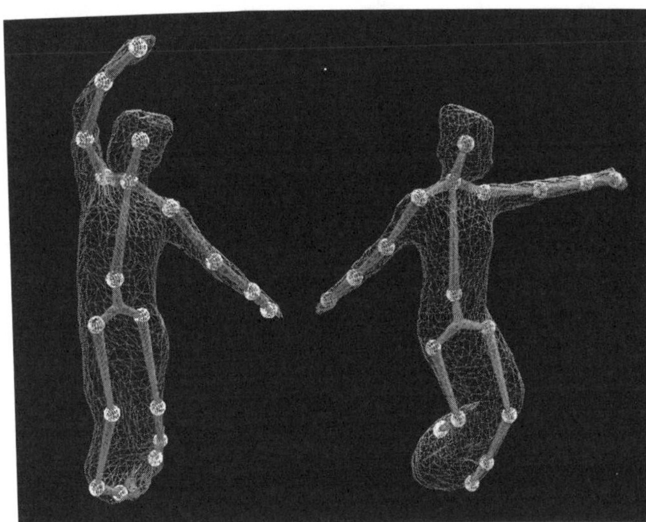

1.1
Four-dimensional video frames of a 2013 choreographic reconstruction of Madge Atkinson's *Mother Earth* (1933, 1935), illustrating the surface mesh and inferred skeletal position. Graphic design by Qizhi Yu and John Collomosse.

The kinetic sphere

The thinking of movement space across various spaces of coexistence (physical, social, economic) provides the main area of concern in Peter Sloterdijk's philosophy of spheres (spherology). In his epic *Spheres* trilogy (see Sloterdijk 1998–2004) he lays a foundation for the different ways of thinking about the human experience of motion in its spherical determination, from microspheres to macrospheres, or from the fetus-placenta to macro-uteri. The representation of spherical models of movement space is by no means new, however. Jorge Luis Borges nailed this sentiment in his essay "La Esfera de Pascal" ("Pascal's Sphere," in Borges 1981). If universal history is the history of a few metaphors, then according to Borges the metaphor of the sphere plays a significant role in the telling of the history of God *ab ovo*, from Xenophanes onward.[2]

Parmenides of Elea plays a key role in this history, since he argued that the sphere model (or Sphairos) gives ideal expression to eternal Being. Because the sphere is always equal to itself, it can be used to express the idea of self-identification and self-generated Being. According to this interpretation, the spherical model illustrates a philosophical opposition between *kinesis* and *stasis*, which Parmenides used to explain one of the basic premises of dialectical philosophy. If the condition of true being is that its reality is unchanging, like that of the sphere, then it can be assumed that change and movement are not real. The argument was provocative: everything we see moving and changing around us is in fact inexistent, in Parmenides' sense of the Real (which we know inspired Plato). Although a number of opponents to Parmenides' doctrine refused to accept such a radical view, the model of the sphere proved appealing. And so, even though he is considered one of the main detractors of Eleatic philosophy, Empedocles borrowed the Sphairos model nonetheless to propose a dialectical pluralism based on two spheres, one that is whole and unified, and one that is dispersed and whorl-like. Like Sloterdijk, Empedocles saw the ontological model not in its static spatial determination, but in terms of its temporal duration; he imagined a process of coming and going of spherical space. Characterized by a cycle of opposites, Empedocles' philosophy involves the transformation of the divine sphere to a nondivine state of disintegration via the agency of two types of soul, and two types of physical movement: attraction (*phylia*) and repulsion (*neikos*). Although I do not wish to pursue this line of inquiry all the way to Pascal's fearful sphere, as Borges suggests one could, it is worth highlighting that the outline of a history of spherology enshrines the idea that movement can be conceptualized—that it can be ideated—through a geometric modeling of space. In other words, because movement is invisible, we need concrete models of space in order to "see" movement; we need to hold tangible spheres and other geometric objects before us to have an analytical spatial architecture to work with, and to be able to visualize the breakdown of movement into component parts.

One can also follow the spherical representation of movement space in relation to the study of anatomical spatial relations. In other words, the sphere model is so general, so powerfully abstract, that its application is not limited only to conceptual models of Being, and to philosophical debates regarding the static or mobile nature of true reality. The idea that one can circumscribe the corporeal body within a sphere can be traced back to numerous endeavors to create a canon of bodily metrics in ancient Greece and Rome. In fact, this effort to represent human anatomy within a spherical model provides the foundation of a formal description of the human body in the Western canon. One example can be found in the work of Roman architect Vitruvius, whose treatise *De architectura* constitutes the basis of a systematic study of architectural proportions based on the circumferential and polygonal representation of a metric body.[3] Leonardo da Vinci's famous illustration of Vitruvius's "Canon of Proportions" has wielded an iconic influence on the representation of movement spaces and the anthropocentric vision of the corporeal body as a measure of all things. The concept of the movement sphere thus persists, and not only through the phallocentric icon of the "well-figured man" (*home bene figurati*), as imagined by Vitruvius (2005). Although the representation of this space is originally two-dimensional and static, as can be seen from the section of Carlo Urbino's *Codex Huygens* pictured in figure 1.2, the iconic representation of motion derived from Renaissance artists like da Vinci, and later Albrecht Dürer, all point toward the ambition to represent human bodies—men, in particular—inside stereotypical or tridimensional space.

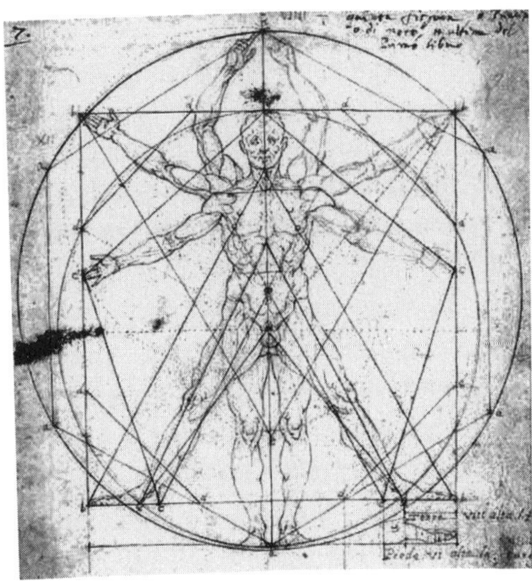

1.2
Image of a Vitruvian Man configuration taken from *Codex Huygens*, a treatise on painting closely related to da Vinci's teachings, by Italian artist Carlo Urbino (ca. 1510/20–after 1585).

The application of solid modeling to the study of anatomical proportions marks the shift from a frame of eidesis to a frame of analysis. No longer confined to a purely philosophical conception, the application of the spherical model to the study of quantitative measure relations of the human body provides a methodological foundation for a number of canonical approaches to kinetometry and anthropometry. In the same way that the sphere provides a key symbol in the telling of the history of God *ab ovo*, according to Borges, the sphere is a seminal space model in the cultural history of movement analysis and measurement, from the ancient pre-Socratic Sphairos model, to François Delsarte's "circle charts," used to describe and measure arm and hand movements in aesthetic gymnastics (Delsarte and Stebbins 1887), to Solomon Nikritin's biomechanical spheres of movement, used to design machinic human motion, to Lincoln Kirstein's spherical models of classical ballet (Kirstein and Stuart 1952), to W. T. Dempster's (1955) "kinetosphere," used mainly in ergonomics and the anthropometry of body action, to the "sphere of movement" used in Noa Eshkol's (1978) system of reference, mostly applied to dance notation. A similar history can be traced in the case of spherical models of gestural movement, going back to the writings of the first-century Roman orator Quintilian. Quintilian wrote of the importance of geometric circumferences in the delineation of gesture in his *Institutio oratoria*, which in turn served as an important inspiration to early modern theories of gestural space organization, particularly the gestural spherical maps conceived by Gilbert Austin (1966, first published 1806) and A. M. Bacon (1875).

In the same vein, Rudolf Laban distinguished between general space and the space within bodily reach. By "kinesphere," Laban meant an imaginary space we are able to outline with our feet and our hands, which marks out the entire orbit of space available to an individual body (1966, 10). Even when we move out of the limits of our original kinesphere, we create a new stance, so that we always carry our kinesphere with us, from stance to stance. Laban had to imagine the kinesphere so that he could "see" movement in relation to space, and so as to find the means of representing it (for instance, in terms of oppositional directions: up-down, right-left, backward-forward)—similar to the dialectical oppositions within the Sphairos model proposed by Empedocles. But in arbitrarily imagining movement within this plane of spatial representation, Laban was not only revealing certain properties of movement, he was also imposing a culturally specific way of seeing movement, and was thus negating other ways in which movement can be made to appear in other cultures of space. One opposition illustrated by Laban's kinesphere, for instance, remains debatable—the relationship between the center and the periphery, or between the bodily navel and the outer reach of the extended human body. According to Laban, the center of gravity of the upright body is also the center of the kinesphere, from where "innumerable directions radiate into infinite space" (1966, 17). The entire model is an exercise in the centering of space and body in motion. The kinesphere model is also an exercise in anthropocentrism.

Dance theorist and phenomenologist Susan Kozel has no kind words to spare for this ideology. Anthropocentrism is "a pernicious elevation of the importance and significance of the human being over the nonhuman world," she writes. "It is the placing of the human being at the center of all structures of value resulting in forms of imperialism, as well as the exploitation of animals, the environment, and anything perceived to be other than human" (2007, 222). Charges like these seem contentious, but they are nonetheless necessary, in my opinion, to question the idea that movement has a center in the body, and that the whole of movement space revolves around an anthropocentric, corporeal subject: a Vitruvian man. The culture of space is underpinned by ideological perspectives that inform the way we see movement, the way we represent it, and the way this system of representation then affects the way we embody our movement. If movement has a center, and if the ideal movement is depicted by a white and athletic young male, and if this is assumed to be a universal model of bodily movement (the Vitruvian canon), how many cultures of movement are then being negated, ostracized, and re-moved from cultural and social convention by this anthropocentric and male-centered hegemony?

A key theme of this book concerns the culturally transformative effects digital technology may have on the representation of human movement, and the changing ways in which this representation can be materialized in the digital era. From this perspective, it seems inappropriate to locate the center of movement space in the body navel or center of bodily gravity. Moreover, it seems inappropriate to speak of a centered space at all. Thus, the attack on anthropocentricism finally kills off any universal position regarding the spatialization of human movement, either as a system that revolves around the corporeal understanding of movement, or as a system that centers on humanistic perspectives grounded on the classical canon of bodily proportions going back to Vitruvius and Quintilian. Because Laban's approach to movement analysis touches on the surface of virtual space, as we will see shortly, it does not fully embrace a virtualization of the body, which is the paradigm offered, for instance, by contemporary motion capture technology. Laban's choreutics can be seen as a language that gropes the virtual. It is a language that focuses on the corporeal body, and the means by which this body can caress the virtual space around it, touch it at the surface, but never penetrate the virtual and never cross this apparently impassable boundary. In sum, the two cultures of space I introduced earlier also define two clear-cut epistemologies: either the virtual subordinates the corporeal body, or the corporeal body subordinates the virtual. Or perhaps we are caught in between, gravitating toward a center of indetermination.

Technological egospheres

If it is true that one is free to move in one's own personal kinetic bubble, then it is also true that one must insert oneself within shared kinetic spheres or spaces of coexistence, as Sloterdijk (1998–2004) points out. Thus, a concentric or co-centric arrangement must come into place between one's own personal experience of movement and that abstract sphere of communication (language) to which we direct ourselves and from where we derive our own sense of identity. This concentric sense of the movement sphere presupposes that one is not experiencing one's own physical space de facto; instead, one is experiencing a sphere caught between physical and mental, between stasis and ex-stasis, subject and object, which Sloterdijk uses as an expansive model to account for a political economy of kinetics. Or as Michel Maffesoli puts it, the model ultimately relates "to the economic sphere, which remains, for the moment in any case, the main fetish of the dominant ideology" (1996, 15). But before turning our attention to the commercialization of the sphere of movement, we need to consider how movement becomes an object of material representation. This brings us back to the transformation of movement via the agency of technology.

22

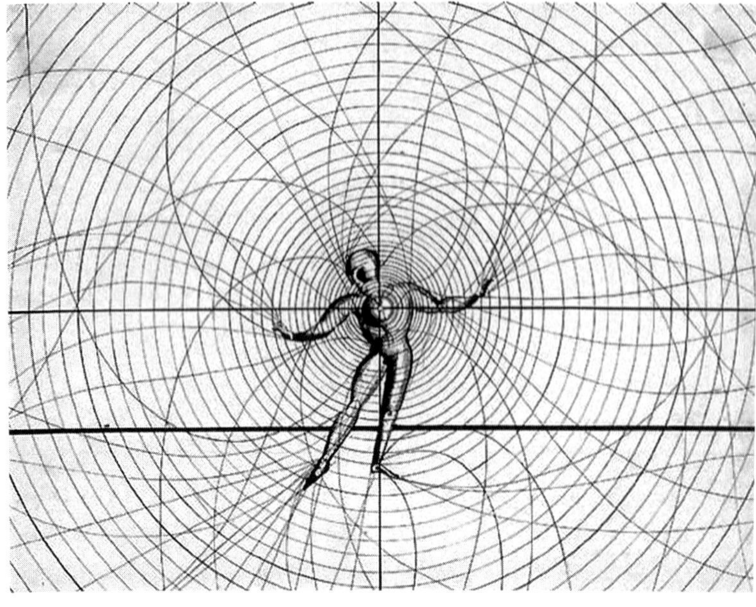

1.3
Oskar Schlemmer, *Egozentrische Raumlineatur* (Egocentric Space Delineation), 1924.

As far back as 1924, Bauhaus practitioner Oskar Schlemmer represented the movement sphere as an "egocentric space delineation," which is the title of a famous pen and ink drawing included in his picture essay "Man and Art Figure" (reprinted 1961). Unlike the Vitruvian ideal of a centered human body, perfectly framed within square and circle, Schlemmer proposed different levels of quadrangular organization and various concentric rings, as well as lines of curvature emerging from a not-so-human subject. The physical delineation of this egospace also seems to define a surface and an implied volume of movement. But unlike Laban's kinesphere, which the anatomical body touches only at given surface points, the surface of concentric rings and curves in Schlemmer's egocentric space delineation is a virtual canvas that does more than provide space for the corporeal body to move in. The space delineation in Schlemmer's drawing can be interpreted as a kind of "second skin" covering both the surrounding space and the subject's body. This second skin covers both the physical and the virtual, both the human body and its geometry. This would imply that subject and space are essentially part of the same thing, in the sense that they are both wrapped in the same virtual skin. Like a polygon mesh in computer-generated imaging, this body is made of physicalized geometry—not just flesh. Schlemmer's synthesis can defeat the meat. It provokes a trajective position halfway between biological anatomy and virtual architecture, which lies at the heart of this artist's vision, as we will see later in this chapter. This idea delineates my own trajectory as well, in the sense that the understanding of movement depicted in Schlemmer's drawing is less stereotypical than that of most anthropocentric depictions. It is less grounded in the anatomical center of movement, and challenges the rather restricted idea that movement involves physical bodies doing physical stuff inside 3D space. From this point of view, Schlemmer's work can be considered a historical precedent in digital movement studies.

Unsurprisingly, this research program was rekindled following the development of computer-aided means of movement design and production in the 1970s. For instance, Delle Rae Maxwell pointed out that Bauhaus performance designs were comparable to computer modeling by primitive solids (1983, 57). Maxwell makes an interesting visual analogy between a volumetric design by one of Schlemmer's students entitled "Man at the Control Panel" (1924) and Norman Badler and Stephen Smoliar's model of the Bubbleman,[4] which was proposed in the late 1970s as a model and software for the computational decomposition of objects into spheres. Although Bubbleman and Bubblewoman had a brief existence not least because alternative technologies and faster computer graphics display devices (e.g., the Silicon Graphics workstations) made them obsolete, it is worth noting that the model produced the first computer-generated images of physical exercise movement (published in *Self* magazine in September 1984). Because Bubble people could be interpreted algorithmically, the Badler-Smoliar software was able to digitally convert three-dimensional object representation from a collection of cross-section outlines to surface points, and from surface points to a collection of overlapping spheres. In the process, the algorithms effected a conversion

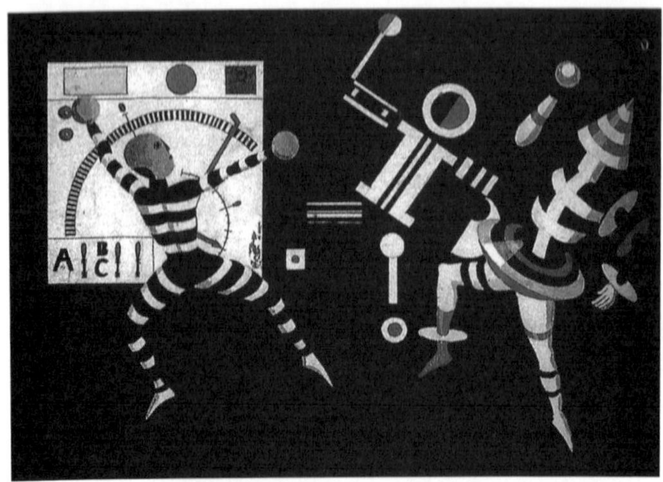

1.4
Man at Control Panel, design for
Bauhaus stage performance by
Kurt Schmidt, based on a concept by
Oskar Schlemmer, 1925.

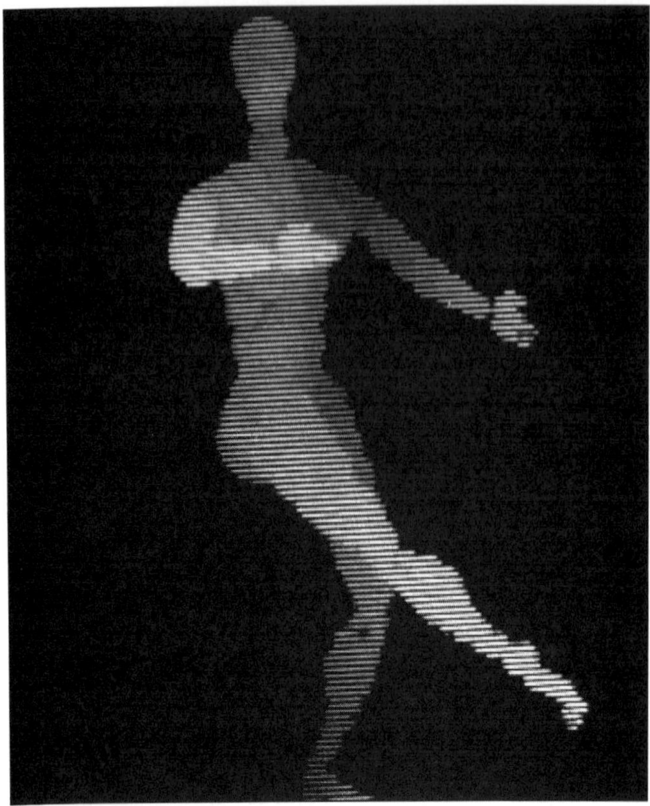

1.5
Bubbleman, a volumetric computer
modeling of the human figure
using about 300 spheres to create
disklike representations of volumetric
bodily figures, created by Norman
Badler and Stephen Smoliar (1979).
Courtesy of Norman Badler.

from surface to volume representation, thus integrating the two cultural approaches to movement space discussed in this chapter.

O'Rourke, Badler, and Toltzis (1979) expanded the notion of a movement space into ancillary fields such as program language analysis and algorithmic analysis, thereby facilitating the representation and communication of movement within electronic contexts. The graphical representation looks lumpy by today's standards, but it was versatile enough to provide a model for the programming of articulated human movement in a computational context. Evidently, the intention of this language was not to provide a physiognomy of the figure or a perfectly realistic rendition of human movement, but to guarantee a representation of computer-readable movement through task-specific operations.

One example of how this model was developed is the Graphical Marionette (1983), a forerunner of today's digital puppetry, due to Delle Rae Maxwell and Carol Ginsberg at MIT. Maxwell and Ginsberg considered the point-cloud figure in its ellipsoidal volume the best means of representing most parts of the human form, even though Maxwell felt the figure still appeared overstylized. By generating points randomly within that volume, they could degrade the ellipsoid shape enough so that it appeared more irregular, and thus more humanlike. I would like to suggest that there is a clear historical link between Schlemmer's mechanical marionettes and the Graphical Marionette developed by Maxwell and Ginsberg. The history of movement unfolding here points in the direction of mechanization and automation, and the design of robotic paradigms of human and posthuman movement. Thus, the notion of the egocentric space delineation (henceforth, egosphere) is also utilized in the field of robotics, and in a way that is not too dissimilar to Schlemmer's models dating back to the 1920s. The term "Sensory Ego-Sphere" (SES) has been put forward to help map the short-term memory structure of robotic humans. This model, which can be described as an interface between automated sensing and cognition, is envisioned as a virtual spherical capsid surrounding a mobile robot.[5] Like the concentric rings that Schlemmer saw connecting his virtual bodies with their surrounding space, contemporary robots are typically designed to understand their own mobility in terms of a global coordinate system, or an egosphere, within which robotic movement is spatially programmed and mapped out.

Although more advanced than earlier models, the egosphere coordinate model poses a fundamental problem when it comes to formalizing the space of humanoid movement. As I intimated above, the sphere is too neat, too perfect, and far too exact to provide a model of the broken and more angular spatial architectures that radiate from the human body. Bearing this in mind, we must leave the sphere to one side and consider a different space machine—a more differentiated model of spatial movement organization.

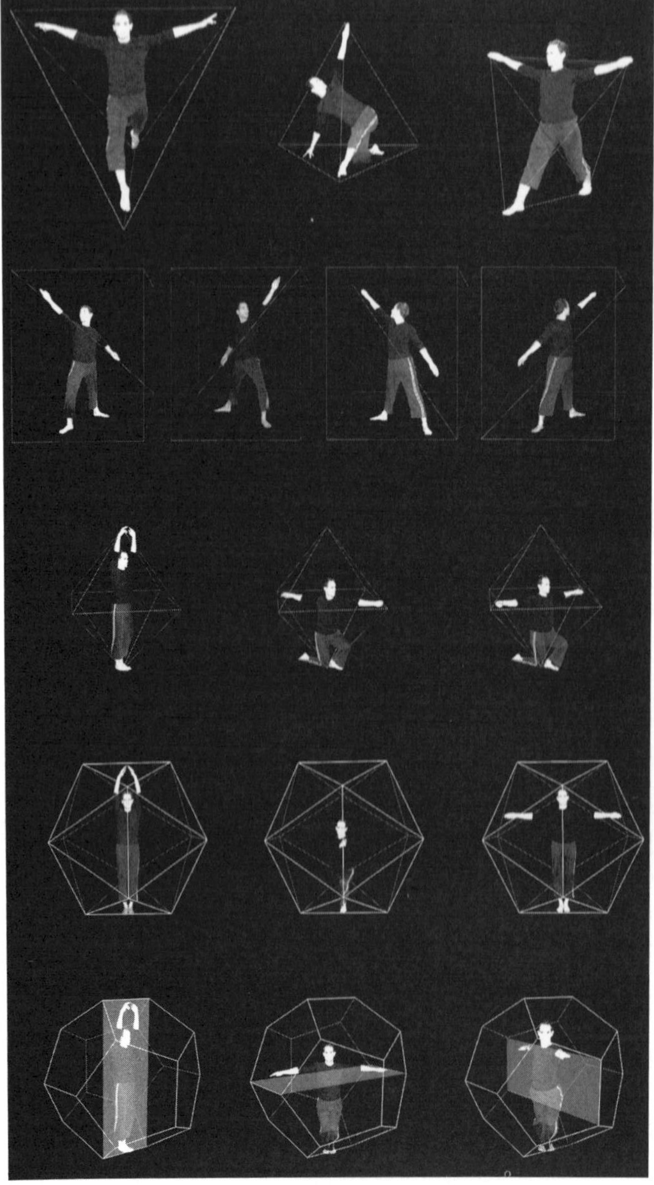

1.6
Composite image of the five models of choreutic space developed by Laban based on the five Platonic solids (tetrahedron, cube, octahedron, icosahedron, and dodecahedron). Stills taken from *Crystallographies* (2012), performed by Nicolás Salazar Sutil with digital artwork by Sebastián Melo.

Crystallographies

In the oddly titled book *Crystal Souls: Studies of Inorganic Life* (1999, first published 1917), German mathematical biologist and spiritual philosopher Ernst Haeckel put forward the idea that crystals are not dead matter but grow and change according to chemical processes, just as living organisms do. The main characteristic of crystalline minerals is their sensitivity to light and heat—their capacity to grow follows from this determination. Crucially, crystalline patterns of growth are determined by a basic rule of geometrical space packing. Haeckel's organic crystallography claimed to reveal a naturally occurring language of space organization. As Christian Bök puts it: "an archaeologist without any mineralogical experience might easily mistake a crystal for the artificial product of a precision technology" (2011, 12). Haeckel's book was a bestseller upon its publication in 1917, and it proved to be hugely inspirational to a young Hungarian student of architecture by the name of Rudolf Laban.

Crystallography can be described as the language of spatial self-organization through the unique arrangement of atoms and molecules in crystalline matter (liquid or solid). A crystal structure is generated as the result of an infinitely repeating array of "boxes" called unit cells. This unit cell functions like a primitive unit in language: it is both self-similar and repeating. Thus, from the simplest possible representation of a molecular structure, molecules are literally composed of unit cells through symmetry operations, much as units of speech make up words in structural grammar. Indeed, according to Bök, "a word is a bit of a crystal in formation" (2011, 12). Mineralogy could be said to perform a wordless language, a language of regular spatial arrangements resulting in crystal lattices that bulk naturally through repetition of the unit cell in three dimensions. In fact, crystalline movement can be represented in written form using a notation system known as the Miller index notation.[6]

The basic difference between spherography and crystallography is that the latter proposes an understanding of space that can be internally differentiated. Unlike the sphere, which is an undifferentiated and boundless space, a cube is a regular space made up of a specific number of points or vertices (eight, to be precise). It is within differentiable space that a discrete language of movement can be generated, across a number of disciplinary domains. For instance, cubic units are found in the language of digital imaging in the shape of the pixel—the smallest addressable element of a picture, or the voxel (volumetric pixel) used in 3D imaging. The sphere and box models illustrate two different ways of applying an abstract object to the design of an embodied architecture of movement. I would argue that these two models of space (spherical and cubic) constitute not only two languages of space, but also two completely different *cultures of space*. Generally speaking, whereas the spherical model is conducive to more abstract ways of thinking space, crystalline models by comparison are conducive to a more concrete way of building movement space and measuring differentiated points in it. Crystallography is therefore a method of construction, a structuring machine that can be used to build and analyze movement spaces.

It is not surprising that one of the most important branches of crystallography is morphology, which focuses on the formation of crystals according to different space systems (e.g., cube, tetrahedron, octahedron). Although he used the term more liberally, Jacques Lacan considered crystallization as the basic effect of discourse, and as a key process in the construction of a subject or ego-ideal via language. And this raises a crucial question, which I will use as a springboard for further analysis. One cannot refer to the inappropriateness of language in terms of a crystalline thought-construction. Lacan argues, "For if, effectively, language was at first some crystallization which was imposed on the exercise of intelligence as an apparatus, why is it not obvious that intelligence would have made language as appropriate as it made, after all, its primitive instruments … ? Why would language not have been something analogous in its own way, if effectively it was the creation, the secretion, the prolongation of an intelligent act?" (1964–1965, 27). This question invites consideration not only of linguistic morphology but also of kinetic morphology, and the way in which the crystalline organization of human movement can be constructed move by move, supporting a language of formalized human movement that is also a secretion or prolongation of a kinetic intelligence.

Choreutics: Moving on the surface of the virtual

Choreutics is the practice of harmonic movement, which can be achieved via a formal motor language involving the articulation of bodily movement paths within different mineral structures imagined (or built) around the body. Laban wanted to turn Haeckel's language of animated crystals into a practical system that would combine elements of dance, therapy, and physical education. Laban looked at the shapes of crystallized minerals as three-dimensional networks (or basketworks) that could support the construction of harmonic sequences of movements. So the aim of choreutics is to formalize the ways in which the body can draw movement pathways along the surface of this invisible crystalline network.

As well as being steeped in the Pythagorean concept of a harmony of form, Laban's idea was also influenced by Plato's theory of the participation of material objects within the *eidos*, or ideal form. Thus, because he needed to work out a movement system based on spatial differentiation, and because the sphere is an undifferentiating space, Laban had to use more suitable geometries to construct harmonic movement sequences. Laban found the five Platonic solids—named after Plato's reference in the *Timaeus*—the most suitable models for his five basic principles of crystalline movement (see figure 1.6).[7] Each one of Laban's models provides a different possibility for the composition of choreutic shapes, which are essentially point-to-point links created by the subject moving within these solids. The points or vertices that make up the solid offer different guiding orientation points, which the choreutic performer can follow with a specified body part (usually the extremities). Thus, Laban's solids work as virtual or physical exoskeletons, which guide the practitioner's construction of movement forms.

Laban explained that the icosahedron is the model that offers the most natural and body-friendly tracks for the composition of choreutic shapes. In addition to *imagining* this icosahedron around the moving body, Laban also *built* physical structures of various sizes to provide practical training and experiential awareness of how to move harmonically. He called these objects "scaffoldings," by which he meant structures that could exist as hypothetical models or as life-sized construction models made of rods and joints. Laban (1956) also conceived and designed a machine called the Chromatic Movement Dial (CMD), which was basically a metal exoskeleton in the shape of an icosahedron. According to Laban's specifications, the CMD could accommodate a person moving freely in space. A dial line would connect the twelve points of this exoskeleton. The user would then follow this line with a chosen pivot point (usually a joint), thus learning to reproduce the correct morphology of harmonic space via a series of predetermined pathways or scales. This apparatus could be applied to a number of kinetic practices, including dance, movement therapy, relaxation, gymnastics, and calisthenics. Laban wrote that human movements "are never complete crystal-patterns, but awareness of harmonious flow resulting from crystalline tendencies increases pleasure in skill" (1966, 114). Thus, the free performance of choreutic shapes inside the CMD would encourage transferable skills and integration of body and mind through movement across various disciplines.

Figuralism and the *Kunstfigur*

As I pointed out earlier, Oskar Schlemmer approached movement arts research—much as Laban did—from a background in the visual arts and architecture. He proposed representing human movement schematically, as part of the graphic system of figural representation that made up the basis of his artistic practice and pedagogy. In a Bauhaus course from the late twenties entitled "Mensch" (Man), Schlemmer used the term "figuralist" (*figürlichen*) to describe the pictorial language of the human figure (Schlemmer 1971). At the heart of his research program was the question of whether abstract space ought to be adapted in deference to the human body, or whether the physical body should take over abstract space. The solution was synthesis. Through the application of classical methods of formal drawing and mechanics, Schlemmer tried to fuse the body with abstract space. The starting point for this integration of man and machine was the language of formal human figuration, which could be applied to a mechanistic/ technological construction as much as to an anatomical construction of human movement. Thus, Schlemmer advanced from formal ways of representing the human body in figural drawing to the craft of making synthetic designs of human automatons, marionettes, and robotlike humanoids on stage, which led to his creation of the applied language of "balletic mathematics" (1961).

As such, figuralism was the basis of Schlemmer's practice not only in the visual arts but also in his work as master of the Bauhaus stage, as exemplified in pieces like the famous *Triadic Ballet* (premiered in 1922, before Schlemmer's arrival at the Bauhaus) as well as the *Figural Cabaret* (1923) and the so-called Bauhaus dances (1923–1929). Using the methodological approach delivered in his "Mensch" course, Schlemmer produced a large number of diagrams, meshes, geometries, and stereometric volumes to help formulate the language underlying his creative practice. Much like Laban's scaffoldings, the methodological tools that Schlemmer applied to his creative practice and teaching provide a concrete idea of how to design, compose, and construct human movement. To sum up, Schlemmer's work involved an understanding of the creative and artistic potential of what he called "the moving figure" (*Bewegtefigur*).

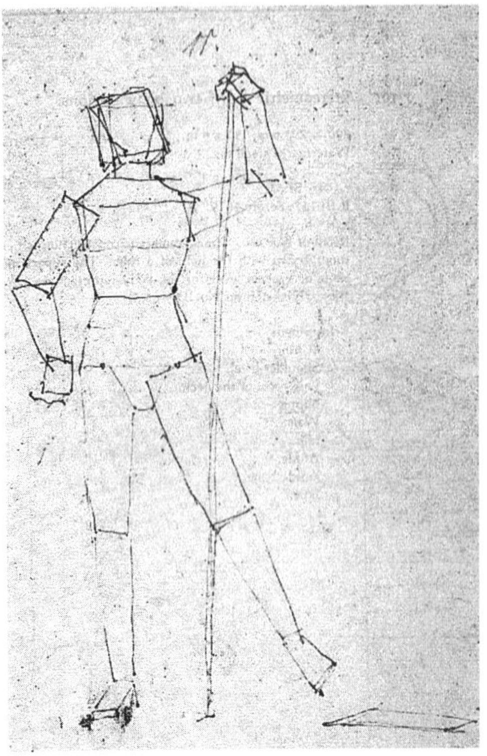

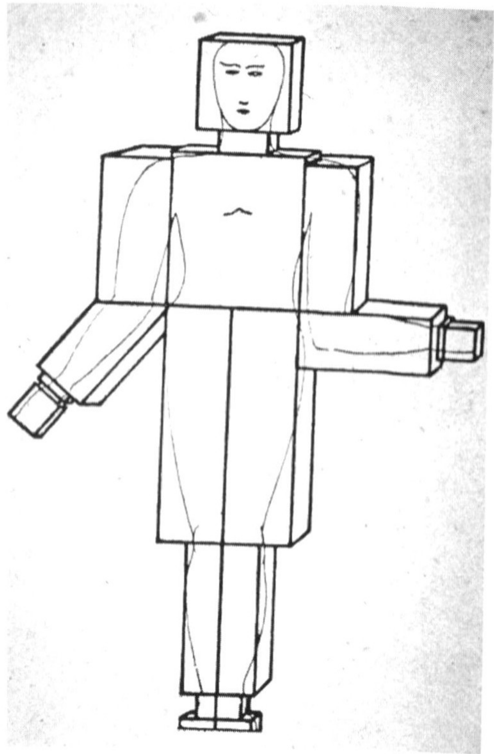

1.7
Albrecht Dürer, *Stereometric Man:
13 Cross Sections of the Body* (detail),
pen and ink, ca. 1523. Nuremberg,
German National Museum.

1.8
Schlemmer's "Ambulant Architecture," one of four models
of the *Kunstfigur* showing how the laws of surrounding
cubic space can determine the design of a moving human
body, taken from "Man and Art Figure" (1925); see
Schlemmer (1961).

At the heart of Schlemmer's vision is the well-known concept of the *Kunstfigur*, or art figure. Essentially, the *Kunstfigur* is a synthetic human: partly bioanatomical and partly geometric. In addition to being an abstract concept grounded on Schlemmer's theory of figuralism, the *Kunstfigur* could also be realized mechanically as a synthetic humanoid: an automaton, marionette, or robotic performer. Thus, Schlemmer proposed four types of *Kunstfigur*: the ambulant architecture, the marionette, the technical organism or mobile, and the metaphysical type. While the marionette model was derived from the *functional* laws of human anatomy and their relationship to space, and while the technical organism or mobile was derived from *motional* laws (rotation, direction, spin, intersection), the ambulant architecture was derived from the laws of cubical space (more on this later). As mechanical constructs, these semiautomated and mechanized humanoids are similar to the visionary model of Aristotle's automaton or the Mechanical Man, a robotic human conceived in the fifteenth century by Leonardo da Vinci and referenced in Schlemmer's Bauhaus notes (1971).[8] Schlemmer's ambition for the *Kunstfigur* was to "free man [sic] from his physical bondage to the anatomical body and to heighten the freedom of movement beyond the body's native potential" (1961, 28). He claimed that the artificial human figure would permit any kind of movement and any kind of position for as long a time as desired. As a result, he believed this synthesis could provide the means of ultimately liberating the body from its physical conditioning altogether, enabling a metaphysical type of *Kunstfigur*. Schlemmer, it seems, was trying to reconcile metaphysics and mechanics. The metaphysical form of the *Kunstfigur* relates to the pure abstractions that this physical being is intended to project or depict—e.g., the star form of the spread-out fingers of the hand or the sign of infinity (∞) of the folded arms—but which are ultimately re-moved, like the movement idea.

As I intimated earlier, the box is a very basic machine. Laban used it to refine his understanding of points that make up harmonic movement in space, and to gain awareness of how to draw choreutic shapes along diagonal lines. Thus, according to Laban, when a body draws diagonal lines in space, this body is effectively creating a virtual box or cubic scaffolding around itself. Being interested in volumes rather than surfaces, Schlemmer put the box machine to use in a very different way. Much like the box language of cubic crystallography or, indeed, like the voxels used in 3D imaging, Schlemmer used the laws of cubic space to make what he called ambulant architectures: robotlike dancers made up entirely of cubes and cuboids. The body can be placed inside a cubic space model in order to reveal symmetry operations, much like the Vitruvian Man, or Albrecht Dürer's notion of man and the magic square, as depicted in his famous allegorical engraving *Melancholia* (1514).

Schlemmer (1990) wrote early in his career that he aspired for a Düreresque mode. The German Renaissance master and mathematician had explored the application of shear transformation to facial variations and had applied a number of other mathematical principles to figural drawing, which are not unlike some of the techniques used by Laban and Schlemmer. For instance, Dürer investigated the various forms that arise from combinations of two-dimensional polygonal shapes—

an experiment that certainly bears a strong resemblance to the study of polyhedral shapes in Laban's choreutic language. Dürer also used massing in schematic drawing, which helped him achieve a perspectival and three-dimensional depiction of the human body. Furthermore, he imagined the forms of all the parts of the body as blocks or boxlike masses, to ensure that his figure drawing subscribed to a three-line perspectival system. The technique also provided different orientations of the box, which might account for basic positions of a body part, including tilting and angling.

Schlemmer's teaching notes at the Bauhaus (1971) contain a number of graphic studies based on Dürer's original works, including a rectangular division of the human body (also known as Boxperson), from 1928. Schlemmer was also drawn to Dürer because the Old Master had paid serious attention to different human biotypes (young and old, male and female, athletic and obese). Schlemmer intended to expand this catalog of biotypes in order to consider different types of synthetic humans. And so, whilst inspired by Dürer, Schlemmer was in fact making a bold move beyond the humanistic approach, leading the way toward what we may now call a posthuman conception of the cubical body. Whereas Dürer's *Stereometric Man* (circa 1523) is not a representation of a human type but a schematic exercise to achieve tilting and angling effects in painting, Schlemmer's plan was to devise a cubic body that could free the human from its own physical anatomy. The *Kunstfigur* can be said to radicalize Laban's so-called "choreosophy,"[9] according to which the soul participates in the activities of the body. Schlemmer did not see the biological human body and its soul as two different things. Instead, he saw them entangled in a liminal ontology, as it were, a being-inbetween that captures the essence of being in movement—a becoming of the human as trajective self, always caught in between: between animal and human, between human and machine, between male and female, between colored and non-colored. The human body, when represented in movement, cannot be only human, nor male, nor white, but is always in between these and other potential modalities of moving bodiliness.

Stereobodies and balletic mathematics

Whereas the disciplines of architecture and the visual arts appealed to Schlemmer as instances of momentary or frozen motion, the performing arts offered an opportunity to return the frozen object back to its kinetic experience. Thus, he embraced the stage as a place where he could materialize geometry in motion. This is why he spoke of his own stage work as an expression of a language he called "balletic mathematics" or "mathematics in motion" (Schlemmer 1961), a kind of technical performance he likened to the geometrically inflected techniques of classical ballet, calisthenics, eurhythmics, gymnastics, and acrobatics.[10]

An important aspect of Schlemmer's balletic mathematics involved the understanding of "space dance"; i.e., a series of full-bodily movements determined by geometrical figures painted on the ground (square, diagonal, circle). Schlemmer also used carpets with various geometric patterns (particularly chessboards) as gridlike lattices on which to coordinate and map his dance. The immediate goal of this method was to discover the different principles that govern objects in space, and to arrive at a purely locational or coordinate understanding of choreographic composition. Based on this simple method, Schlemmer staged a trio entitled *Space Dance* at the Dessau Bauhaus in 1926. The patterns of the costume corresponded to the shapes produced by the dancing automaton as it moved on a diagrammatized dance floor. Using planar geometry as a basis, he could then project the formal structures into the volumetric space of the stage, and thus determine both the movement and costumes of the dancers in relation to the floor. Schlemmer acknowledged that coming to dance from painting and sculpture allowed him to appreciate movement "all the more because the expressive range of painting and sculpture is restricted to the static, the rigid, to movement captured in a fixed moment" (1990, 283). Because static postures and the tableau representation of motion are not sufficient to create works for the stage, Schlemmer's language of balletic mathematics rested "partly on the fundamental theories of geometry and stereometry, transposed into new intriguing materials; and partly on the basic laws of the human body, which is both a being of flesh and blood, mind and emotion, and a remarkably well-functioning apparatus of joints" (283).

In his dance *Box Promenade* (1929), Schlemmer creatively applied the notion of the stereobody to a choreographic experiment. Over the course of this piece, three performers were given the task of creating different spatial arrangements of boxes and bodies on stage. The dance is a reminder that the performer must engage in a technical problem: in this case, finding fundamental relations between abstract objects and concrete physicality, so as to make a synthetic figure that is neither entirely physical nor entirely abstract.

The emphasis on these formal elements of choreography seems a world apart from current computer-generated aesthetics, where the language of solid modeling is effaced. Computer-generated images of moving bodies often disguise the underlying geometry from the final rendition, in order to convey a more realistic or hyperrealistic aesthetic effect. Today we do not see the formalisms hidden under layers of gloss. By hiding the underlying geometry, and by dressing it up with flesh and flash, computer-generated imaging supposedly induces a sense of believability within digital frameworks. Despite the stylistic difference which seems to relegate Schlemmer's work to a historical period obsessed with geometrical aesthetics, the language of figuralism represents a clear antecedent to the emergence of computer-aided movement design in a digital performance context. As I will show in part IV of this book, although formal motor languages have been largely effaced, and although we no longer see the language underlying the glossy aesthetics of digital imaging, Schlemmer's history is a lesson that shows the beauty of form and movement in its most skeletal and geometric simplicity. Schlemmer's experiments are to this day a rallying cry against "the fad and aesthetic form, which can hold its own against the perfect utility of functional objects and machines" (1990, 135).

2

Observing movement through time

Earlier I barred the dimension of time from my discussion, and in doing so I pointed out that I would rather treat movement space in a physical determination involving only three parameters. Of course, this is missing the point: movement involves the *temporality* of space. Movement is not only spatial but also spatiotemporal. This was a problem for both Laban and Schlemmer, whose writings are distinctly silent on the question of temporality—which is why they will not provide a suitable framework in this chapter. Instead, I will draw on the work of French physiologist and experimental photographer Étienne-Jules Marey, particularly his scientific study of time in human movement. From an architectural perspective, movement could be said to be all part of a founding proxemics that accentuates the vividness of the spatial framework (Maffesoli 1996, 133). But movement is relevant beyond the issues of proximity and distance. My intention is to call on the founding *chronemics* of movement observation.

E. T. Hall (1966) theorized human communication in terms of the proxemics and chronemics displayed in everyday behavior, according to which culture-specific behavior could be determined by personal uses of space and time. Throughout this book, I will address this categorical distinction, but not without some degree of reservation. Movement occurring in physical space can be seen to be ongoing, and it is determined by physical proximities and distances—hence, proxemic movement. On the other hand, movement occurring along instantaneous moments is parsed, or broken down into frames, shots, steps—hence, chronemic movement. However, as we will see, this division is conceptual and arbitrary, since space and time are entangled in movement. Thus, space engenders its own temporality (duration), and time produces its own spatiality, for instance in terms chronological lines and timelines. In sum, although movement has been addressed here in terms of two separate categories (space and time, or proxemics and chronemics), it is important to understand that movement lies between them, in the unstable conditions of space-time.

To clarify this argument, I will briefly consider two very different notions of rhythm: Laban's proxemic notion of "space rhythm" and Marey's chronographic rhythms. Following this brief clarification, I will trace the idea of a chronemic observation of movement—that is, movement observed first and foremost from a temporal determination—and the development of the medium of time writing, or chronography. I will then follow the historical development of this medium into cyclography, a technology of movement inscription pioneered by Soviet physiologist Nikolai Bernstein to describe short and continuous movement cycles. These two case studies will help steer the discussion toward a consideration of how technological mediation can lead, historically and culturally, toward an increasingly abstract determination of time within movement studies. And here is the crux of the matter: two epistemologies of movement emerge from this division. From physical space

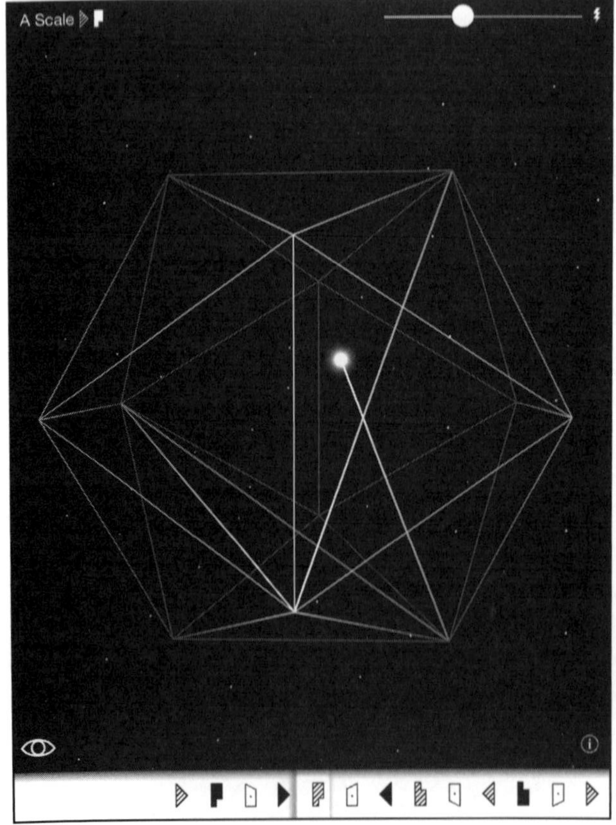

2.1
Laban A Scale. Still from *Moving Space*,
an app developed by Brenton Cheng for
iPad and iPhone (© 2013 Center Moves).
Courtesy of Brenton Cheng.

emerges an epistemology in which movement is typically seen as a proxemic phenomenon, in which physical bodies draw unceasing paths while moving. From the chronemic appreciation championed by Marey, an epistemology of movement emerges that sees movement no longer in terms of continuous physical distances and proximities, but in terms of intermittent speeds and transitions.

This leads me to the question of space rhythms. According to Laban, when moving inside a virtual architecture, the body draws directions that make up polygonal or spatial rhythms following one another in linear succession, thus allowing for infinite variations, deviations, and deflections. An example of this is Laban's notion of the movement scale. Space rhythms are configured into an A scale, as shown in figure 2.1, when the subject moves from one point to another in a specific twelve-point sequence defined by Laban. The movement is continuous along the subject's kinesphere, and it is only punctuated by spatial points of orientation that reroute the movement along the subject's chosen pathway. Now, the conception of movement is clearly proxemic. To create these rhythms, the subject has to move along uninterrupted spatial distances, touching points in this invisible surface surrounding the body. The main property of movement, while performing the scale, is the distance covered by the moving body from one point to another.

The properties of distance and proximity are abandoned in a chronemic representation of movement. When looking at movement from the point of view of abstract time, there is no continuous distance. If my intention is to record movement temporally, say the movement times of a subject performing this A scale, what counts is not the proximity or distance from one point in space to another, but the intervals between one moment in time and another. A sequence in time can be thus chopped into instantaneous frames of movement. From this chronemic determination, the language of human movement is not only defined in the way Laban and Schlemmer defined it. We also keep track of movement in a chronemic way—for instance when we count, or when we punctuate the passage of time with sounds, as in the ticking of a watch or the clicks of a metronome. The moment a body enters durational space, it also enters into a relationship with a chronemic behavior, which dictates the way in which different moments and intervals are reckoned with as quantitative determinations of motion, which are in turn coupled with qualitative determinations such as speed, sustain, attack. or delay. But how is this representation of movement times achieved? How does this temporal determination of movement also enter the plane of representation and language?

Like the arms of a clock, the human body can start to perform time as soon as it moves at regular or time-specific intervals. Insofar as spatial movement emerges from a bodily anatomy that is made up of discrete extremities (two arms, two legs), those body parts can stamp their own quantitative measure relations on the canvas of durational space. In other words, when one moves in kinespheric space, numerable relations or space rhythms are created naturally, as it were, by the alternate sequence of moving body parts. Thus, the basic unit of timing in locomotion is stepping. Similarly, a base unit of timing in dance is the step. The same applies to other units of timing like the feet: while the foot is a body part, it is also a standard unit of measurement in the durational arts (dance, poetry, oratory). The function of the foot is to create an abstract recognition of time while referring back to the corporeal body. In effect, the foot can also leave a print, which is why it can be considered a prime modality of time writing or writing with the feet (odography). In sum, feet become a natural symbol, which is directly extracted from the activity of physical contact between body and space, or by the marking of body-time in space, and which is then assigned a value (even a meaning) within the domain of representation, say as an object of natural movement notation. Relevant parameters of kinetic time can be visualized as the conventional mark is drawn. Insofar as the mark is indelible, insofar as it stays for the eye to see, movement time can be materialized and then analyzed or even conceptualized within the realm of eidesis.

The function of time marks is liable to different cultural systems of representation. Chronemic determination is particularly relevant to a study of digital forms of movement representation found within technologies like motion capture, or what I call "e-motion" (online movement), which will be discussed at length in part IV. Given this creative evolution of time marking and time punctuation, it is important to note that the process of making marks offers opportunities not only for repetition but also subversion. As Carrie Noland writes: "We can leave our marks in the wrong place, invent private or countercultural mark systems, or use mark making as an exploratory project, investigating how our bodies might move differently and thereby achieve materialization and cultural legibility in unexpected ways" (2009, 215). For the time being, what concerns me is the conventionalization of the mark, and the process by means of which the mark becomes a social convention, a symbol that can be floated over to the domain of socially convened representation and language.

Chronographic code

Étienne-Jules Marey's book *Le mouvement* (1894) is grounded on an understanding of the temporality of corporeal movement, and the graphic recording of movement times using novel capture technologies. Marey achieved a representation of movement times using two distinct technological media that he pioneered: chronography and chronophotography. Chronography was a written record of movement times (similar to a notation system), whereas chronophotography yielded a photographic record of movement times. Writing on this same subject, André Leroi-Gourhan (1993) argued that in human beings the treading motion that constitutes the rhythmic framework of walking is accompanied by rhythmic movements of the arms, and "whereas the former governs spatiotemporal integration and is the source of animation in the social sphere, the latter has to do with the individual's integration in what is not a time-and-space-creating but a form-creating system" (310). Leroi-Gourhan's insight is hugely useful to help us understand Marey's work and the role Marey's research program will play in the context of this investigation. I will address Marey's work in two separate sections, one dealing with the rhythmic frameworks of movement time and the other concentrating on movement form. Here, I will consider the rhythmic framework of time-dependent walking, which Marey explored via the medium of chronography.

Unlike chronophotography, chronography is a nonphotographic medium that Marey pioneered to record duration and sequence of movement in terms of periods of contact and displacement. Specifically, he used chronography to notate periods of foot contact issued by a walking or running subject. Marey's study of the human gait can be interpreted as a juxtaposition of an abstract sense of progression (metronomic time) and a physical progression (human gait), which enabled him to accurately measure and record the basic modalities of human and animal locomotion.

Le mouvement begins with an exploration of magnitude and the way in which time can be represented in graphic form as a segmented line. Marey argued that it was necessary to write time in this geometrically explicit way because "[linguistic] language is as slow and obscure a method of expressing the duration and sequence of events as the graphic method is lucid and easy to understand" (1895, 2). He championed the idea that the "graphic method" was the most natural way of expressing durational movement, especially because, as opposed to word-based language and symbolic notation, the graphic record could convey directly to the mind the meaning of complicated rhythms. Since he was committed to a scientific enterprise that demanded unequivocal systems of representation, Marey justified the use of his graphic method by arguing that the technological medium would bypass naked-eye observation.

Marey came up with an ingenious needle tracing device attached to the feet or hands of a moving subject via pneumatic tubes, which could automatically detect the moment when right and left foot alternately touch the ground and register this physical stimulus onto a piece of paper wrapped around a cylinder. The transmission of air along the tubes enabled the physical stimulus to be recorded onto the scroll, yielding a real-time record of live movement: the rising and falling movements of a walking subject would trigger the tracing needle to rise and fall at various periods and intervals, producing a written record that corresponded exactly with the physical action. Marey proposed two ways of scripting movement times: either in terms of dashes (similar to the Morse code) or in the form of a continuous curve, the variations of which expressed different temporal phases. This distinction between a discontinuous and a continuous graphic record was applicable not only to Marey's chronographic technique but also, as we will see presently, to the chronophotographic study of movement forms.

Marey also realized that time signatures created naturally by biped or quadruped tempos also involved a consideration of the *sound* of movement. Temporality, according to Marey, is punctuated and marked audibly by physical displacement of the feet, which becomes the body's standard unit for marking movement time via sound. Marey illustrated three experiments in his book *Le mouvement* involving the visual and sonic record of the human pace using his odographic notation. He attached his chronographic device to a pacing man, a pacing horse, and the moving hands of a piano player. In

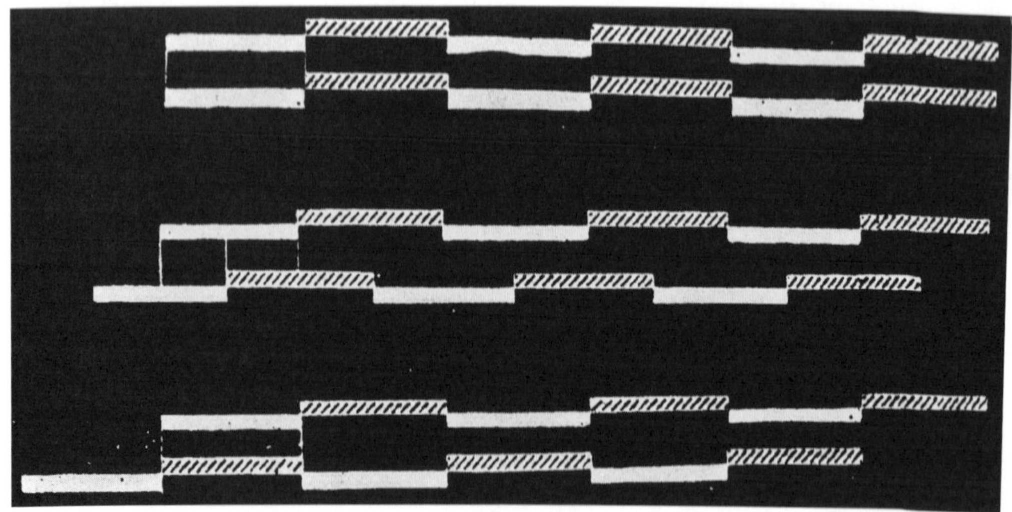

2.2
Three examples of a chronographic
record produced by Étienne-Jules
Marey showing the paces of a horse—
amble, walk, and trot. From Marey's
Movement (1895: 9–11).

providing the means of writing the patterns of human and animal footfalls, or the patterns of hand-falls in the case of the piano player, Marey's odographic and chirographic records showed the key moments when the body touches its supporting surface. More importantly, his time-writing technology provided the means of showing how different bodies produce different temporal patterns, and how bodies perform transitions between one pattern and another (for instance, how a horse alternates from trotting to galloping, or how a soldier shifts from walking to marching). Setting aside the intended application of this research, which was to provide scientific means of improving various modalities of locomotional performance in sports, horse racing, and the army, Marey's work opens up a discourse of movement through its material representation. His capture media suggest that movement may be rescued from an often invisible and inaudible determination. Motion sensation, for Marey, is not enough. To extract a discourse out of movement, it is necessary to hear it, to visualize it, and to think it in its material representation. Only from this material understanding of the temporality of movement can an analytical discourse come about.

Finally, Marey also showed how novel technology could be used to yield this materiality. For example, he acknowledged that while chronography provided the means of expressing the actual sequence in which horses' feet strike the ground, the technology gave no information as to the place on the physical ground struck by the feet. In other words, it showed no sense of proxemic space—only a representation of pure temporality. To address this problem, he compiled records of horse hoofmarks on the racetrack, then created a table of six parallel tracks comparing an ordinary walk, a long stride, a quick walk, an amble, a jog-trot, and a gallop. Once again, because he was concerned with the tempo of the movement—rather than its space—he made the decision to cut out and stitch together different spatial strips, creating a temporal situation in which different tracks are placed alongside one another. Ultimately, the idea of cutting and stitching strips of durational movement illustrates just how different the chronemic paradigm is from the proxemic approaches discussed in part I. Indeed, Marey's experiments are an example of how technology may afford ways of recomposing movement through the editing of time. Thus, he paved the way for a modern understanding of movement representation in terms of technological capture systems capable of manipulating durational movement—what I will refer to in terms of time control technology, or *chronokinesis*.

Cyclographic times

Building on Marey's initiative, advances in the scientific account of live movement were carried out by Wilhelm Braune and Otto Fischer in Germany (see chapter 3) and Nikolai Bernstein in the Soviet Union. Bernstein believed Marey's methodological innovations formed the basis of a rigorously scientific quantitative investigation of movements with the aid of technological mediation. Inspired by Marey's technical achievements, Bernstein pioneered a number of novel graphic technologies in the 1920s and 1930s that could illustrate every phase of time-dependent movement while

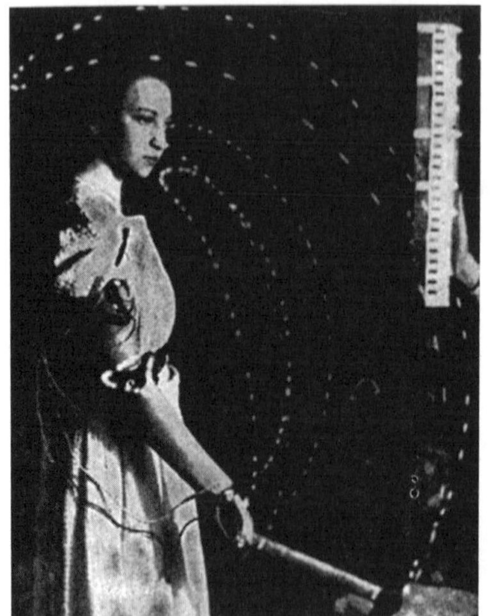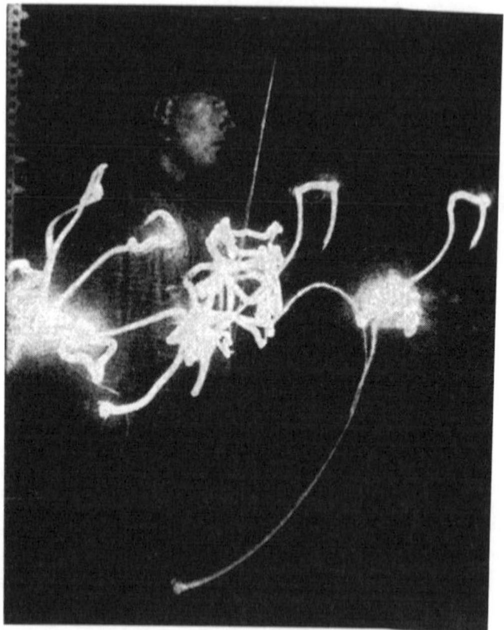

2.3
Chronocyclographic method of rational-
izing hammering motion, developed at
Alexei Gastev's Central Institute of Labor.
From Fülöp-Miller, *The Mind and Face of
Bolshevism* (1927).

directly representing the interrelations between successive phases. Whereas Marey was concerned with recordable *phases* of timed movement, which could be defined by quantitative and qualitative changes, Bernstein spoke of movement *cycles*, which were tridimensional representations of continuous movement times. To fully explain these processes, I will carry out in part III a detailed examination of the pathways of specific moving objects. But for now I will outline the evolution of a temporal parameter within represented movement, particularly in relation to the cyclographic technology developed by Bernstein and his associates.

Bernstein's team applied two significant technical developments to the observation of time parameters. The first is the use of electric light bulbs as marker points, or what are now referred to as moving light displays (MLDs). Fischer and Braune had experimented with these in the late 1890s, using Geissler tubes attached to a subject. Bernstein's second improvement was the use of long-exposure photographic techniques, which, unlike Marey's time-lapse photography, allowed the capture of a durational rather than instantaneous period of time. A cyclographic representation of a walking or running subject would thus appear on the sensitized plate as a series of luminous displacements. So, rather than considering the passage of time in terms of discontinuous points of contact, as Marey had done, Bernstein could observe the continuous passage of time over the course of a movement cycle. Long exposure times enabled the MLDs attached to the subjects to be captured and recorded as continuous movement curves known as cyclograms. Although cyclography became widely used in a number of technical contexts, it became most prominent within the study of industrial movement and labor, not only in Bernstein's research program in the Soviet Union but also in the cyclographic studies of Frank and Lillian Gilbreth in the United States, conducted as part of their time-motion studies of industrial labor. The Gilbreths also developed their own movement notation system based on the reading of cyclograms—albeit, unlike Marey's code, their therblig notation was encumbered by a horoscope-like array of symbols.

Bernstein spoke of "movement geometry," a language that led to the expression of each point of a free body in tridimensional space. To achieve a direct representation of this movement geometry, however, he had to develop the technological means. To this effect, Fischer and Braune's chronocyclograph was used as the basis for a new optical motion capture system at the Laboratory of Photocinematography (led by Nikolai Tikhonov), housed at Alexei Gastev's Central Institute of Labor (CIT) in Moscow. Tikhonov and Bernstein captured CIT cadets using photographic sequences of images of selected lines or points on the body. The drawback was that small, complex, and repetitive movements whose trajectories always came back to the same starting point could not be easily recorded. And because these were precisely the types of movement CIT directors wanted to investigate, Bernstein and Tikhonov used an improved version of the cyclograph apparatus developed by Braune and Fischer in the 1890s. Unlike chronophotography, cyclography could capture micromotions and cyclical movements.

Bernstein combined the advantages of the cyclographic method with new recording techniques that could register live movement in terms of motion curves or waves removed from the photographic print and representable as abstract graphisms on paper, which could be mathematically analyzed. The method was known as kymocyclography (literally, the writing of wave cycles). What Bernstein's kymocyclograms showed, in effect, was that the variation between movement trajectories and their complexity decreases significantly, even in richly innervated systems, under the action of human movement automation. As such, motion capture technology and the underlying mathematical language provided a scientific validation to a state-sponsored initiative to automate and mechanize industrial labor following a Soviet Taylorist ideology. Science and technology of motion were thus applied to a cultural transformation of human motor into machine motor. Representation was yet again the means of developing an eidetic and political discourse to carry out this cultural reprogramming of the human kinetic experience (Salazar Sutil, forthcoming).

Finally, it is important to note that Bernstein's contributions lay not so much in the physical issuance of motor activity, but mainly in the coordination of human movement and posture by the central nervous system. One of the main pioneers in the field of motor control and motor learning, Bernstein argued that it was necessary to attend to the coordination of neurophysical human movement in both its spatial and temporal determinations. He described the neurophysical issuance of a motor program based on exact and time-dependent formula. In other words, Bernstein hypothesized the existence in the central nervous system of a naturally occurring language of neural motor planning (see chapter 11), which involved the arousal of nerve tissue via the activation of a dormant or latent code. He then assumed that the motor system must unfold at this neural level as a temporal structure involving stamped-in connections between elementary engrams, creating either a chain or comb logic. This chain then assumed an engrammatic form, which Bernstein considered to be a structural physiology of movement at the neural level—or what he called the "motor program" or "motor image" (Bernstein 1984a).

Bernstein's insights lead me to an important conclusion: the representation of the temporality of movement, and the formal construction of a morphology of movement, are not only relevant to the external and largely arbitrary representation of movement as language. Before movement is expressed in material form as a culturally specific inscriptional medium, it is programmed (it is precoded and prewritten) by the brain according to a natural language of movement that is subsequently read and performed by the body. Thus, the creation of a temporal structure of movement and the coding of this information occur at the level of an internal motor program before they exist in external, culturally determined languages of movement representation. Before the graphic language of movement come natural neurophysical codes. Likewise, before movement time is represented or performed, it exists as the temporality of thought.

Chronography to chronokinesis

Marey's chronograph apparatus and chronophotographic guns can be viewed historically as two very different types of motion-recording technology that developed quickly over the second half of the nineteenth century. On the one hand, the chronograph is a stimulus-responsive apparatus that records physical movement by means of a needle-point pen, similar to a long line of medical technologies including the myograph, the cardiograph, the cyclograph, and the dynamograph—ancestors of modern-day medical technologies like eMRI. On the other hand, Marey's chronophotographic gun, a refined version of Muybridge's chronophotographic technology, is part of a different tradition of technological artifacts devoted to the capture, recomposition, and projection of illusionary movement—ancestors of modern film. That Marey was able to apply his physiological research to these two types of technologies indicates that, at the time, there was no clear disciplinary differentiation between these technological advances. It is easy to forget that Marey's work was intended to be a scientific contribution, since, from a contemporary perspective, cinematographic media is often considered part of the artistic and creative industries. Yet the historical trajectory of motion-recording technologies tended toward specialization, with a further distinction between medical technologies of motion recording and more creative technologies. In addition, there has been a significant shift in the material conditions of movement studies, as is clearly evidenced by the evolution of Marey's research program in the early decades of the twentieth century. Whereas his chronographs and chronophotographs evidence a historical period of technological enterprise devoted to the automated recording of movement, current technologies have moved away from the pure record and the need to improve the quality of recording. Current technologies can be seen less as recording instruments and more as instruments of control—especially in the computer era. One way that Marey's technologization of movement vision can be historicized, therefore, is in terms of a definitive shift away from a mediation of movement through symbolic language and notation. Today's machines are perhaps more properly considered as instruments of chronokinesis, or time control, which can carry out communicational instructions directly through physical signals, thus bypassing the more removed process of symbolization. The passage from technologies of recording to technologies of control is discussed in part IV of this book, where I argue that computer-aided technology has radically changed the technological mediation of movement and, by extension, our whole culture of movement, especially in the digital context. According to this conceptualization, the defining factor is the enhanced power to manipulate data that computer-aided technologies can afford.

Marey's chronographic apparatuses were capable of registering corporeal movement times chronometrically (i.e., as linear time), but today current developments in image-based and code-based motion recomposition have greatly expanded the possibilities of time control. Instead of registering time as a segmented or continuous line, time-manipulative recording technologies can now afford tridimensional stereoscopic samples of fully embodied time. Computer technology can offer almost complete control over any parameter or axis of movement. Leapfrogging from the rudimentary chronographic record, 3D digital tools afford the splicing, looping, cutting, pasting, and general nondestructive and nonlinear manipulation of time data within a stereoscopic and variously scalable environment. In addition to the technical specificity of different software tools used for 3D motion animation and modeling, chronokinetic technologies have a smooth interoperability that enables a flexible means of combining and synthesizing existing digital platforms.

The term "chronokinesis" is borrowed from science fiction, where time travel and manipulation are a common convention. Chronokinesis is found, for instance, in a great number of fictional characters possessed with psychic, time-controlling powers. The word has its roots in Chronos, the god of time in Greek mythology. However, other mythological traditions are also populated by heroes and deities possessed of the power to control time. The Marvel Comics universe, a rich and eclectic synthesis of world mythology and comics fiction, has featured a number of superhuman beings possessed with time manipulation superpowers, such as the Greek-inspired character of Kronos. Kronos is said to exert control over the souls of deceased mortals, and thus is capable of animating artificial bodies or inanimate matter. The definition of "chronokinesis" in the science-fiction context comprises different forms of time manipulation: e.g., slowing, speeding, stopping, or even reversing time. While science fiction can reference Einstein's physics to support the validity of their heroes' powers, the capacity to change the movement of time need not be a subject only of science fiction. In fact, the power to control time is a key feature of motion-editing and composing technologies.

The graphic design of 3D characters and objects in virtual reality relies, in theory, on those very same powers: namely, slowing, speeding, stopping, or reversing time. But chronokinetic technology can do much more. Within this technological context, character animation software suites like Studio Max (1995–present), Maya (1998–present), and MotionBuilder (2008–present) are examples of how the virtual production of 3D objects and 3D movement enable users to efficiently manipulate spatial and temporal data with great reliability. Advanced character animation technology for virtual production enables users to capture, edit, and play back sampled movement in responsive interactive environments, optimizing the display and control of virtual movement. Rather than just recording and analyzing real-time movement, as Marey's chronographic technologies did, these motion-editing suites provide productivity-geared workflows—i.e., the means of fabricating virtual movement within the framework of motion-specific industry production. Chronokinetic control thus provides movie- and animation-makers with the necessary and comprehensive tools not so much to record as to invent or create movement in an extensible, industry-oriented production platform. In this context, contemporary technologies of movement and time control have enabled the emergence of an industry of movement composition—a commercial kinetopoiesis—that supports the design and production of animated graphic imaging.

And this brings me to a concluding remark: technologies do not only transform *how* we express movement in cultural form. On the other hand, technology does not only impact on the ideologies behind the expression of movement, for instance, by debunking the humanist and masculinist perspective. Technology can also help define *why* we represent movement. Marey needed to find a means of materializing movement, of seeing it in order to read it, because he wanted to understand movement scientifically, and apply this knowledge to improved physiological research in a number of areas including sports and the military. Our need to represent movement today is also dictated by the need to fashion an industry out of movement. Technology is an important factor in determining this shift of practice, this reconsideration of the reasons why we need to represent ourselves in motion. Why do we need ever-changing technologies that can help us see and read our movement? Clearly, because technologies afford enhancing ways of composing movement, of manipulating and controlling represented time and space, and because more powerful ways of seeing, of composing, of designing movement boost a contemporary understanding of smart, mobile, and kinetic economies, where industry players can capitalize on the technologization of motion. Thus, technology can help propel the wider cultural shift of practice from motion discipline to motion control, and from a modern science *of* motion, to an advanced capitalism *in* motion.

3

MOVEMENT FORMS

Form analysis

The preceding chapters paid attention to corporeal movement within tridimensional models of movement space, and what I referred to as the chronemic determination of movement. What follows is a concern for the actual representation of movement forms. I will focus, therefore, on the invisible mark that corporeal movement leaves in its wake. So if the previous chapters dealt with the canvas (i.e., surfaces and volumes), this chapter focuses on the actual brushstrokes. Building on the investments of chapters 1 and 2, I will touch on three key approaches to the representation and analysis of movement forms: graphic drawing, chronophotography, and computography. One fundamental question these graphic media and their respective technologies raise is this: What if we could visualize a passing movement, as opposed to the human body that moves? To do so, one would have to imagine that when we move, we stroke the air that surrounds us, cutting invisible linear pathways through the air. Three different ways in which this invisible mark—this movement form—will be considered, are as trace, as trajectory, and as route.

Although the mediated recording of movement forms is a modern phenomenon, the *idea* that movement can be captured as a residual line is ancient. It finds its prephotographic substrate in the ancient conceptions of movement trace, going back to the paradoxes of movement first proposed by Zeno. The form of movement poses a formal problem. Because the line is continuous and Zeno's arrow is only at a single point of its trajectory at any moment in time, the arrow must be still, even when moving: hence the paradox. What flows from this example is the direct link between form and formalism. From the visual line of an arrow, one can think up a formal problem: formed images elicit abstract or imaginary forms that can, in turn, provoke problems of formal logic or mathematics. This argument underpins my entire discussion: the point of visualizing movement is that one can express an ideal form of movement through optical media. One can see in recorded movement evidence of further abstraction, which helps communicate not only physical intentions but also a kinetic rationality—or even thought itself. Thus, movement becomes a carrier of our voluntary physicality, as well as a medium for the expression of our innermost intellectuality.

Laban (1966) defined the traceform as referring to virtual shapes the body could express in a kind of "form-writing." Like the trajectory of Zeno, which connects the formed image with an abstract mathematical formalism, the traceform is a medium that integrates body and mind. Laban added: "understanding forms with the brain only, or responding to [these forms] with feeling only, has the disadvantage of giving a purely intellectual or sentimental pleasure, without the benefit of their integrating power" (1966, 112). These forms integrate the physical and mental into a holistic mode of thinking—what one might call total movement. In fact, choreutic forms also connect the moving subject with a spiritual sense of interiority, which is why Laban spoke of traceforms as "snail shells of the soul" (115). He concluded that the binding and loosening processes in nature, leading to change between stability and mobility, are not only reflected in the essential forms which our movements take; "they are also the basic content of a language of movement. In order to speak and read this language one must experience [its] alphabet" (114). There are many ways in which one could compile a movement alphabet, as we will see later on. For instance, one can identify the primitive linear forms that movement lines can take (straight, curved, twisted, and rounded). These lines provide basic units of kinetic composition—they are the letters, if you like, that make up more complex morphological structures of scripted or graphically represented movement forms.

The difficulty of studying traceforms and analyzing their intrinsic properties is compounded by the fact that these forms are invisible to the human eye; thus, the traceform poses a problem that is inherently mediological. How can a movement form be visualized? How can we see the writing that is produced during form writing? What kind of communication does this virtual writing help convey, and to what effect? To begin with, I will consider the representation of movement forms as linear traces or strokes created by individual limbs, which can be subsequently visualized as light displays, or luminous lines left behind by a moving body. This visualization of the movement trace is largely the remit of photographic recording, especially via the use of long exposure times. And it is somewhat paradoxical—albeit highly pertinent to this inquiry—that long exposure times should blur objects in motion while retaining the clarity of objects at rest. By the early twentieth century, long-exposure techniques had made their way to scientific and artistic motion research, and to the capture of moving light displays (MLD) attached to human bodies. This medium is today known as light painting or light drawing, and it has an extensive genealogy going back to the chronophotographic studies of Étienne-Jules Marey with photographer/gymnast Georges Demenÿ in the late nineteenth century. Anton Giulio Bragaglia's futurist experiments in photodynamism are perhaps the earliest record of the application of the technique to art photography (more on this to come).

Although it is not possible to generalize about the use of form-writing and light-drawing and the many different applications that the medium has rendered over the years, this chapter intends to show how the materialization of the movement form provides a necessary means for observing and analyzing movement, and thus reprocessing it as an object of material thinking. The passage from form to formalism is central to my understanding of how technology transforms the way we represent our own movement, and how it is possible to evolve language and script out of human movement via specialized technological means.

Finally, it is worth stressing that the medium is treated here as a modality of motion representation that is somewhere between writing and drawing. Although within artistic circles the technique is traditionally referred to as "light painting"—a medium closely associated with the works of Man Ray and Pablo Picasso's collaborations with photographer Gjon Mili—the drawing of traceforms can also be discussed as a form of writing or as an invisible calligraphic medium issued by the entire body, particularly within Man Ray's conception of "space writing," Laban's (1966) treatment of human traceforms as "form writing," and William Forsythe's "room writing" (1999). According to Laban (1966), traceforms are more than just a core compositional element in the visual arts, for the audible arts such as music and oratory also rely on nonvisual types of traceform, which give shape to sounds and rhythms. Thus, form writing is a multimodal system that integrates music and dance, visual and audial form.

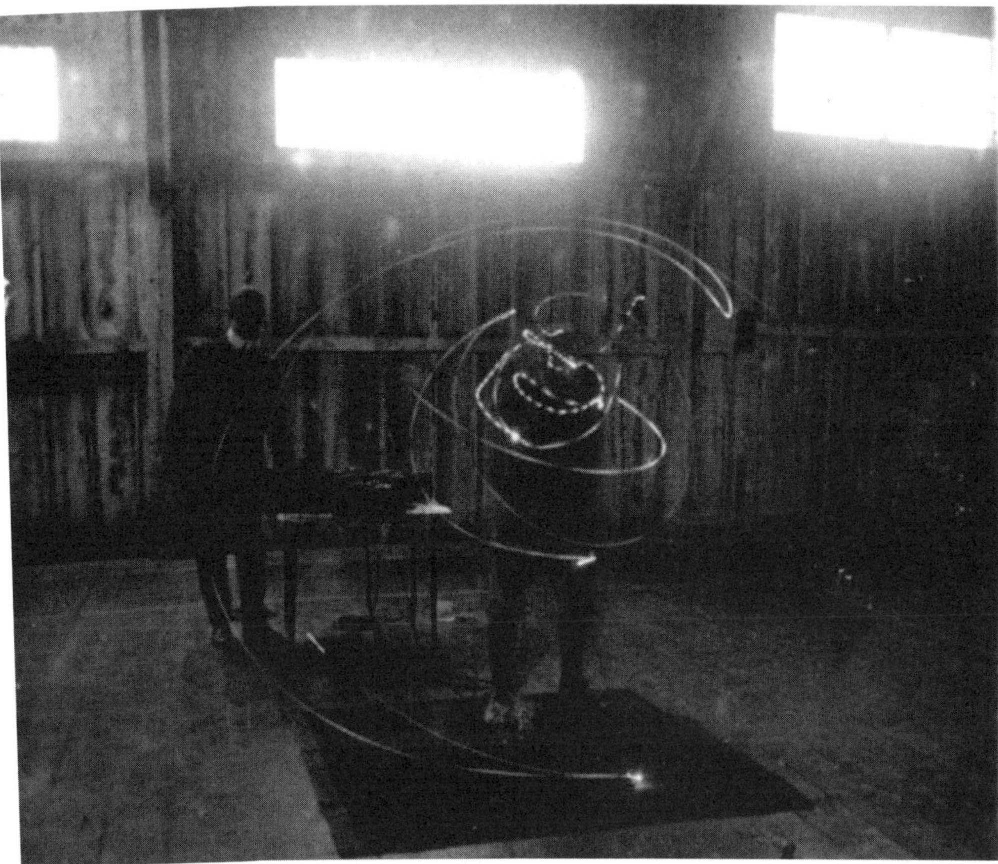

3.1
"Chronocyclegraph of Roger [Howey?], champion golfer,"
c. 1915. Frank B. Gilbreth Motion Study Photographs
(1913–1917). The Kheel Center for Labor-Management
Documentation and Archives in the ILR School at
Cornell University.

3 MOVEMENT FORMS

The chronophotographic trace

According to Marey's graphic method, the observation of relative motion demands a standstill in the unceasing stream of movement. The illusion of a standstill is based on the snapshot or saccadic perception of the human mind, which is able to seize only single phases of an uninterrupted flux. But if human memory is the only faculty left to perpetuate motion, and human memory is incapable of coping with the retention of large amounts of movement data, then an artificial means of connecting preceding and succeeding snapshots is necessary to reconstitute progression. Instead of relying on the chronograph for this permanence, Marey relied on a technological medium developed by English photographer Eadweard Muybridge in the late 1870s known as chronophotography.

Muybridge's chronophotographic instrument was intended to solve basic observational problems elicited by the study of animal locomotion. American industrialist and horseman Leland Stanford approached Muybridge in 1876 because he was interested in developing a scientific approach to gait analysis after having read Marey's book *Animal Mechanism* (1879, first published 1873). Stanford commissioned Muybridge to conduct a scientific experiment using automatically generated photographic sequences that would help recompose the image of a horse's locomotion, and in the process provide an accurate method for the improvement of horseracing performance.

Muybridge's famous 24-frame series of Stanford's running stud, presented in fast motion on his zoopraxiscope in 1877, showed that durational photography could provide an objective vision of movement, breaking down the continuum into discrete units and positions that enabled the scientist to study specific movement sequences (e.g., a galloping horse) at a fine-grained level of detail. Marey improved Muybridge's chronophotographic technique by developing his own experimental equipment. Perhaps the best-known of Marey's many devices was the chronophotographic gun, an instrument capable of shooting 12 consecutive frames a second, all of which were recorded on the same film.

Marey's ambition went beyond photographing movement sequences, however; he wanted to develop an estimative scientific method that could recover the exact positions and motion pathways of designated reference points located on his moving subjects. A mathematical calculation of movement based on graphic records was developed using a method that would subsequently be known as photogrammetry. The term, coined in 1893 by German architect Albrecht Meydenbauer, was originally used to refer to a photographic image documenting buildings and important cultural heritage sites, but it was later expanded to include the analytical and photo-mathematical study of moving objects in Sebastian Finsterwalder's "Geometric Fundamentals of Photogrammetry" (1899). (Incidentally, this line of work can be described as the methodological basis of contemporary motion capture methods of movement analysis.)

Like Muybridge's pioneering work in the United States, Marey's chronophotography removed optical sensation from human observation, in this case to delegate vision to an automated and mechanized process. Light exposure would be captured by a sensitized plate rather than by human organs (i.e., the eye). Rather than embedding an image onto the retina, the photographic image was chemically processed and artificially delivered onto sensitized material (film or print paper). To represent movement forms in the material medium of a chronophotographic print, Marey faced two main technical problems. The first was how to accurately capture a subject in motion. He discovered that when the captured subject is shot against a black backdrop, no impression is left on the sensitized plate because the subject is not lit. If the subject is properly illuminated, however, or if parts of the subject are illuminated, then the photographic shot will leave a record in the sensitized plate. The second problem Marey faced was how to actually record the movement forms themselves, rather than the subject's whole body. In addition to eliminating the background exposure to make his targets easier to find and measure, Marey introduced retroreflective targeting to track specific body parts, thus producing more abstract representations of movement where the target and background exposures were almost completely independent of each other. So, by dressing the subject in a black body suit and attaching reflective tapes along bodily extremities to represent specific limbs, Marey could effectively capture the skeletal forms of a moving subject as though it were geometry in motion—a process he called "chronophotographic geometry."

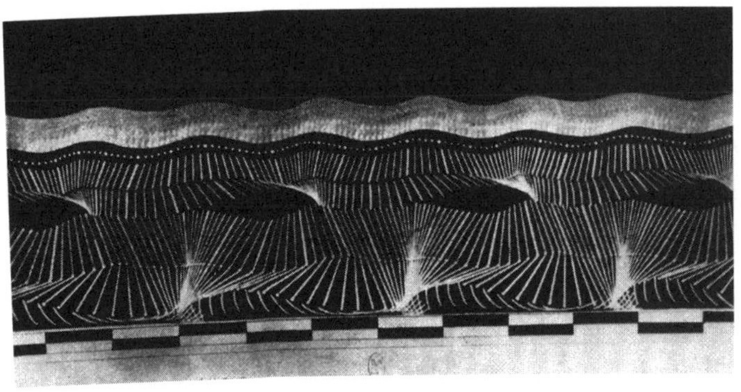

3.2
Étienne-Jules Marey's geometric
chronophotograph of Georges Demenÿ
walking, 1883.

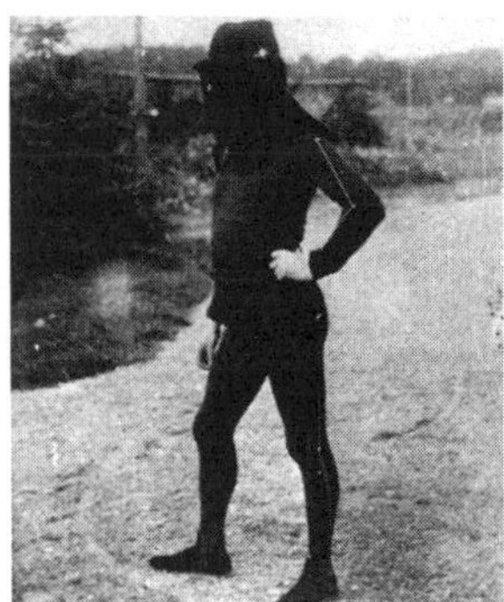

3.3
Georges Demenÿ in the black suit
with striping and points for geometric
chronophotography, 1883.

By adopting Muybridge's chronophotographic technology and developing it into a photogram-metric study of skeletal tracking, Marey achieved the technical and technological means of seeing the underlying structure of human movement and representing it in graphic form. Chronophotographic trace capture could thus be described as a kind of palimpsest—writing inscribed over the photographic image. By following the process described, Marey could obtain a curved traceline of movement or a geometric representation of the bodily structure of movement, which could be effectively super-imposed over the photographic image of the human body. Peter Weibel calls this "opseography," or "writing over the seeing" (1996, 341). By placing a diagrammatic layer over the photo image, Marey could move beyond an image-based observation of the trace and identify the underlying kinematic formalism. Thus, there are two visual layers to his chronophotographic representation of movement: one is the photographic capture image, and the other is the diagrammatic writing he obtains from using his novel photogrammetric technique, which can then be expressed in more abstract terms as a purely mathematical representation. Once again, the passage from form to formalism is achieved in order to illustrate an essential structure underlying human movement. This said, Marey maintained that geometry ought to be considered an experimental science, not an abstract branch of mathemat-ics. Thus, he wrote that the conception of a geometrical straight line "did not evolve from man's brain as a purely abstract expression, but rather entered therein, on seeing a stretched thread or some other rectilinear object" (1895, 24).

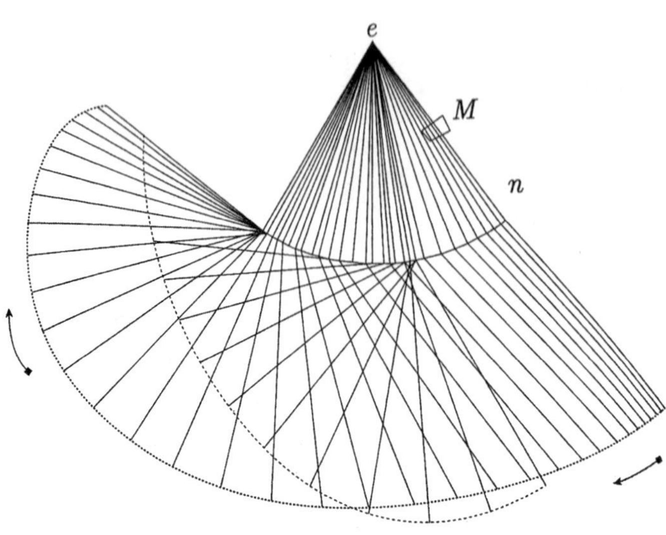

3.4
Articulated pendulum, after a chronograph by Étienne-Jules Marey (1894). Diagram taken from Zalamea (2012). Courtesy of Fernando Zalamea.

Colombian philosopher Fernando Zalamea (2012) draws on an 1894 chronophotographic print produced by Marey to express the idea that chronophotographic geometry can be developed into a more abstract mathematical formalization. Weibel's notion of opseography can now be pushed further, so that in addition to writing on an image, one can derive mathematical languages from a movement image. Zalamea uses Marey's visualization as a conceptual model that explains the historical development of mathematics from static to dynamic conceptions of line and space—from immobile to mobile mathematics. In other words, mathematics evolved, according to Zalamea's chronophotographic model, from a simple and inarticulate language to a highly articulated and movement-specific series of synthetic languages. According to this author, whereas the top part of the pendulum determines knowledge of movement in terms of a fixed frontier (e.g., classical geometry), the lower part harbors a sophisticated articulation between webs and scales of concepts and models (e.g., modern and contemporary geometry). Zalamea argues that the chronophotographic visual model helps explain how contemporary mathematical thinking opens itself up to the curvatures characteristic of the living and the animated—indeed, to the mobile base of mathematics: "the kinesis, the movement, the transformation, or the gait, let us say, of concepts governs all of mathematics" (2012, 330). According to this reading, mathematical ideas refer to a method of positions, to a becoming or a peregrination, which means that mathematics opens itself to the study of living movement.

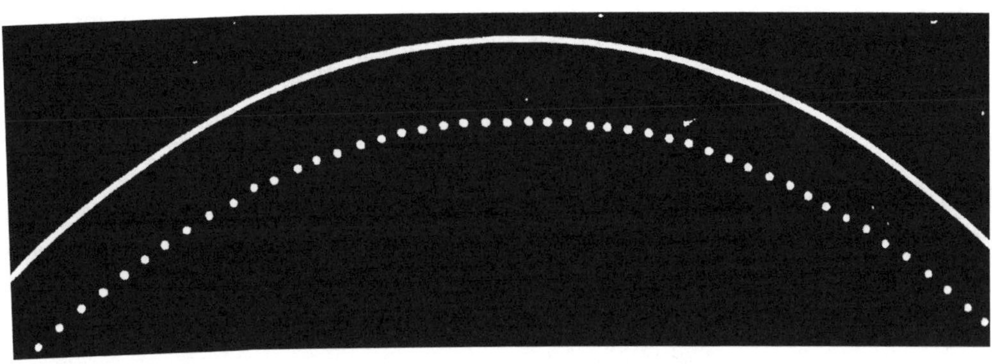

3.5
Simple trajectory and chronophotographic trajectory of a shiny ball
moving along a dark backdrop,
taken from Étienne-Jules Marey's
Movement (1895), 55.

Although Marey himself commented that the mathematical study of his chronophotographic records would be rather complicated and of limited interest, he also acknowledged that the movement of certain bodies typically produces forms analogous to mathematical forms. And even though Marey's analysis stopped short of reading the language laid over the image as opseographic mathematics, he nonetheless recognized that the language he could extract from the image was not verbal but formal. To illustrate this point, in the early 1890s he photographed the flight of a ball—an experiment that is in many ways similar to Zeno's problem of the arrow in flight. Marey knew that if he shot his illuminated ball against a black backdrop, a continuous impression would be left on the sensitized plate. But he added a variable. He did not photograph the continuous path of the ball but a path broken at regular intervals. Thus, he wished to categorize movement in terms of two recorded modalities of the movement form. Marey used the terms "simple trajectory" and "chronophotographic trajectory" to refer to the same distinction between continuous and broken lines of recorded movement that he had previously announced using chronographic technology. These lines written on the photographic print show that, in addition to a movement space and a movement time, understanding of movement is refined by an awareness of the resulting form—and that form can be excluded from space and real time in order to be treated as an independent object of abstract thought.

Computing trajectories

One of the shortcomings of photogrammetry is that it conveys a two-dimensional account of movement. By means of triangulation, a technique that involves taking photographs from at least two different locations, a so-called line of sight can be projected from the camera to determinable points on the captured object, which can be mathematically intersected to produce three-dimensional coordinates. Tridimensional coordinate measurement is a major step toward modern methods for motion capture and analysis. Progress in this area is due to German physiologist Wilhelm Braune and mathematician Otto Fischer. The leap from a graphic to a computational approach was achieved only a year after Marey first published *Le mouvement* (1894). Braune and Fischer's *The Human Gait*, today considered a classic on gait studies, was published in its first version in 1895. It stands as the first modern computational approach to the study of movement trajectories, half a century before the emergence of the electronic computer. Whereas in contemporary photogrammetry, computer algorithms are typically employed as customized tools for the minimization of error, Fischer and Braune had to compute their data manually, or with a mechanical calculator, which made their approach not only error-prone but also highly dependent on technological improvement.

Fischer and Braune's experimental work is divided into two key stages. A chronophotographic capture studio equipped with a four-camera protocol yielded x, y, and two z coordinates of selected points on a subject's body. Mathematical modeling was then used to describe the images as three-dimensional coordinates, or as kinematic equations (I will return to Fischer and Braune's equations of motion in due course). To recover the exact positions and motion pathways of designated references in this tridimensional setup, the points located on the moving subject were not reflective tapes, as in Marey's laboratory, but Geissler tubes, which had to be suitably taped to the subject to prevent electrocution, and which were designed to flash intermittently (26 times per second) to provide a chronophotographic trajectory.

The computational approach produced a vast amount of information about the whole extent or range of a movement form: the amplitude of particular points of the body, the limits of the changes of the angles of articulation, the distribution of the trajectories of the movements in relation to surrounding objects, and the exact forms of these trajectories. Using this data-rich approach, and by turning the images into mathematical variables, Braune and Fischer claimed to have obtained the full transcription of the process of movement. Through their work, the methodology had evolved beyond a literal opseographic approach. So, whereas Laban's traceforms and Marey's traces preserve their identity as optical forms, Braune and Fischer's computational trajectories lose this identity in order to be identified as graphical computations of a function. This consolidation of a numerical and tabular representation of the movement form provides far more abstract realizations of the movement stroke than Marey's chronophotographic geometry.

An improved computational study of movement trajectories was also developed, as I pointed out in the preceding chapter, by Nikolai Bernstein in Soviet Russia. The spatial data acquisition through mirror registration pioneered by Bernstein and his collaborators provided a refined version of Marey's chronophotography. Bernstein's method for calculating motion pathways using this protocol was called cyclogrammetry, which is effectively a tridimensional photogrammetry. To evaluate cyclograms, Bernstein constructed two-dimensional charts (similar to Braune and Fischer's tables) that used a parallel coordinate system rather than standard Cartesian coordinates.

What concerns me here is not so much the details of how the computation was carried out and to what effect, but the evident co-relation between the development of technological mediation in the observation of live movement and the rise of an increasingly mathematized language of human description and analysis. The introduction of high-end technological apparatuses to capture movement at increasingly fine-grained levels of detail and at much improved levels of resolution provokes a profound historical shift in the understanding of human movement in three significant ways. First, trajectory computation abstracts the movement form to the extent that trajectories yield numerical or algebraic descriptions of movement rather than visual descriptions. Second, because this knowledge is quantitative in nature and there are greater capabilities for information gathering, movement analysis must account for such vast volumes of numerical data that the study of human movement became too difficult for humans to process without using computers. Third, due to the many possibilities of capturing and quantifying any physical movement at fine-grained levels using high-end technology, the field has evolved into considerably more specialized and discipline-specific studies of human movement.

This three-pronged effect of the computational approach can be glossed further. The cultural tendency to turn scientific photographic imaging into mathematical and computational formalisms is in turn marked by a tendency to understand movement not only as human bodily motion (i.e., a physical activity such as locomotional gait) but also as social, cultural, or economic motion. A trajectory can refer both to the lines left behind by a tracked point on a subject's body and to basic patterns of individual or collective behavior and opinion. At this higher level of generalization, movement trajectory can refer to consumer behavior, to patterns of financial fluctuation, and to any number of nonphysical trajectories occurring in an abstract sense of movement space. Methodologically, however, trajectory computation can address both concrete and abstract determinations in much the same way: through the collation of quantitative data over a period of capture time, which is analyzed using customized mathematical models. A computer system is perfectly capable of performing factor analysis on referendum data, consumer behavior data, or a dataset derived from physical movement. Thus, trajectories and patterns of movement explain the way groups of people think, the way they act, the way they consume, and the way they physically move in stereospace.

Braune and Fischer's work may well have been hampered by miscalculation, but this is perhaps the only major difference between their work and contemporary approaches, at least from the methodological point of view. Furthermore, their computational approach questions the reliability of human calculative agency, at least in terms of processing significant amounts of quantified movement information. In turn, the quantitative method has made the science of movement fully dependent on computerization. This computerization of the knowledge of movement further reinforces quantification, provoking a circular loop where the production of complex data demands sophisticated computational analysis tools, which in turn produces further data complexity.

Trajectory analysis has moved a long way since Marey's trace studies in the late nineteenth century. While Marey's work is referenced today mainly for its historical merits, the accuracy and specialization of this science is questionable, especially when compared to the physiological and biomedical sciences carried out now. Whereas the nineteenth-century science of movement produced a wide array of disparate motion research programs that were conducted largely in the name of physiology, contemporary research has become considerably more area- and problem-specific. It is not easy to generalize the study of human movement in a contemporary context, not least because of the greater number of subfields and subdisciplines devoted to different ambits of human movement research. These are spread over wide areas of expert application including sports science, dance science, military science, biomedicine, biomechanics, robotics, computer vision, geographic mobility and transport, and surveillance and security, to mention but a few. Nor is the crossover of expertise between these disciplines straightforward, given the degree of area specialization. Integrating motion research in the computerized era is extremely difficult, even from the broad perspective taken here. Technology has empowered disciplines to see human movement at such a level of detail and with such granular understanding that the plan of integration is, in many cases, all but wishful thinking. In fact, the more science and technology continue to drive the specialization and minutiae of movement knowledge, the harder it becomes to zoom back to a perspective that can be shared between disciplines. There is hope for integration, though, and scientific-artistic experiments today can draw on Marey's work if in need of inspiration.

Multidimensional tracewriting in C8's *Flatland*

The spatiality of writing is an issue that preoccupied French paleontologist and archaeologist André Leroi-Gourhan. In his book *Gesture and Speech* (1993), this author argues that Western alphabetic writing is two-dimensional because of the linearity of spoken language. Written language, which leaves linear traces in space, is subordinated to spoken language, which is linear in time. Leroi-Gourhan associates this linearity with the linearity of rational thought. This spatial determination of language can be questioned, however, by adding further dimensions to thought, from which one might expect further dimensions of language to emerge. We return to an idea I brought up in the introduction, and which I borrowed from Rodolfo Llinás (2002): linguistic language is part of a larger category that includes motor languages. In other words, speech and words are only one fraction of the entire production of language generated by the human brain, and which includes motor languages. Rational thought is only one portion of the entire thought production of the human brain, which also involves physical thinking.

In a similar vein, Leroi-Gourhan (1993) challenged the purely linear fashion in which language is represented in its linguistic form (i.e., as lines of sound or as lines of words), in order to champion the concept of "multidimensional graphism," which he considered to be a primitive mode of inscription incorporating phonetic, visual, and kinetic elements into a more synthetic type of script. In his discussion of Chinese writing, Leroi-Gourhan argues that at least one-half of any given character in this script form is pictographic, while the other is phonetic. He also describes parasitic images in this system, which can cause the reader's thoughts to stray in a manner irrelevant to the real object of notation. Leroi-Gourhan further suggests that the images conveyed by Chinese pictography are worthless as images, and yet give us an inkling of a mode of thought based on diffuse multidimensional configurations. Rather than functioning as an imprisoned language within linear phoneticism, the scripted Chinese character opens up multiple ways of thinking by mixing phonetic and visual associations.

It is also worth noting that Leroi-Gourhan discusses multidimensional graphism in relation to a primitive mind. After all, gesture, which he argues underpins spoken language, can be regarded as though it were an atavism of language. Gesture tends to throw us back to former ways of expressing thought, returning us to a prosody of grunts, guttural noises and hand movements, onomatopoeia, clicks, flicks, beeps, and taps. This throwback is in no way meant in a pejorative or indeed a progressive sense—language in a digital-era context is changing toward a recovery of dynamic gesture and gestural interfaces, thus challenging alphabeticism and linear speech. If gesture is a throwback, it is also a forward throw; gesture is a language of the past as well as a language of the forthcoming digital era—gesture is an atavism for the future.

Multidimensional graphism, according to Leroi-Gourhan's theory, enables a modality of written inscription that is nonlinear, in that it starts from no single bodily source. If we return to the geometric understanding of movement in terms of a shift from point to line, then one could argue that the reason we produce lines of speech is that the movement of sound originates from a single point—the mouth organ. Speech is a form of communication that can be imprisoned, to borrow the term from Leroi-Gourhan, within a single sensory modality. Speech is primarily sonic, whereas written language is primarily graphic or visual. Multidimensional tracewriting, on the other hand, originates in any part of the multidimensional body, or in various parts simultaneously. Furthermore, multidimensional tracewriting is a cross-modal form of script, in the sense that it can mix different sense schemata. For instance, as Leroi-Gourhan points out, Chinese pictograms combine images, ideas, and sounds. We can expand the possibilities of mixture here to a combination of different technologies of writing, so that in addition to creating script that is hybrid in a sense-schematic way, tracewriting can create script that combines various technologies of inscription, and not only handwriting. The exploration of a multidimensional writing technology is, for instance, one of the main intentions behind *Flatland*, a digital dance theater piece I created along with the artistic collaborative C8 in 2012, based on E. A. Abbott's novella of that title from 1888.[1]

Our most immediate source of inspiration was not experimental photography, however, but Abbott's original text, where the notion of a "luminous wake" (1992, 60) is used to refer to the trajectory that a physical object leaves behind when moving, and which can be visualized in terms of a linear form. The "luminous wake" refers specifically to the movement forms left behind during the rise of a 3D character (Sphere) out of the 2D world of Flatland. C8's production opens with a dream sequence, in which the character of Square, played by Sarah Rogers, is dreaming of a passage from the flat world of linear thought and linear movement forms to a universe of complex nonlinear arrangements of gesture. It is worth taking a moment to ponder the terms I use: wake and awakening. The wake is the form that a moving body leaves behind, but as this body moves and leaves a wake in its path, so it awakens the body to a new reality, a new dimension of kinetic being. C8 was interested in developing a system capable of representing this luminous wake using more than a single technological medium (time-lapse photography). In other words, C8's ambition was to combine a mechanical approach to the parsing of movement (time lapse and long exposure) with a computational approach. This piece proposed a mixed-technology setup for the creative composition of traceform writing, comprising four strands: (1) time-lapse photography, (2) algorithmic visualization (using a Jitter package for MAX/MSP), (3) slit scan video, and (4) Microsoft Kinect motion capture.

By attaching a moving light display (a portable LED) to the extremities of the dancer's body, we could record traces of movement using time-lapse photography. This camera setting enabled us to capture the moving light attached to the dancers' wrists and ankles, and to represent graphically Abbott's notion of the "luminous wake." In addition, because the sequences were shot in darkness, what we obtained in the final video image is the sight of a gesture without its body. Here is the first step toward a removal of the gesture and the kinetic form from its concrete materiality and physicality, in order to enter the domain of abstract representation. The question is, what level of physicality remains, if any, as we progress into this domain of abstraction, and as we move from form to formalism? I will return to this question in chapter 12.

Unlike the historical representations of cyclography discussed earlier, C8's goal was to produce imagery within an artistic and creative context, or to be more precise, to develop a technique germane to the digital media arts. Thus, the optical gestures derived from C8's photographic capture were subsequently treated as a computer database. *Flatland*'s multidimensionality points to the possibility of writing in a hyperspatial domain. By treating the different images as data inputs in a Max Jitter software setup, C8 recombined the unitary gestures using looped operations, provoking a random process of movement recomposition. In other words, we fed each single luminous wake or traceform into the computer engine, which looped them randomly and rendered them into algorithmically recombined images. One could argue that in this way, the original captured gestures were turned into hypergestures. Rather than being generated by the body, these hypergestures were excluded from the body, and then fed as data to the computer, where they were subsequently looped to produce a heightened degree of visual complexity. What C8's digital version of a multidimensional tracewriting points to is not the disappearance of the body, but the survival of the bodily gesture across different planes of representation and technological media. Even if the body's presence disappears, the bodily gesture remains, and with it an essential trace of the body. Thus, the atavism of bodily gesture also reveals its endurance within computational forms of mediation and within complicated data processing operations.

Although most of the looped images of the dancer's movement curves were complex, some of the compositions created algorithmically appeared fairly uncomplicated to the eye, as we can see from figures 3.6 and 3.7. Because the process of composition was left to the computer and to a process of trial and error, the modality of writing we explored in this project is not controlled entirely by the writer, author, composer, or choreographer. This agency is shared between humans and computers, leading to more aleatoric ways of generating kinetopoietic structures. The result was a language that is entirely alographic. What I mean is that the computer yielded cryptic visual configurations and hypergestures that convey thought before rational logic—or else thought before the representation of straight lines and before the linearization of thought from A to B to C. C8's hypergestures were like a series of hieroglyphs that provoke expressions of thought whose logical meaning could

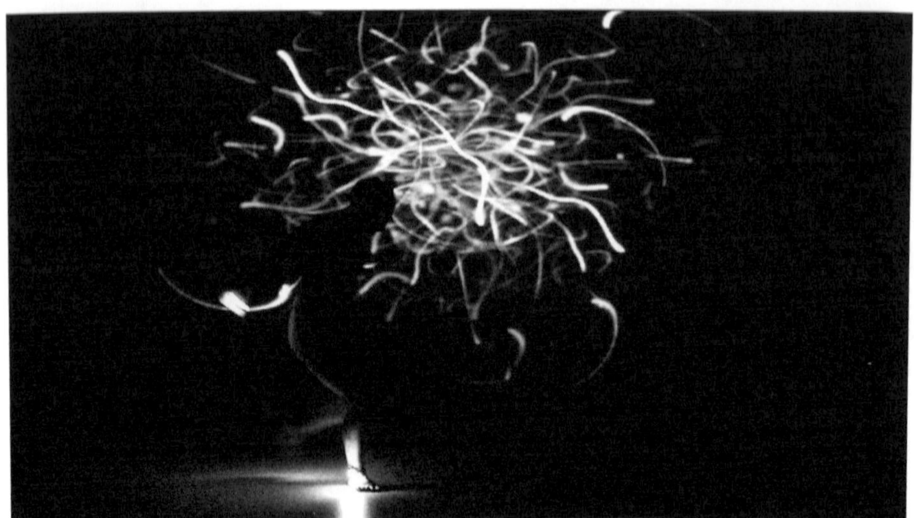

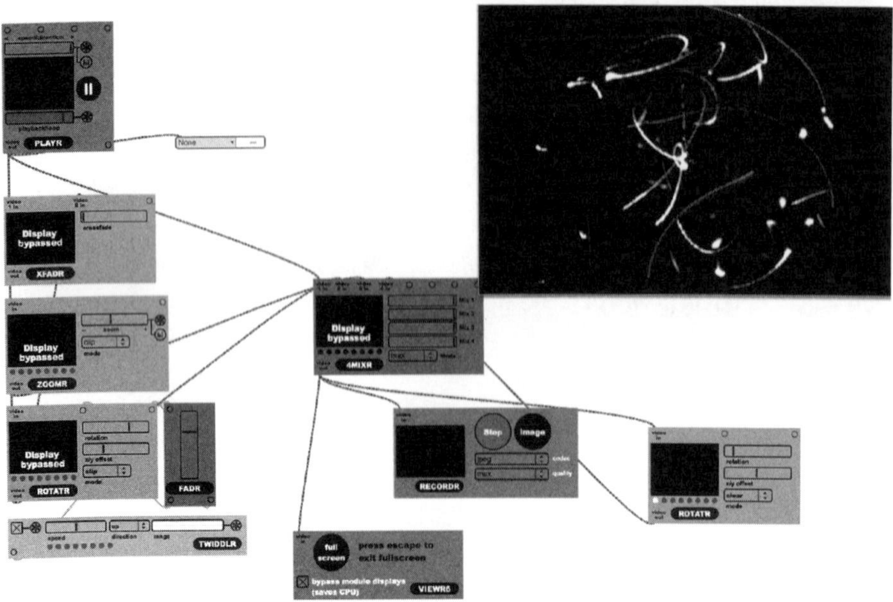

3.6
Still from C8's *Flatland* (2013). Performer:
Sarah Rogers. Directed by Nicolás Salazar Sutil.
Video by Sebastián Melo.

3.7
MAX MSP Visual Programming language
workflow for C8's *Flatland* (2013).

not be fathomed by rational thought, but only through physical thought. By allowing the language to emerge from more sources than one (i.e., the whole body rather than the mouth), and by mixing various processes and technologies of representation, C8's computographic representation of the looped gesture or hypergesture performs the idea of multidimensional graphism as a kind of gestural alogography—a language or protolanguage that is still babbling and groping toward logical signification, but which ultimately escapes it or supersedes it.

William Forsythe: Tracewriter

Earlier, I mentioned that the dialogue between different scientific and artistic disciplines of movement research is today fraught with a number of difficulties. There are exceptions, of course, and one is the interaction between the disciplines of computer science and dance. Within this context, American choreographer William Forsythe must take credit, particularly in terms of combining mathematical, computational, choreological, and choreographic skill sets into a collaborative effort aimed at studying and creatively representing human movement in the medium of dance. Forsythe's research is perhaps best known from his *Improvisation Technologies: A Tool for the Analytical Dance Eye*. Originally published in CD-ROM format in 1998 and later as an interactive DVD, *Improvisation Technologies* is an opseographic study in Marey's tradition, insofar as it is based on the idea that one can write over the seeing of movement (see Weibel 1996). In this case, one can create graphic animations over a source video. *Improvisation Technologies* is thus a collection of short video clips that show Forsythe illustrating a series of basic kinetic formalisms used in his choreographic practice. Each demonstration is overlaid by an animated computer-generated line that graphically depicts the traceforms and virtual shapes performed by Forsythe. Originally developed as a training tool for new members of Ballet Frankfurt, *Improvisation Technologies* has become a well-known example of the computational approach to dance studies, and it is widely referenced within the literature.

What is significant about this project is not only its cross-disciplinary and cross-modal examination of corporeal movement analysis. It also reveals what Laban (1966) had referred to as an inner vision of forms, which exists prior to any concrete realization in choreographic, architectonic, sculptural, or indeed musical morphology. Forsythe's formalisms could be said to be the consequence of an inner vision of movement, what I will define later in this book as "innermotion." Forsythe calls this "physical thinking," a faculty that is activated by the mental and physical processing of kinetic formalisms. This thinking informs specific choreographic techniques developed by Forsythe over the course of his work as a ballet and contemporary dance practitioner. He also expands on Laban's notion of form writing by producing a set of opseographic exercises that show bodily movements that are less balletic and less choreutic, and thus more liable to torsion, to decenteredness, and to disharmony, but which can nonetheless generate rich written signs over the visual record. As such, one could argue that Forsythe is a creative writer as well as a dancer. Or rather, a traceform writer.

One of the many writing techniques featured in *Improvisation Technology* is "room writing." In room writing, Forsythe applies a technical understanding of the bodily traceform to a free-compositional technique, so that the traceform can be used to scribble and write freely on the virtual canvas of a kinespheric room. According to Forsythe, room writing involves imagining surround architectures through the reduction of objects to their geometric content. Thus, a doorknob can be described as a circle, a door can be described as a rectangle, and so on. To draw such objects, one must arbitrarily choose a point on the body that is carrying the movement line, usually a joint or pivot point. In Forsythe's example of room writing, one can use the elbow joint to create two arcs that make up a doorknob (circle), and one's forearms to delineate the contours of a door (rectangle). The object of the exercise is to bring about a dynamic transformation of the dancer and the dancer's virtual space. In Forsythe's illustration, the aim is to brush aside the doorknob or push the door over, and to take the body of the dancer off balance.

We can expand the concept of the room so that it refers to a more abstract space occupied by a mover, rather than an imaginary habitational room with doors and doorknobs. To write onto an abstract sense of room is precisely what contemporary trajectory computation can do, as I conceptualized it earlier. To write trajectories over the changing patterns of people's attitudes, trends, and beliefs via data analysis is one way of abstracting the sense of kinetic room available to human movement. From this perspective, technological tools for the analytical eye are widespread across many fields of kinetic practice, not only dance. A shift from a virtual sense of the room, as featured in *Improvisation Technologies*, to a more abstract room created by pure data is precisely the direction Forsythe takes in a later work, *One Flat Thing, reproduced (Synchronous Objects)* from 2009.

One aim of this project was to put together a transdisciplinary team of specialists to create an online digital system capable of interpreting dance choreography in terms of abstract data. From the strictly choreographic perspective, *One Flat Thing, reproduced* is an ensemble piece that examines the principles of counterpoint. According to Norah Zuniga Shaw's definition (2009), counterpoint can be defined as "a field of action in which the intermittent and irregular coincidence of attributes between organizational elements produces an ordered interplay."[2] The piece is thus conceived in terms of three interwoven structural systems: movement material, cueing, and alignments. "Alignment" here refers to short instances of synchronization between dancers in which performed actions share some attributes but not necessarily all. Forsythe's piece is therefore constructed as a system of liaisons, an apparatus of physicalized logic bound by analogous choreographic shapes, related timings, or corresponding directional flows of movement. Whereas the clockwork mechanics of *One Flat Thing, reproduced* are hard to visualize with the naked eye, given the invisibility of the choreographic traceform, the piece is conceived as a digital object, at the center of which is the effort to animate these invisible shapes and structures.

Developed at Ohio State University by Palazzi et al. (2009), *Synchronous Objects* is a web-based tool first used to interpret *One Flat Thing, reproduced*'s counterpoint as computational data. By combining information derived from two different views (top and front), *Synchronous Objects* was able to generate three-dimensional data for each dancer's location, which was subsequently visualized using inventive computational instruments created by the developers. The result is a process whereby visual complexity can be simplified to single units of a traceform structure, via basic algorithmic computations of movement trajectories. As in C8's case, the result is a choreographic rendition of hypergestures and hyperrhythms that arise from the treatment of the visual input as purely computational and quantitative data.

This data dance is intended not to document or reconstruct an original dance piece, but to reinvent it. In turning the original dance into visualized statistical, geographic, and kinematic data, and thus synthesizing the concrete movements of the dancers with abstract parameters obtained via trajectory computation, the dance speaks to the profoundly kinetic (and potentially choreographic) nature of data. As the authors themselves point out, although quantification requires a reductive process that necessarily obscures certain aspects of knowledge (the dancers' intentions, performance quality, and kinesthetic awareness), quantitative data also reveals key aspects of a movement (in this case, structure). *Synchronous Objects* ultimately interprets the formal thought and physical intelligence of a dancer at a greater level of mathematical and computational complexity. The project website confirms this idea, particularly when the authors admit they had to put together a multidisciplinary methodological framework drawing on dance, design, computer science, geography, and statistics in order to carry out this work. The project triggers the question: Is all data danceable? Can any body of data be visualized aesthetically and artistically to produce an aesthetic appreciation of the beauty of endlessly moving information? Is the entire stream of data in the World Wide Web imaginable as an immense choreography of electronic traces of movement?

INNERMOTION

INNERMOTION

PART II

INNERMOTION

4

The mug joke

Up until now I have discussed the representation of movement space only via the language of classical geometry. When Aristotle pointed out that "in mathematics motion is a fiction" (1961, 443), he was referring to solid geometry, which within the classical tradition involves a language of frozen structures. Thus, Aristotle presented a description of the structure of bipedal movement in terms of an isosceles triangle—the brachylogy becomes a little easier if we consider that isosceles means "equal legs" in Greek. Whereas previously I considered how geometric objects without duration (solids) help represent movement in stillness, my intention now is to recruit a modern model of mathematical space in order to tackle a different model—one that can represent objects and bodies through change and through movement.

Henri Bergson's theory of duration provides a starting point for the radical shake-up of solid geometrical thinking, at least in the philosophical literature. According to Bergson, the representation of motion in solids is a vain attempt to represent movement: "never can these solids strung upon a solid make up for that duration which flows." Bergson added: "What we actually obtain in this way is an artificial imitation of the internal life, a static equivalent which will lend itself better to the requirements of logic and language" (1983, 4). Beneath linguistic representation, however, lies a sense of continuity and duration, which Bergson argues cannot be cut or broken down (unless we turn movement into language). This critique of solid geometric thinking, which feels so at home among inanimate things, is also an invitation to consider categories of language beyond the linguistic regime. Perhaps in taking up Bergson's critique we are getting closer to that general category proposed by Llinás (2002)—and mentioned in my introduction—according to which linguistic language may be seen to be part of a broader program of constructed languages that include morphological movement, and which are controlled by the brain. If the logic of solids manages to secure only a representation of external and static images of moving objects, then what is needed to integrate the knowledge of human movement is an awareness of that "internal life," which Bergson associated with duration. How can we gain access to that interior universe using only linguistic language and rational thought? How can we see the entrails of movement, the flow of physical thought before it curls up into morphologically constructed movement languages?

To address this problem, I will distinguish two fundamental levels of human motion, which for the sake of argument I will define as "innermotion" and "outermotion." Whereas outermotion concerns the external representation of movement as language, which I tackled in part I, innermotion concerns deep structures of formal movement, before these become rigidified in crystalline language. My intention is thus to discover the prelinguistic base of a movement system, in order to argue that underlying the language of movement is a deeper layer involving the more fluid and flowing forms of motional thinking. My intention is to unpack this double-decked theory in three stages.

First, I will introduce the reader to general topology, a mathematical model of space that overcomes the shortcomings Bergson identified within solid geometry. To distinguish general topology from other branches of mathematical topology (especially networks, which I will consider separately later on), I will address this discipline strictly in terms of one of its core functions: continuity. The main argument of this chapter is that the relationship between inner and outer can be represented in cultural theory as a continuous mapping from one domain of movement to another, thus creating the envelope that is integrated human movement. In other words, topology helps us to understand the relations between inner and outer determinations of human movement, rather than the purely external determinations conveyed by solid geometry.

Next, I will provide a preliminary case study drawing on Jacques Lacan's topological theory of language, which will provide a distillation of this chapter's basic thesis. In Lacan's view, language is the outer layer of the subconscious, which is the deeper mental landscape of the psychic subject. From here, I will turn to focus on psychological topology, a theory that is best exemplified by the experimental films of German-American psychologist Kurt Lewin. Finally, I will flip the methodological approach of this argument on its head. Instead of addressing the psychology of movement, I will move on to the subject of movement psychology. At this final stage of my discussion, I will focus primarily on Rudolf Laban's idea of topological movement and his theory of efforts, which accounts for the internal dynamics underlying external movement. To conclude, and drawing on my own collaborative practice, I will refer to *Labanimations* (2012), a series of three short dance videos that explored the question of how to visualize the dynamic and continuous duration inside external movement.

This leads me to the first stage of my analysis: topology, which is one of the most misunderstood mathematical ideas to have entered cultural and media studies. Topology is not the antithesis or dialectical opposite of geometry. Rather, general topology is a major branch of mathematics dealing with a number of ideas related to space, all of which are generalized in relation to properties that are preserved under continuous deformation or continuous functions. In fact, topology is a modern theory of geometry, a mathematics that is the implicit expression of abstract motion. To provide some degree of disambiguation, I must add that the title of this section refers primarily to the mathematical idea of a map, or a topological mapping. In mathematical topology, a mapping function is a core concept involving continuous input and output relations between two different spatial domains (e.g., two sets or groups). So, when an object from one domain is injected onto another in a continuous fashion, one calls it a mapping. It is this core idea of general topology that cultural theorists have mostly latched onto when they speak, for instance, of a topological turn in cultural theory (see Lury, Parisi, and Terranova, 2012).

Despite a rather restricted use of the term, cultural theoretical topology typically helps articulate the concept of foldedness, which can be generalized in an extramathematical sense to theorize processes involving continuous influences from one domain to another; in this case from innermotion to outermotion and back. Although input and output relations typically involve two domains (i.e., two groups, two sets), topological maps do not portray two spaces, but one space that changes between two or more domains. In other words, a topology describes one thing (one map) which is continuously changing from one state to another, what in the most clichéd of typecasts—to the point of being a mug joke—is often explained with the example of the coffee mug and the doughnut. For a topologist, a coffee mug and a doughnut are the same. Why? Because one shape can turn into the other following a process of continuous deformation. What concerns the topologist are not the two different shapes (coffee mug and doughnut), but the process in between that leads to a continuous deformation. This is why topology is sometimes referred to as "rubber-sheet geometry:" it is a study of objects subjected to rubbery distortion, and to mappings that allow one object to turn continuously into another. So the topologist bites the coffee mug thinking it is a doughnut.

For the present, the joke is intended to help conceptualize a passage from the domain of external movement space to the domain of purely internalized movement, which I will address in subsequent chapters. The joke can be used as a memorable example of how human movement is in fact a map in which thought is turned into physicalization, and physicalization is turned to thought. Like a topological map, human movement is a continuous mapping of inner to outer and outer to inner determinations. Movement is the outer appearance of an inner thought, which is connected continuously to this outer expression by an uncut process from mental to physical formations and back.

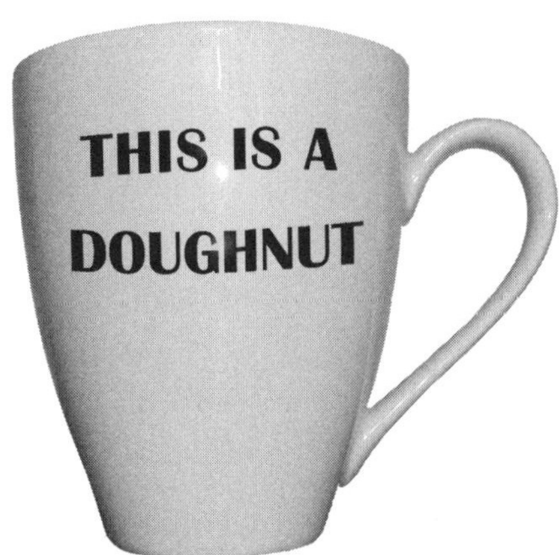

4.1
Mug joke illustrating a popular definition of
mathematical topology. Photoshop design
by Carolina Sequeiros.

Lacan's Moebius band

A. J. Deutsch's science fiction short story "A Subway Named Moebius" (1958, first published 1950) follows the mysterious disappearance of a train in the Boston subway network after the introduction of a new rail line that causes the topology of the network to become infinitely complex.[1] The train's disappearance can be explained by the rail network's infinite number of connective possibilities, which turn the system into a giant hyperdimensional Moebius band, twisting the railway into an other-dimensional track. The premise of the story is that by a supposedly topological rule of thumb, things in the phenomenal world can be made to vanish via an interdimensional twisting operation. But what does science fiction topology have to do with the subject at hand, one might ask? Of course, the mathematics in Deutsch's short story is completely fictional: a train running along a Moebius strip will not, by any mathematical or physical rule, disappear.

In cultural theoretical modeling, topology is also conducive to a kind of fiction: the fiction of concepts. Cultural theoretical topology thus typically addresses the concept of cultural dynamics as a continuous process of bidirectional change. Of particular interest here is Jacques Lacan's Seminar XII (1964–1965), in which the maverick French psychoanalyst and psychiatrist introduced his students to a topological schema for the study of the psychic subject. Lacan discussed topology in terms of identification. For Lacan, the problem starts when the subject becomes and names itself *through* and *in* language. He saw language as a place, a site, wherein the subject is effectively realized. It is clear that the Lacanian self is conceivable in a spatial sense. The space is constituted not by psychological factors, but by the foundations of a language system. Lacan explored this spatialization in relation to four key qualities: indetermination, deception, certainty, and desire. These constitute fundamental ways in which identification is driven along the spatiality of language.

Lacan began Seminar XII with the assumption that the language with which subjects identify themselves is not merely an inanimate object—a lifeless structure. For Lacan, the subject is always a fading thing under a dynamic chain of signifiers. He referred to the construction of a language as a "scaffolding" (1964–1965, 21–22), a term that is, of course, central to Laban's choreutic language as well. Because the objects of language cannot be understood without the subjectivity used to animate them, there is no such thing as pure scaffolding, a pure structure of language. Language machines and tools have been created to be used, and so as to be transformed and evolved by use. In Laban's terms, no choreutic scaffolding can exist without a body or bodily subjectivity that will bring the structure into existence. Like the ensouled crystals of Ernst Haeckel (1999), language is a crystalline system of structures that conform, that are constituted morphologically, within linguistic as well as movement languages, and which continue to evolve organically and according to social, cultural, and environmental conditions of use.

An uncanny similarity between Laban and Lacan can now be detected, way beyond surnominal similarity. For a start, Lacan's thinking is fiendishly cryptic at times, in the same way that Laban's is unwieldily esoteric. In Lacan's examination of the structural analysis of subject identification, the linear structure of concrete discourse and the chains of signification can be ordered and harmonized—just as in Laban's theory of space harmony. Moreover, Lacan's harmonic structures of language can be represented or at least given shape in some sort of notation medium, which Lacan called the "stave," drawing on musical notation. As we will see later on, Laban's system of movement notation also relied on a movement stave.

Instead of advancing a formal system of psychoanalytical notation, however, Lacan proposed the topological modeling of the psychic self. Again, Lacan took his cue from the spatial determination of the psychoanalytical subject. Insofar as one cannot sustain discourse except from an exceptional place—the location of the subject—the subject must thus be spatialized. Lacan called this "the plunge into three-dimensional space of intersubjectivity" (1964–1965, 47). So the study of the subject is by definition a stereotypical analysis, to use the term I put forward earlier in this investigation—except that the objects plunged into this stereotypical space are ever changing by their participation in language, and thus cannot be expressed in the static system of representation of solid geometry. In addition, Lacan proposed to go beyond studying the concrete part of language—what he called "master words"—and turned his attention to what he called the "hole of language," or the suturing of language. This definition of what lies inside and what lies outside language provokes, once again, a move toward a topological way of thinking. In Lacan's view, this ought to be the crux of psychoanalytical interpretations of the psychic subject.

It is clear that Lacan saw language as defined primarily by linguistics, as opposed to movement. His analysis, however, is general and conceptual enough to allow a migration of terms beyond linguistics to a study of movement languages—hence a connection with Laban's work. For instance, Lacan claimed that language is inadequate and insufficient vis-à-vis thought. Language is at first the crystallization imposed mechanically or technologically on the exercise of intelligence; it is a crystalline formation of thought, a compact arrangement of letter-to-letter or word-to-word links making up discontinuous arrangements of thought in the solid spatiality of technologized discourse. Lacan spurs on the debate: "why would language not have been something analogous in its own way to thought, if effectively it was the creation, the secretion, the prolongation of an intelligent act?" (1964–1965, 27). Thinking is an intelligence trying to find itself in the inadequacy that language imposes on it. To this effect, it is not written language (notation), which could best represent the subject as an object of thought: only another object of thought could do that. What best represents thought is a mathematical abstraction: hence the need for mathematical models. Topological objects appealed to Lacan as thinking machines available to thought before entering the plane of the symbolic and therefore before the inappropriate arbitration of word-based language.

In the same way that word-based language enters the real (in the Lacanian sense) and embeds structure within it, so the subject enters language and deforms its crystal structure. In entering language, the subject encounters and passes through an opening—the "hole" Lacan speaks of. What psychoanalysis uncovers, according to him, is the passage from subject to object, from thought to language. It is a strange passage by which, to quote Lacan, "one comes to the between-the-two" (1964–1965, 36). From the subject's perspective, on the other side of the divide is pure and potential language. In the interval, which establishes a correspondence between the inside and the outside, is the world of the dream—Freud's subconscious. Lacan thus helps articulate what is perhaps one of the central premises of this book—movement and language are not the same. Nor are thought and linguistic language the same. Thought is the source of linguistic language, and thought is the source of movement language, from ballet, to choreutics, to gymnastics, to acrobatics, to our own motor-acquired vocabulary of everyday movement. This being "between the two"—between the subject and the object of language, between I and not I—is what provokes the ever-changing topology of self-identification.

74

To provide a visual aid for these abstractions, Lacan held up a Moebius strip to represent to his students the idea of a passage from inside to outside via the continuous surface of self-identification. The importance of the model, he explained, is that one should be able by a certain movement along the band's surface to get from any point of signification to another, so that meaning and the crystallization of a subject's identity are essentially part of a continuous deformation of possibilities. Lacan told his students:

> **the signifier is essentially structured on the model of the aforesaid Moebius surface, ... namely, that it is on the same face, constituting the back and the front that we can encounter the material, the material which here is found to be structured on a phonematic opposition and this something which is not translated but which passes, which passes from one signifier to another in its functioning, in the functioning that belongs to language. (1964–1965, 30)**

The subject is identified, or self-identified, through its existence in language—and not only linguistic language in the way Lacan conceived it. This fictional topology also leaves us with a model of the moving subject, the "I" who expresses its own sense of self via movement. The subject is in the process of becoming itself through its identification with both linguistic and movement languages. We become ourselves insofar as we learn to move in particular ways, insofar as we train to dance, to do sports, to run, to jog, to crystallize a way of moving in relation to gym training, army training, school training, and so on. Insofar as learning motor skills evolves into subjective patterns of embodied movement identities, who we are at any given point in life is expressed in the unique ways in which we walk, stand still, or hold our bodies, the way we carry ourselves in movement. And here is the crux of the matter: both the subject and the crystalline and rigid structure of language exist in a Moebius-like surface. I cannot hold the Moebius strip in my hand to illustrate the point as Lacan did in his seminar. Instead, we must imagine the Moebius band. When a surface strip is made up of two sides, inside and outside, and the surface is twisted, it is never facing in or out but is always changing from one side to the other. This is precisely, according to Lacan, the relationship between subject and language. Neither is static and fixed—not least because they are bound to each other in a relation of difference. Subjects that come to be in language are changed by the continuous twist provoked by language, while language that is embodied by the subject is deformed by the twists of subjectivity.

In Lacan's terms, the subject can exile himself as a result of this situation. In a more kinetic context, the self becomes ecstatic when it learns to move outside its own perceived sense of self. By embracing ecstasy, we learn to evolve beyond a present state of kinetic being, even beyond a present ontology of movement. By moving in "ex-stasis," we break with our established sphere of kinesis, we provoke a rupture of the sphere in the sense proposed by Empedocles and Sloterdijk, thus creating new spheres of movement. Understanding movement from the outside, say from the ecstatic position of digital technology, is one way in which the ontology of human movement can progress to a new sphere of movement and movement representation. Before I turn my attention to the ecstasies of technology, however, I must return to Lacan's argument. When we understand that this sense of outside is connected continuously to our interior self, the subject manages to put himself in a state in between the two. Lacan went on to say that while some might call this "intersubjectivity," intersubjectivity in fact concerns a subject that understands another subject: "that a viscount encounters another viscount, that a policeman encounters another policeman" (1964–1965, 47). The topologies discussed in this chapter are not intersubjective at all. Rather, we must return again to Virilio's "trajective" to find a more appropriate term. As I pointed out in the introduction, in addition to representing the discrete division between subject and object, between movement and language, the trajective is also a trajectory, a path, or a way between. Lacan argued that one had "to trace the paths" of the subject, which he believed to be the main purpose of psychoanalysis (1964–1965, 22). The trajective can be thought of as a band along which we move continuously from subject to object. We are never one or the other, we are never the two put together side by side in a dialectical superimposition. We are always walking along a surface that is changing between subjectivity and objectivity. What is happening in this process of self-identification through language—which is simultaneously a process of deobjectification of language through self—is not a cut, or a translation. Movement is not translated into language only once and for all; it is invented continuously into language. Movement is invented as a language of architecture, of dance, of music, of animation—each evolving infinitely like the subway named Moebius.

Topological psychology via Kurt Lewin's films

Kurt Lewin's book *Principles of Topological Psychology* (1936) offers a number of interesting contributions to a Gestalt theory of topological movement. Lewin's contributions are of interest to me especially because they provide the foundations for a psychological model of movement space. This framework is significant in the context of this discussion for two reasons: the model provides a description of the dynamic interplay between person and environment, or internal and external space, from the point of view of field forces, or forces that are conceived to be psychological forms of movement. Crucially, these forces influence a situation either by driving movement of an individual to a goal (a helping force) or by blocking movement (a hindering force). Secondly, this theory is grounded on the proviso that because of their spatial determination, these fields can be mathematically described in a topological constellation of constructs. What matters here is not the fact that Lewin drew on mathematical topology for a language and a means of representing psychological movement. More importantly, he did not use a static representation of purely external space (using the language of solids), not least because he saw movement as a dynamic and evolving relationship between a changing individual and its changing environment. Thus, he could conceptualize movement in terms of two temporalities—that of the individual evolving from childhood to old age, and that of an environment changing according to social and cultural factors.

Also central to Lewin's analysis is his theory of locomotion. Lewin argued that one moves psychologically through regions of the life space, and thus one is continuously crossing different kinds of boundaries (physical, mental, social), which characterize the permeability of psychological space. He distinguished between particular kinds of locomotion: bodily locomotion, mental locomotion, and social locomotion. For example, a prisoner stuck in a cell is confined by prison walls, which determine this prisoner's bodily locomotion. His capacity to imagine himself outside prison is delimited by the boundaries of thought (mental locomotion), and by restrictions on the prisoners' social interactions set by prison authorities (social locomotion). I will return to these categorizations of locomotion later on. What concerns me more immediately is the sense by which these categories of locomotion help Lewin understand movement from a dynamic perspective.

Inevitably, Lewin grappled with the question of how psychological dynamics could be represented. Because he intended to identify pathways connecting internal life space and external social space, Lewin's preferred model was the Jordan curve. In the mathematical language of topology, a Jordan curve lies closed in the plane, but without self-intersecting. Every Jordan curve divides the plane into an interior region bounded by the curve and an exterior region containing all of the nearby and faraway exterior points. Given its high level of abstraction, the model helped Lewin represent the connection between mind space and physical space, or between physical space and social space, in a vast number of ways involving various aspects of an individual's psychological life. The Jordan curve was intended to illustrate an abstract space that comes into existence through the marking of inner-outer boundaries, which the individual must necessarily cross. Lewin cautioned that symbolic representations should not be seen to correspond primarily to a static situation, but should be viewed as a momentary situation in a continuous process. In other words, in order to reveal how a person's psychological space is dynamically changing in relation to changing field forces and changing boundaries, it is not enough to draw a single diagram. What is needed is a sequence of diagrams—a kind of filmstrip or animated representation of the diagram to show how an individual changes over time in relation to ever-changing environmental conditions. Arguably, it is this need to observe psychological locomotion through moving images—through knowledge in motion—that led Lewin to use film as a medium for the exploration of topological psychology.

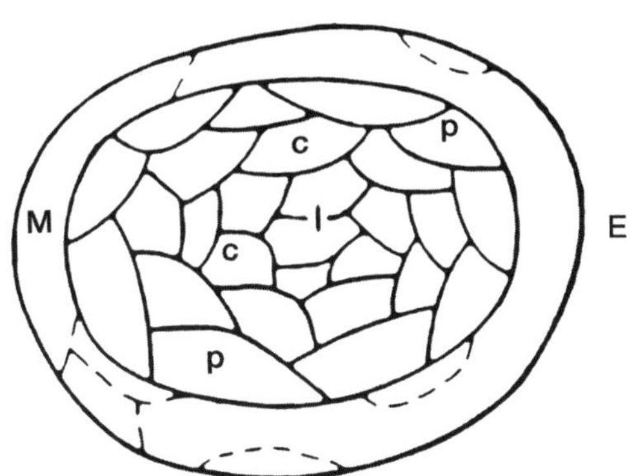

4.2
Topology of the person representing M, motor perceptual region; I, inner-personal region; p, peripheral parts of I; c, central parts of I; and E, environment. Adapted by the author from Kurt Lewin's *Principles of Topological Psychology* (1936, 77).

Lewin knew and was personally inspired by Russian film director Sergei Eisenstein, himself an associate of the so-called Vygotsky circle, an informal personal network of scholars associated with psychologists Lev Vygotsky and Alexander Luria. Film media played an important role in the advancement of Lewin's theories, for it provided him with the means of identifying (or framing) a field force, recording it, and analyzing it. The films are also powerful artistic statements. The subject matter of these films is worthy of attention. They focus on a very specific human biotype, and a very specific movement type. The Lewin films focus primarily on the subject of children's movement.

The films show instances when children take their first steps toward a language of movement. Moreover, the work reveals that the language of movement performed by children is not the same as that of adults. For example, Lewin's short film *Walking Upstairs for the First Time* (1924) explored the notion of boundaries in children's walking, particularly crossing thresholds or going up and down stairs for the first time. These films show that human movement is not a fixed system, but that it evolves organically. In the same way that word-based language is an organic system, according to Lacan, psychological movement is something that grows in us. Lewin's insights also bring to mind the convention in children's fantasy literature of the child's capacity to animate things around them, especially toys. Lewin's films pose a hugely interesting question: Why do children see the world via an animational imagination, and why do they experience movement differently?

In his film *Field Forces as Impediments to a Performance* (1925), Lewin showed the difficulties encountered by several children as they attempted to sit down for the first time on a rock. The film exploits a conflict: in order to sit down, the children must first turn around and thus make a movement contrary to the direction of the goal. To be able to sit on the rock, the girl in Lewin's film has to lose sight of the rock—hence the conflict. Lewin's most substantial film is *The Child and the World* (1931), directed by Eberhard Frowein. This film is significant because it shows the evolution of a child from birth to about the age of ten. As one of the first experimental films on psychological movement to include sound, the film is also of significance in that it conveys the sonic perception of movement by the child. By immersing the eye and ear of the viewer within a child's perspective of the world, the film allows viewers to understand a world that is intensely animated, which is perceived by the child as the magic of motion. The film takes us through a number of emblematic moments: from a baby discovering the possibilities of self-motorization and shaking a rattle, to a toddler watching cars and trams go past his window, to the menacing shadows moving on the walls of a child's bedroom at night.

Showing movement from a child's perspective, and being able to show that a child moves and perceives the kinetic experience differently from an adult, ultimately reveals that movement grows in us as our bodies and minds grow. Movement representation is not confined to a static diagram linking inner and outer relations: it is a faculty that we acquire, that we cognitively evolve, and that we train and refine throughout our lives. From the perspective of a child, at least according to Lewin's films, movement is the way in which knowledge of the world can be accessed before worded language. To learn to move is to learn how to insert oneself within a structured understanding of the world, and thus to enter a world where things have been deanimated or demystified by convention— that is, by language. Once inside that structural and ordered world of movement, our kinetic identities continue to change and evolve, sometimes helped toward new goals, sometimes hampered. But because movement is ultimately liable to physical conditions, the ongoing transformation of our kinetic identities first awakened in childhood must eventually wane. Just as movement grows in us and crystallizes into more rigid kinetic identities as we grow up, so movement decays in us, degenerating into an unintelligent senility. I am reminded of Samuel Beckett's wheelchair-bound character of Hamm, in the play *Endgame*, who calls out a sad eulogy to movement: "Why was it so long coming. ... If I can hold my peace, and sit quiet, it will be all over with sound and motion, all over and done with" (1990, 126). This topological enveloping of inner and outer movement—this ever-changing and growing kinetic identity—finally shrinks into a knot, a knuckle, a self that is prostrate and silent. Hamm has become kinetically unintelligent, incapable of creating expressive and meaningful representations of a moving self. Like him, the childhood of movement depicted in Lewin's films will be lost, and the children will become invalids, reliant on walking-stick technology to keep moving, or rather, to keep an artificial sense of movement going on inside.

Topological movement theory

As opposed to a psychology of movement, Laban explored the field of movement psychology. In particular, he was interested in the relationships between expenditure and recovery of movement energy, which formed the subject of his unpublished book *Effort and Recovery*. Left unfinished at the time of Laban's death in 1958, the manuscript deals primarily with Laban's understanding of movement economy and movement work psychology. As part of his research into motor control and the neurophysical issuance of movement, Laban also addressed the mental and bodily aspects of effort as a compensatory relationship. In what remains of this chapter, I will call on Laban to reinforce the idea that integrating inner and outer domains of movement can be represented through topological models, and I will expand on the possibilities of developing a topological vision of these relationships through film and videographic media.

In "Topological Explanations, Qualitative Aspects," intended as chapter 4 of his book *Effort and Recovery*, Laban addressed his theory of efforts explicitly in terms of a topological determination. As in a previous book on the subject (coauthored with management consultant F. C. Lawrence), Laban wanted to analyze certain physical movements in relation to fundamental properties of effort expenditure and recovery. This line of thought originated in the observation of industrial movement in a number of key factories in postwar Britain, with the goal of developing a theory of movement economy that could help workers become more efficient and effective. The manuscript exemplifies a shift in Laban's research, and a move toward the development of a kind of experiential movement psychology based on simple observational methods that could be applied in a number of related fields, including therapy, consultancy, and management profiling. Each chapter in this book would have contained an observational case study exhibiting a certain principle governing the relationship between effort and recovery. The case study in Laban's chapter on topological relations describes a meeting between three people, two of whom had quarreled, and depicts the resolution of the quarrel and the recovery of a harmonic relationship via the mediation of a pedantic instructor.

According to Laban, there are two directions in the flow of energy: the inverted tendency toward recovery, and the everted tendency toward effort, or practical action. This inverted flow and everted counterflow of energy produce two types of forms. One, which we have already addressed, is the traceform: the outer dimension of a movement form. The other involves what Laban (1966) called the "shadow form," i.e., forms that show the inverted direction of an animational flow, and which are almost imperceptible actions that convey the recovery of energy by the body. Unlike traceforms, which are performed in the space outside the body, Laban's shadow forms are "inversions of the flow constantly interpolated into the everted flow" (1953, 119). To represent a dynamospheric form, one has to consider positions that are constantly changing according to emotional, psychological, and sensory dynamics affecting the internal formation of movement. In other words, dynamic movement, in Laban's theory, refers to a complex array of continuous emotional, psychic, and intellec-

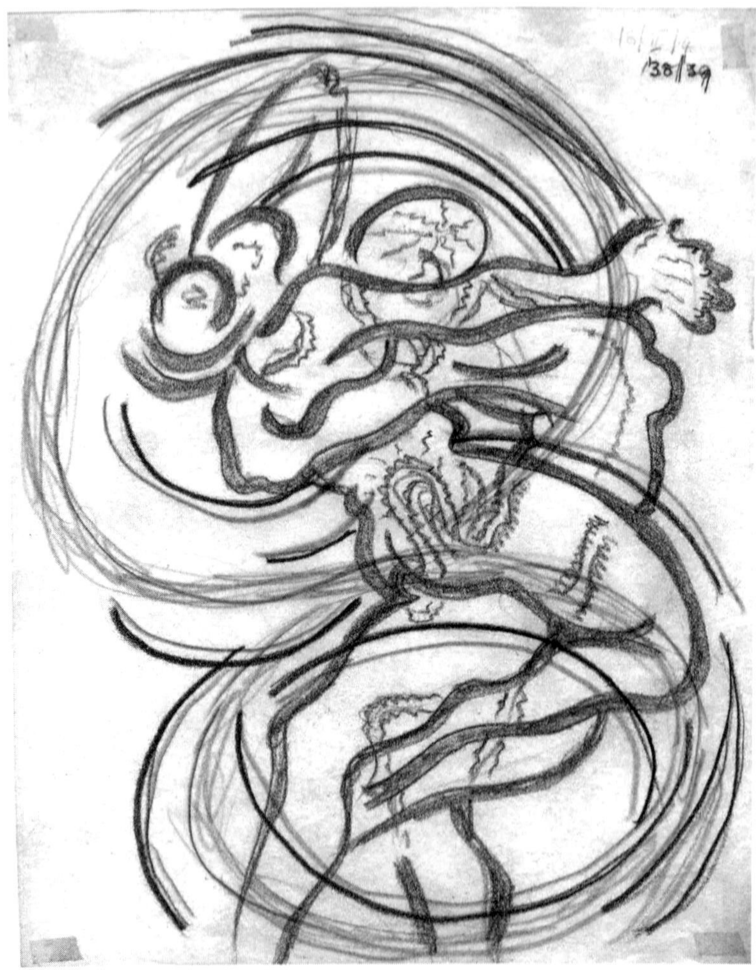

4.3
Figures in Lemniscate, c. 1938–1940.
Drawing by Rudolf Laban in black
and red crayon of two figures copulating
within a figure-eight loop. Laban Archive,
National Resource Centre for Dance,
University of Surrey, L/C/3/100.

tive forces that constitute the inside of outwardly performed movement. So, whereas traceforms are the expressions of visible movement in outer space, and can be accounted for in terms of point-to-point and numerable relations, shadow forms are interconnected spatially with one another by uncountable transitory positions.

Echoing Nikolai Bernstein's theory of the topology of the motor field,[2] Laban argued that to understand the process of effort and recovery or the spending and reinvesting of energy, one has to pay attention to qualitative properties. Thus, functional industrial actions like hammering or drilling could be examined in terms of measurable properties. This is precisely what Bernstein had tried to do in his application of cyclographic analysis to industrial movement in 1920s Russia. But when it comes to understanding qualitative differences and reversions into opposites, Laban argued the contrary: "Yardsticks, stop-watches, and other measuring implements fail utterly" (Laban 1953, 120). Rather than finding support in the language of solid geometry, which as we have seen is the basis for the choreutic shaping of harmonic movement, Laban's theory of efforts drew on mathematical topology. According to him, this is a language where nonmetric spatial relationships are investigated, especially those related to properties that are not altered by questions of size or shape.

As two examples of operations that might exhibit a topological relation, Laban argued that a right-hand glove can be turned inside out in order to fit on a left hand, and that the furry hide growing on the outside of an animal can be inverted when turned into a coat. Both cases illustrate a property-preserving relation (right-handed to left-handed and outside to inside). Both cases also exemplify, following two different operations, that the objects in question remain functionally the same. Laban then applied this logic to actual motor actions in order to describe definite movement functions, such as circuit movements where inside and outside are transformed one into the other, or where left and right are transformed seamlessly as part of the same continuous action. Take a function like feeding, for instance. Whatever the size and shape of the organism, feeding remains essentially the same: the goal is to incorporate an external element (food, nutrients) into an internal digestive system, which then must externalize the residual components. Feeding actions are therefore constant functions. The same applies to sex. Regardless of the size of the bodies involved or the duration of the action itself, sexual activity is generally experienced as a qualitative sensory exchange between two or more bodies.

Laban expressed the topological relationship of sexual intercourse in terms of a Moebius-like movement pattern. Sex is a motor activity involving differentiated bodies that are folded one onto the other by the act of penetration. This activity is defined by its intensive rather than quantitative determination. The quantitative determination of the bodies involved—exact size, magnitude, or proportion—is not necessarily relevant, nor is the extensive determination of the movement—for instance, how many singled-out moves are necessary to complete the act or how long these movements take. Unlike choreutic movement, which can be broken down into point-to-point intervals, effort movements are intensive and can be observed only in terms of continuous phases. Thus, the intensive properties of efforts are said to decline or peak, as in the case of sexual intercourse.

Finally, Laban conceived his theory of topological movement to understand not only non-metric space relations but also nonmetric time relations. He wrote that time appears as an experience of change from one position to another. As opposed to the progressive duration of movement times, which Marey found to be essentially chronometric, Laban spoke of the "protension" of time. Protensity is a nonmetric relationship, a positional property independent of any size or length of duration. Laban wrote that waiting for someone is an excellent example of protensity: "It is irrelevant whether the waiting has a longer or shorter duration, or whether it takes any exactly measurable period of time at all. It remains waiting, and it is implied in any kind of sustainment of the production of a change" (1953, 139). The same applies to the time taken by feeding and sex: fast food and quick sex undermine the basic premise of their protension.

Videography of the dynamosphere

Laban represented the inner and outer domains of human movement in two ways. First, he proposed conceptual and practical models, such as the so-called seven-link chain, which is similar to Jacques Lacan's Moebius strip.[3] To represent the formation of inner dynamics, Laban (1966) was also inspired by topological models such as knots, lemniscates, and what he called the "inverted circle." These furnished him with basic models of the dynamosphere, which can be defined as the inner dimension of the kinesphere. These models also supported Laban's interpretation of fundamental inner forms involving relations of opposition (opening and closing, or stable and labile), which determine the continuous mapping function involved in the inner dynamics of human movement. The other way Laban managed to represent the inner and outer domains of human movement is through the use of graphic media, especially drawing, sketching, and film.

Crucially, Laban experimented with the medium of film to visualize the dynamospheric mood of human movement. His unpublished script "Film about the Harmonious Movement of the Human Body" (1984) is structured into five short sequences or dances. These five sequences progress from an inner determination of movement (dynamosphere) to an outer determination (kinesphere), resulting in a cultic dance. Laban describes a figure that appears against a dark background, who breathes, walks, bends, and stretches. A close-up shot of limbs and torso reveals details of these external movements. Laban writes: "The dark background becomes spatially articulated. One can see the inside of a crystalline cavity. Movements are adapted to the spatial articulation" (1984, 1). But as the space starts to transform and becomes less rigid, less crystalline, so the movements of the dancer become continuous lines drawn into the space by limbs (arms, torso, legs), becoming visible as "shining circles, clusters of rays and rotating ribbons" (2). Within this swirl and blur of movement, other figures suddenly appear until a larger group is formed. Laban then superimposes images from nature—clouds, water, branches of trees—and prescribes the use of time-lapse to superimpose the image of an unfolding flower. Next, mechanical bodies reveal "free space-motifs, twisted bands and lemniscates" (4)—that is, dynamospheric forms characterized by their continuous deformation or topological function. Human movement changes into natural patterns, which in turn change into machinic movement. The point of this imagery, it seems to me, is that the inner dynamics of movement is a common reservoir of forms shared by human and nonhuman kinetic entities. Eventually, the forms become "schematic shapes, structures and architectures" (3). The script concludes with a section entitled "Film-thoughts," which explains the thinking behind the film's visuals. Here, Laban argues that the intention of the piece was to integrate logical thought and poetic pictures to represent "what is in between, [which] is neither fish nor flesh" (5). The film demands a concentration on the flow of pictures and on a mapped flow from the spatialized architecture and language of movement to its inner sense, and back again.

Laban added:

This logic is the logic of movement. These pictures are movement pictures. A film with text. The text should neither explain pictures nor divert from them, but supplement them. Logic has a marvelous flow. It should, however, not be misused for the establishment of theories, but for the sharpening of the understanding of constant flow and for its integration. (1984, 6)

As we have seen, Laban's film begins with an external structure, a crystal. The film then shows the inside of this crystal, and it provides a number of associations between the representation of this internal logic of movement in humans, in natural patterns, and in machinic movement patterns. What matters are not the different external representations of movement but the internal sense, what Laban calls "the logic of movement." This logic is inside language, and it features dynamic stresses that contain the emotional, affective, and psychic contents of total movement. To be able to see (or think) the inside of movement, and thus to be able to integrate the inner and the outer, a topological mapping is needed that reveals something that is neither fish nor flesh—movement that is made simultaneously of the continuous and deformable forms of free thought as they approach the structures and syntax of an external language. This, then, constitutes the logic of movement, according to Laban, and this is an idea I want to highlight, since I will take it up again later.

It is worth pointing out that Laban's film experiment can be compared to Anton Giulio Bragaglia's futurist experiments in photodynamism,[4] which according to the Italian avant-garde photographer was developed to challenge the analytical and external representations of movement produced by Marey and his chronophotographic geometries. Like Laban's logic of movement, Bragaglia's photodynamism was intended to reveal images in a distorted state via the medium of long-exposure photography, in order to show how objects are inevitably transformed in movement. Bragaglia wrote: "We seek the interior essence of things: pure movement; and we prefer to see everything in motion,

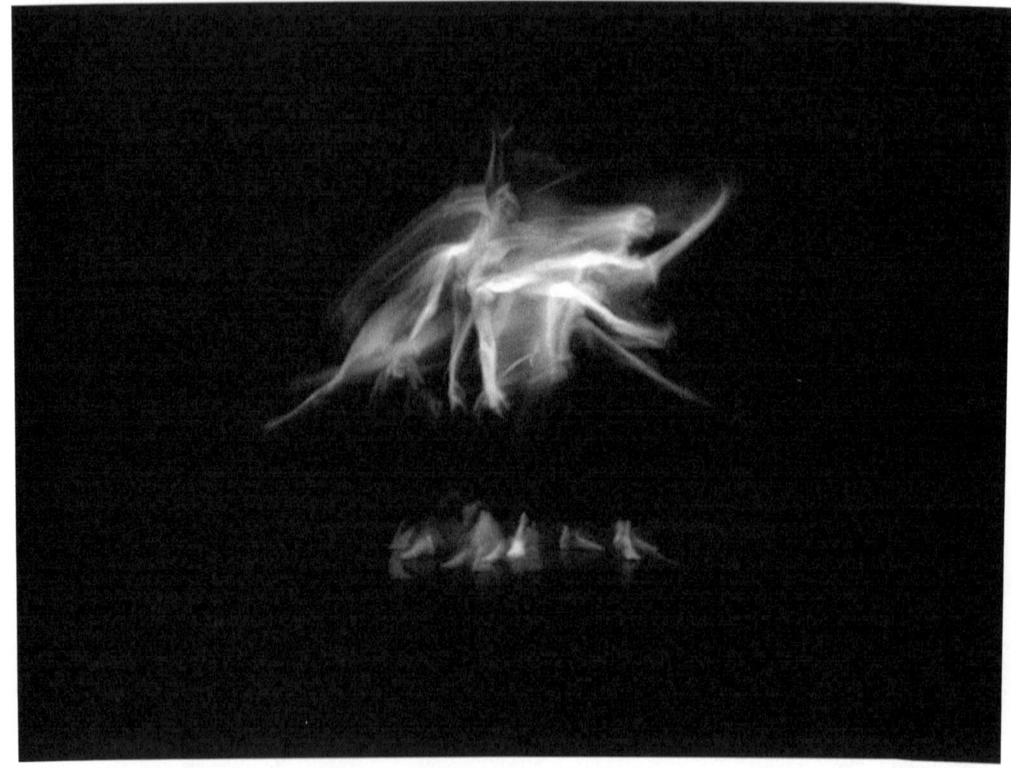

4.4
Still from *Labanimations* (2012). Concept by
Nicolás Salazar Sutil. Choreography and
performance by Melina Scialom. Directed
by Sebastián Melo.

since as things are dematerialized in motion they become idealized, while still retaining, deep down, a strong skeleton of truth" (1973, 42). Both Bragaglia and Laban show how a technological medium (in this case long exposure) can help us see movement from the inside out. This ecstatic vision of movement leads, as Bragaglia himself implies in his manifesto (1973), to a unique technological vision that transforms the way we see the world by giving us vision (knowledge) of a world that exists in motion, of a world that whirls.

Labanimations (2012) is a series of three short videos inspired by both Laban's film experiments in time-lapse cinema and Bragaglia's futurist photodynamism. Conceived by the author, directed by Sebastián Melo, and choreographed by Melina Scialom, this project was prompted by a series of questions Bragaglia raised about the failures of Marey's analytical vision of movement. But exactly how does Bragaglia's photodynamism provoke the means of seeing movement from the inside? And to what extent can variations in speed, direction, and intensity be used in time-based media in order to avoid the trap of mimicking the interiority of movement? Perhaps long exposure times can enable a set of strategies which, although not attempting to completely reveal the inside, at least reveal a more dynamic, less rational and more intuitive representation of innermotion. *Labanimations* demands an attention from the viewer that resists the purely external representation of fixed shapes and frozen poses.

The focal point for this project was a set of three original drawings by Rudolf Laban.[5] Although the drawings are distinctly geometrical depictions of human movement, upon close inspection they also reveal dynamic linear and color patterns, evincing an internalized sense of movement. In order to reimagine the drawings, we used long exposure times to create a motion blur that would bring forth a dynamic content. In other words, our aim was to imagine the inside of these drawings, and to express the inner content through a dynamic medium. Taking the drawings as a starting point, the dancer performed a sequence that consisted of one single phrase repeated for 20 to 30 minutes in a loop. Unbroken repetition enabled the performer to enter a state of fluidity or continuity.

In attempting to recover the dynamic content of the dancer's movement while having to efface the choreographic structure itself through motion blur, *Labanimations* highlights the basic problem of motion vision: the camera is always set at a distance from the moving object. Vision is always projective, and therefore *Labanimations* is a projected (and thus fictional) sense of the movement's inside. The swirling continuities and continuously deforming virtual volumes that are created by the photographic medium do not reveal the interior of the dancer's movement, but rather show the optical effect that her movement has on the camera. Inevitably, this piece is intended to show not so much the power of the camera to *see* the movement as its failure to connect with the object at a kinesthetic level, and its irrevocable condition as an external eye. The videography then points back to the original drawings, and reveals that these too are externalized representations of lived inner movement observed by Laban himself.

But there is a (Moebius) twist in this argument. The photographic eye is an external and artificial organ that sees superficial effects. Yet it manages to pick up more than external structures of movement. Time-lapse manages to record also dynamic qualities like speed, direction, weight, intensity. These properties belie an internal sense of movement. Thus, we were reminded that movement is never entirely inside or outside, but that the logic of movement, which is supposedly an envelope of inner and outer, cannot be segmented or divided. The connection between what goes on inside and what appears to the eye externally is continuous. In being able to capture these dynamic and inner moods of movement, the long-exposure camera eye is capturing an image that is at once outside and inside—it is enabling a way of seeing that is topological or at the very least maps the way from inner to outer and back.

We can now look back at the various theoretical perspectives touched on in this chapter and offer an integrated theory of total movement. Unlike the purely external representations of spatialized movement discussed in earlier chapters, the internalized production of movement at the level of kinetic thought and kinetic dynamics (emotional and psychic contents) undergirds the complex constitution of integrated human kinesis. If we expand Lacan's notion of self-identification via linguistic language to a notion of self-identification through kinetic language, we can then argue that once the subject enters the domain of objective kinetic representation, that is, once the subject articulates formalized movement in dance, in sports, in gymnastics, in military movement, in kinetic art, the subject is liable to the same process of self-identification or crystallization of the "I" that Lacan identifies in the case of linguistic language. We are defined by how we move in these formal kinetic disciplinary contexts. Unlike linguistic language, however, the languages of movement are less linear and more complex. What lies inside physical movement is also, as Laban has shown, a complex dynamospheric realm, where emotional, psychic, and intellective stresses, moods, or dynamic efforts are stored. Finally, the expression of our sense of self via movement, via formally articulated movement, leads to a construction of movement selves that is not only confined to the physical realization of kinetic action. Languages of movement also form spaces of kinetic self-identification and communication that make up a social space—a social kinesis, borrowing on Lewin's theorization. Here, then, is a theory of integrated human movement that begins to consider the complexity of human movement as a conduit to the crystallization of multidimensional selves in motion—selves that can be continuously reidentifying themselves from childhood to old age, given their condition of trajective in-betweenness. Neither inner nor outer, neither mental nor physical, neither fish nor flesh, neither object nor subject, movement is always the hole, the passage in between. Movement then becomes a map, a conduit to connect the inside of a human and technological system with its outside, through a constant function (the logic of movement).

Finally, if movement then crystallizes with habit, with repetition, with routine or regular training, and if the kinetic self becomes rigidified within a movement convention, what has concerned me throughout this book is the possibility of intervening in this process of congealment and breaking away from the forces that rigidify the kinetic self. The creative potential of movement within the movement arts, or what I call kinetopoiesis, can be utilized to break away from this rigid state of routinely trained and habitual kinetic self-identification, in order to consider possibilities of kinetopoietic intervention, or a troubling of kinetic normativity, through the rupture and revolutionary knowledge of a movement ecstasy. To be outside oneself is to learn to look back inside and to see ourselves moving as though for the first time.

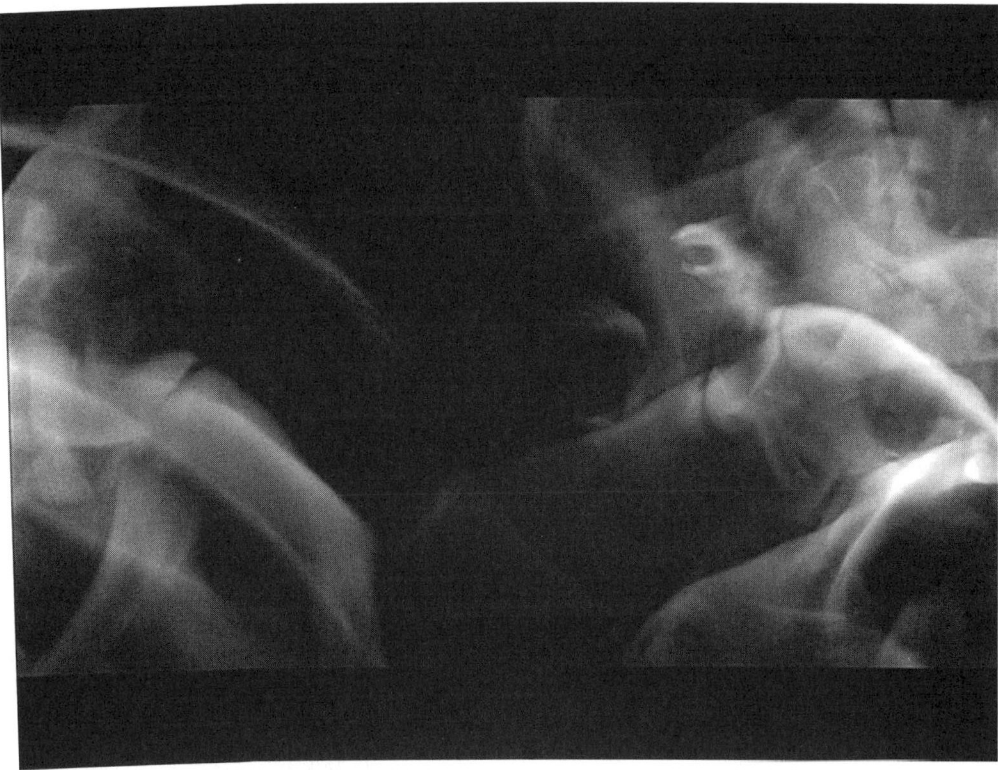

4.5
Still from *Labanimations* (2012).
Concept by Nicolás Salazar Sutil.
Choreography and performance by Melina
Scialom. Directed by Sebastián Melo.

5

Movement to pensement

This chapter addresses a distillation of the book's overall research question: How does a language of physical movement arise from an internalized mental activity? To what extent is physical movement an externalization of mental action? Motor activity—or what Colombian neuroscientist Rodolfo Llinás calls "motricity" (2002)—cannot be divided from mental activity—or what he calls "the mindness state." In Llinás's view, this mindness state "is the product of evolutionary processes that have occurred as actively moving creatures developed from the primitive to the highly evolved" (2002, ix). In fact, according to Llinás, "what we call thinking is in fact the evolutionary internalization of movement" (35)—an idea that resonates with Lewin's conception of an individual's internalization of environmental conditions within the life space, or indeed Laban's notion of a transference between kinesphere and dynamosphere. In what follows, I will describe this transference as a passage from movement to what I call "pensement."

The Latin language has two words for the verb "to think": *cogito* (a term made famous by Descartes's famous dictum) and *pensare*, which is synonymous with "measured deliberation." For the present purposes, *cogito* is a conceptual dead end, if we mean a Cartesian separation between thought and sensation, body and mind. Thus, we are left with *pensare*, a term that refers to a concrete action or physical doing as much as it does to a mental activity. In order to reach a decision, one often finds oneself balancing or weighing up an argument, for instance when we draw a line between the pros and cons of a certain decision. So *pensamentum* is a situated way of thinking. Moreover, it is a spatialized way of thinking, insofar as it derives from the separation or spacing of elements into contrastive units; it requires a specific context in which separate entities of thought are being balanced out or weighed against each other. It also requires a performance of sorts, in the sense that one performs this mode of thought in order to extract a result (hence the etymon *-mentum*, which applies to Latin words to denote outcome). This concept of pensement is more appropriate than thought (*cogito*), and prevents my thesis from hinging on a Cartesian body-mind split. Rather, the type of thought I have in mind touches on what I earlier referred to as physical thinking. More specifically, "pensement" refers to a modality of thinking that is not re-moved from bodily, sensory, or indeed from kinetic experience. In fact, as I imagine the term, "pensement" is a premotor activity; it is the thought behind movement.

My discussion of pensement begins with the activity of counting numbers and producing numerical progressions via movement. I will show different ways in which movement can be internalized numerically, in accordance with different types of numbers and different types of progression (especially cardinal, ordinal, and binary). Subsequently, I will address the activity of making abstract liaisons or connections of logic via movement. My intention is therefore to refine the idea

I modeled in chapter 4 about topological relations between innermotion and outermotion. Rather than dealing with the emotional inner content, I will home in on a very particular sense of inner-motion as an expression of physical thought (pensement). This chapter asks: How do the body and embodied activity generate their own modality of thinking through measuring, numbering, and connecting ideas at the level of physicalized logic?

Counting on the body

Film director Peter Greenaway noted in his book *Fear of Drowning by Numbers* that "counting is the most simple and most primitive of narratives—1 2 3 4 5 6 7 8 9 10—a tale with a beginning, middle, and an end and a sense of progression—arriving at a finish of two digits—a goal attained, a denouement reached" (1989, 23). The idea Greenaway applied to his theory of film, particularly in his film *Drowning by Numbers* (1988), is simple: counting can set a film narrative in motion, thus bypassing conventional dialogue-driven narrative. Greenaway shows that counting does not have to be conceived in an abstract way. *Drowning by Numbers* includes different concrete physical activities that involve numerical progression; for instance, rope-skipping, star-counting, the singing of number songs, the playing of number games, or in the case of the film's main plot, the counting of mariticides, or murders of husbands, committed by a grandmother, her daughter, and her niece—each named Cissie Colpitts. There is a relationship here between abstract number entities and material realizations of the number in physical life. The counting symbols used in this film represent a pattern of time, whose progression across the lives of three women leaves an indelible and countable trace in their lives.

Returning to Lewin's idea of an infant's understanding of movement, he argues that children have no concept of abstract numbers. They acquire numbers by counting fingers (finger math), or by counting stones or abacus balls, or by counting flights of stairs. Thus, the value of a number stems from a physical progression involving a movement that is made up of repetitions. This is what Italian artist Mario Merz (1989) called the "flight of numbers"—a sense of progression at once material and abstract. This integrated sense of numeration can be related both to movement and growth, which is why Merz typically used the Fibonacci number sequence to illustrate the point: in nature, as in architecture, material things grow according to a given numerical progression.[1] Conceptual artist Mel Bochner, who was closely associated with Merz's Arte Povera movement, expressed a very similar idea in his *Theory of Sculpture*, a series of sculptural works that addresses the connection between counting and the physical arrangement of stones in space. Bochner argued that without the object, there would be no number. Likewise, without the numerical progression, the object would not move. After pointing out that the Latin word for "counting" is *calculus*, which translates as "stone," Bochner then adds: "by juxtaposing the numbers with the stones [one] forces a confrontation between matter and mind" (2013).

On the side of a corporeal semiotics of number, Brian Rotman has argued that there are numerical languages whose significance, value, and strategic or instrumental interest do not derive from their meaning. Rather, the value of numbers resides in the fact that they take place and they have actually occurred or have been performed within a particular operation or calculation. Rotman (1993) argues that when counting goes on infinitely, say from 1 to ∞ (1, 2, 3, 4, 5, ...), this dot-dot-dot ideogram (...) imposes a myth of disembodiment on the counted number. Challenging this metaphysical understanding of counting and the axiomatic method it distilled, Rotman claims that the disembodied counted number is a culprit in the proliferation of a fantasy that for centuries remained free of critical examination, and which was assumed to be true. By recognizing this endlessness, according to Rotman, one could see the fantasy as fantasy.

Because Rotman's argument is staged in terms of an opposition—God mathematics versus body mathematics—the idea that one can bring the body back into the languages of number and geometrical space presupposes that, historically at least, the body left, and that it was subsequently taken over by this God agency. But the body need not be brought back as though it had been lost; physicality has always been inside numbers. Consider the example of the child learning elementary arithmetic. For a child, numerical calculation stems directly from the activity of raising and lowering fingers, and thus her knowledge of arithmetic emerges through a reckoning of numbers as physical entities before these numbers assume an abstract identity. Even in classical Greek mathematics, which aspired to ascend beyond the body, ancient numbers were rooted in the counting of pebbles— what Plato called the aesthesis of number (*arithmos aisthetikos*), that is, the sensory and physical domain of number. Classical mathematics was never completely disembodied; classical notions of number and geometry achieve a level of abstraction only insofar as they derive from this aesthetic or physical domain. Still, Rotman's argument is helpful in trying to unpack my own: when seeking to extract formalisms from form, numbers provide a natural system.

Rotman has also proposed (2000) that a modern understanding of iteration and extension, or what he calls "counting with non-Euclidean fingers," can produce a different configuration of the most basic mathematical element—a number—and by extension, its most simple arithmetic functions. According to Rotman, non-Euclidean counting and the non-Euclidean number emphasize not the immateriality of infinity, but the embodiment of the counter—the materiality of the one-who-counts, and the materiality of writing and signifying. Georges Ifrah (2001) reinforces this point by arguing that numbers grew alongside a certain materiality used to inscribe them and a certain physicality, or even the mannerisms, employed to communicate them. Yet I would argue that this corporeal sense of mathematics is not historically tiered or divided into Euclidean or non-Euclidean chronologies: counting with the body is natural. If we are to believe a universal history of counting such as the one proposed by Ifrah, human beings have always counted, or at least have always learned to count, with their fingers or bodies. Progressing by numbers is an actual way of internalizing a physical process and giving it a mental description, a numerical form. As Rotman said in this regard:

Mathematical symbols, then, relate to these inner moves as writing does to speech, or better as stage directions and script do to a play: they are instructions, in other words, which allow the performance to be re-created, to be communicated and repeated in and out of the head. These internal performances are waking dreams, rigorously controlled thought-experiments. Mathematicians imagine symbolically coded simulacra of their embodied selves, puppet agents or avatars which they cause to inhabit and perform actions within virtual worlds, within, that is, internal idealized spaces, that are abstracted and fictionalized fragments of the actual, external activities of their bodies. (2011, unpaginated)

It should be clear by now that the passage from movement to pensement can be achieved by the transference of progression from an embodied movement to an abstract movement. To sum up, the "numerical progression" alluded to in the title of this chapter moves in two ways at once: toward an embodied pattern of movement, and toward abstraction. In what follows, I would like to focus on how this internalized progression from physical to mental determinations, or from bodily sequences to internally counted numbers, constitutes a basic language in the construction of formalized movement in the movement arts, especially dance.

Shut up, I'm counting!

Dance is a good example of the connection between movement and counting. Generally speaking, dance comprises the basic skill of counting steps, or counting actions that are strung together in a numerical or quantifiable sequence. A time signature in dance is often (but not necessarily) aligned to music. But what does the dancer dance to, when there is no music to provide a time signature? The answer is, typically, counted steps. What a dancer counts are the indivisible units of a dance phrase or section, in order to string these together into an intelligent and rationalized progression, for instance from 1 to 8. This would make up a standard 8-count dance phrase. In addition, a dancer can count along a musical measure, either in 4/4 time (1, 2, 3, 4, 1, 2, 3, 4, …) or in 3/4 time (1, 2, 3, 1, 2, 3, …)—a classic example of which is the waltz. Because each one of these measures is made up of individual counts, dancers must cluster musical measures exponentially, so that 2 musical measures will make up 8 dance counts, 4 measures will make up 16 counts, 8 measures will make up 32 counts, and so on. Whoever thought formal dance involves a mindless body ought to think again.

Dance counting highlights the need to connect the body to its pensement, so as not to rely on pure stylization, or the misconstrued impression that dancing is prancing. Dance counting relies on structured and ordered patterns of temporal units. Whether the count is explicit, or whether the numbers are hidden under the musical incidence, does not alter the fact that dancing can be considered a way of counting with the whole body. Of course, dancing is much more than that. Counting steps, however, is a good place to start.

As a choreographer committed to revealing the basics of dance movement—i.e., the core elements of repetition and variation—Lucinda Childs is content with letting the count do the dancing.

Childs's interest in working out choreographic works by counting stems, much like Bochner's *Theory of Sculpture*, from a desire to understand dance as a conceptual art form. Childs is, of course, well known for her pioneering work with the Judson Dance Theater, where alongside Yvonne Rainer and Steve Paxton she laid the foundations of what is now known as postmodern dance. In addition, there are strong ties between her work and the burgeoning minimalist and conceptual art movements championed by Bochner and Sol LeWitt in the visual arts, or by composers like Philip Glass and Steve Reich.

Untitled Trio, from 1968, represents the starting point of Childs's inventive exploration of a choreographic calculus—the term is here used in the sense put forward by Bochner, meaning a materialized form of counting. But rather than counting stones, Childs was concerned with the counting of fairly complex choreographic time structures carried out by a dancer (counter). Childs's works of this period are also referred to as "silent" works because her dances did not feature musical accompaniment. However, one could argue that these "silent" dances are in fact accompanied by a music of numbers, for movement is music, even if it carries no sound—at least in the neo-Pythagorean sense of the term *musica*.[2] But if there is no sound, some other medium must come to carry the music—and that medium is number. Childs made no attempt to hide or simplify the number underlying the dance movement. On the contrary, her ambition was to make the numerical progression explicit, so that the audience would know from the outset that in the absence of sonic music, the dancer can dance to the eidetic music of numbers.

Childs choreographed *Transverse Exchange* (1976) to make up exactly 1,449 counted steps. The piece featured five dancers drawing out parallel lines with runs and jumps while a counting progression unfolded in the process. The choreography is composed arithmetically: eleven-, eight-, and five-count phrases are repeated (added up) to make up 1,449 dance steps. The dancers are counting on this sum, which becomes their arithmetic dénouement. Likewise, in *Figure Eights* (1976), Childs explored the idea of time crossing by having two sets of eight counts: from 1 to 8 and from 8 to 1. With eyes closed, and thus forced to connect to the sound of a metronome, the dancer performed both counts simultaneously, so that while one arm marked an ascending time sequence, the feet performed a descending time sequence.

Lucinda Childs's collaboration with minimalist composer Philip Glass and conceptual artist Sol LeWitt is most emblematic. Their collaborative work, entitled *Dance* (1979), saw performers punctuate entrances and exits in relation to a visual counterpoint provided by video footage of the company rehearsing passages from the piece. Performing on a lattice floor in order to reinforce the numerical progressions in a spatial sense, Childs's dancers cut the stage in pairs on horizontal paths with increasingly complex combinations of 12-count, 24-count, and 48-count phrases. Much like Glass's score, or Le Witt's décor, the spatial patterns for each of the three sections that made up *Dance* had an underlying and unchanging diagrammatic pattern, which highlighted the cumulative variations in phrasing of each movement.

Although *Dance* had a score by Glass, the performers were not dancing to the music, any more than they were dancing to the space—to the grid floor or the rhythms of LeWitt's video. The dance, as concept, is representative of that double movement I spoke of earlier: at once physical and mental. In watching Childs's dancers, one sees two categories of movement issued at once. The difficulty does not lie in the numerical complexity of the progression, for mathematically the counts are elementary. Likewise, the movements of Childs's dancers are far from the technical sophistication of classical ballet. And yet it is the double thought process that makes the entire performance a feat of endurance. To think in two ways simultaneously questions the way in which I have staged this chapter's main argument. It is not that we think from movement to pensement, as though these were opposite sides of a thinking spectrum. The human body-mind is a polyrhythmic, polytiming, and polythinking organism: it does not only produce one thought, one formalism, one language at a time, but indeed as many as a programmed body is able to carry with it.

Childs's idea that one can dance a series of nonstandard times, for instance through time-crossing, or through simultaneous time counts, has prompted my own exploration of counted dance. In addition to exploring the idea that one can think various progressions at once, I have explored the possibility that one may count different types of numbers at once. My exploration has focused on counting with noncardinal numbers. In other words, rather than dance-counting to eight using cardinals (1, 2, 3, 4, 5, 6, 7, 8), I have explored dancing using ordinal numbers or binary numbers, or a combination of binaries and cardinals, to expand the possibilities of that polyrhythmic thought process found in Childs's silent dances. For instance, in *Ordinal 4* (2010), a piece Brian Rotman conceived and wrote in the mathematical language of category theory, the arithmetic dénouement achieved over the course of the choreographic structure was intended to reach both a final sum (like Child's 1,449 counts) and a proof of concept that remained true to the basic axioms of category theory, as indicated in Rotman's score (see below).

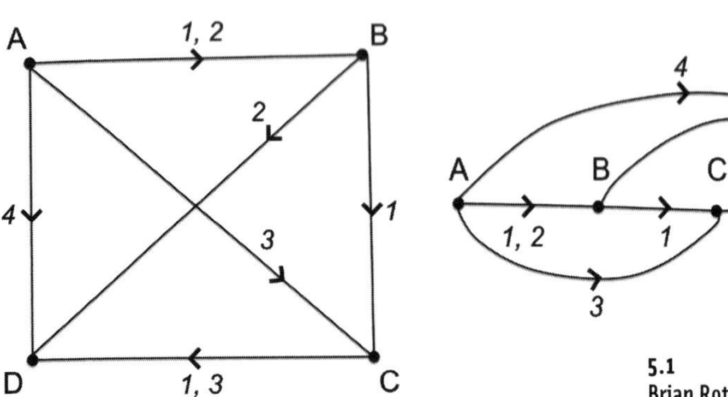

5.1
Brian Rotman's diagrammatic instructions for *Ordinal 4*. Courtesy of Brian Rotman.

It is worth pointing out that mathematical categories use only two entities: objects and arrows. Objects are static, whereas arrows relate to basic operations indicating the mathematical movement, or mapping, between objects. The intention in *Ordinal 4* was to perform a category-theoretical representation of the number 4 by interpreting the mathematical object as a choreographic position and the mathematical arrow as a transposition, or movement. Crucially, the dance count does not refer to a progression of cardinal numbers (1, 2, 3, 4). Ordinal numbers involve an order, a list, a ranking, or a grading: 1st, 2nd, 3rd, 4th. Thus, the task of dancing and counting to ordinal numbers is to situate the mental object—the counted number—within an ordinal system where units are related to one another in terms of predefined criteria of organization. In Rotman's diagram, 1, 2, 3, and 4 refer to the four performers in the dance. The arrows symbolize the routes they must follow in this prescribed mathematical category. Also in this diagram are four stages or positions (A, B, C, and D), which each dancer must go through. These four edges of the diagram symbolize the ordinal progression: 1st, 2nd, 3rd, and 4th, which if obeyed fulfill the axioms of this mathematical category. Rotman (2011) argued that any dance piece (or musical composition) could embody a variety of types of movement structures, choreographed and emergent, at many levels. Not all such structural elements need to reproduce a mathematical entity; all one needs is a distinguished feature, a core or dominant element. In this case, the distinguishing feature is of course a category theory diagram of ordinal 4, which four dancers performed by obeying their prescribed routes, and by starting and finishing their progression in unison. And because the diagram is an abstraction, it does not have to be interpreted as a ground plan for the blocking of actors/dancers on stage. In other words, the diagram does not have to be interpreted as a bird's eye-view of the locomotional movement of four dancers walking a straight line or a quadrangle. The structure is abstract, and so it can be performed in many ways other than in locomotive space. The dancers could perform the same structure in sonic and gestural space, as well as in a space where all three previous spatialities are combined. Thus, when choreographing Rotman's diagram, I asked the dancers to walk the diagram, to vocalize it, to perform facial gestures to illustrate it, and then to perform all three tasks simultaneously in the fourth and final iteration of the structure. Thus the dancers reach a fourth iteration, which is a choreographic realization of ordinal number 4. In this way we got to the numerical dénouement of the piece.

The intention in *Ordinal 4* was to fulfill three elementary axioms of category theory, which translate to three basic rules of performance: (1) four dancers must cover the four possible trajectories that make up the category by moving from one point to another, fulfilling their common identity. (2) The four performers each follow an assigned composition of arrows, which means they are also differentiated by the unique paths taken (this, in more simple terms, amounts to the four different characters they play). Finally (3), the four dancers achieve associativity, in the sense that the movement 1 + 1 + 2 would be the same as 2 + 1 + 1. To dance a category (denoted as C), Rotman's instructions were:

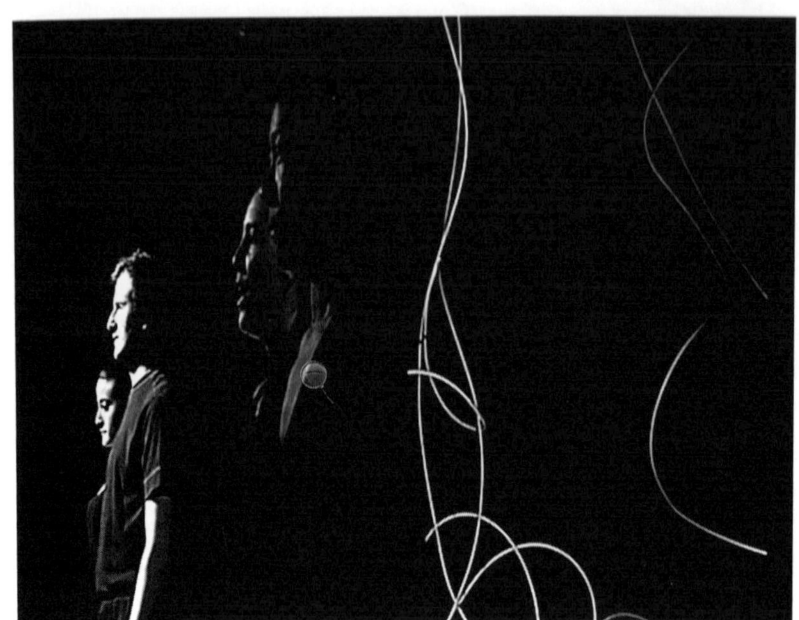

5.2
Ordinal 4, performed at Goldsmiths College, March
2009. Choreographed by Nicolás Salazar Sutil.
Performers: David Alonso, Jack Lawless, María José
Pantoja, Wei Ting, and Ana Paulo Oliveiro.

Four regions of (physical and/or gestural) space A, B, C, D are designated. There are four dancers labelled here 1, 2, 3, 4. They all exit A. Dancers 1 and 2 go to B along identical paths; from B dancer 1 goes to C whilst dancer 2 goes to D; dancer 3 goes from A to C, and then dancer 3 and 1 go on an identical path to D; dancer 4 goes from A to D. Dancer 1 and dancer 3 arrive at C simultaneously, all four dancers arrive at D simultaneously.[3]

Rotman is inviting us to look at diagrams borrowed from category theory in a way that is not so discipline-specific—so that the activity of representing the diagram need not be the sole preserve of mathematicians. According to Rotman (2011), category theory diagrams can be read as "a sign for transformation, change of state, movement along a path, a flow of information." An immediate goal therefore presented itself in the choreographic performance of *Ordinal 4*: "to demonstrate that these axioms can be danced by dancing a particular category whose diagram of arrows of necessity incorporates them." It is important to point out that in writing this "mathematext," Rotman was inspired by similar examples of mathematical dancing found in the anonymous seventeenth-century play *Blame Not Our Author*[4] or Beckett's geometric mime *Quad* (1981), which I discuss later. Rotman's piece highlights that the creative imagination of a mathematician stems from the first vision of a structure or an order, before structure crystallizes in a formal mathematical language (categories, in this case). That first vision of the structure is common to other disciplines. The first image of a choreographic movement can be a kinetopoietic structure very similar to the structures imagined by a mathematician, an architect, a musician, a sculptor. As the structure is revealed to the artist in the orbit of pensement, it exists in a domain of creative thought that is shared by various disciplines of creative composition. What *Ordinal 4* reveals, therefore, is the possibility of connecting creative minds (mathematicians and choreographers) by accessing that common vision of "pensed" movement.

Binary bodies

In 2010 I developed a short choreographic exercise and practice research project entitled *Binary Flesh*, along with my artistic partners at C8.[5] The goal of this exercise was to dance with ones' fingers. More specifically, we wanted to accomplish a silent dance that would be performed to the music of a binary number count. The dancer was asked to perform an "age" (31 years) by using a technique known as binary finger counting. This technique makes use of the hand (five finger digits) to create a strip of binary numbers using two basic finger positions: folded and outstretched. By combination of these two positions along the five fingers (or rows), a human hand can count binary numbers up to 31. Thus, the sequence below shows five rows representing finger positions (pinky, ring, middle, index, thumb): 0 indicates the finger is folded, and 1 indicates that the finger is outstretched. The binary number sequence was used as a choreographic score, in which the final outcome, the dénouement, was to count up to the age of 31.

00000 = 0	01000 = 8	10000 = 16	11000 = 24
00001 = 1	01001 = 9	10001 = 17	11001 = 25
00010 = 2	01010 = 10	10010 = 18	11010 = 26
00011 = 3	01011 = 11	10011 = 19	11011 = 27
00100 = 4	01100 = 12	10100 = 20	11100 = 28
00101 = 5	01101 = 13	10101 = 21	11101 = 29
00110 = 6	01110 = 14	10110 = 22	11110 = 30
00111 = 7	01111 = 15	10111 = 23	11111 = 31

The dancer was then told to perform the binary progression illustrated here by alternating between two given *bodily* positions. In Position 1, the dancer stood with the right arm outstretched and the right hand illustrating a binary number, while in Position 0 the dancer crouched and did not move or count. To fulfill the dance count, the dancer was thus asked to crouch and stand—to move along this two-state sequence of bodily movements—until she had finally counted a cardinal sequence of 31. The sequence of 31 standing-crouching movements was carried out while simultaneously counting binary digits with her right hand as shown above. As in Childs's *Figure Eights*, the aim of this binary number dance was to provoke a situation in which the dancer was forced to think in more ways than one. Not only did the dancer alternately stand and crouch up to 31 times, thus having to accomplish a countable series of basic physical movements, but she had to accomplish two mental sequences simultaneously. First, she had to vocally count from 0 to 31 in cardinal order, and then she was told to count with her right hand (silently) by placing her fingers in the positions given in the progression shown above, thus obtaining a binary finger count from 0 to 31. The piece was accompanied by two video projections. One showed a dancer/counter moving along a binary sequence in a different tempo from the live dancer, thus creating a sense of visual counterpoint from the audience's perspective. The other video image showed a prerecorded close-up of the dancer's hand depicting the 32 counts that make up a binary finger count (00000 to 11111)—albeit in random order. This binary number count highlights the idea that two-state operations, which I have referred to elsewhere as counterpoint, can be used to create an iterative temporal structure. In other words, the binary progression can be used as a narrative, in the same way that a cardinal count from 1 to 100 provides Greenaway an opportunity to devise the narrative of a film. In the digital era, progressions are often relayed and performed in terms of binary strips, like the one used in C8's performance of *Binary Flesh*. So the cultural narrative that these particular numbers evoke (binary digits) is not entirely removed from the contemporary history and materiality of representation. As the language of universal computing in a digital-era context, binary digits have enormous cultural and historical relevance today. Numbers evolve with the technologies used to represent them and the techniques used to perform them. As the numbers change, so does the mental (and indeed physical) performance of externalized (danced) numbers.

To sum up, there are different types of number (cardinal, ordinal, binary, complex, irrational, fractional, and so on) because each one affords a different modality of expression and representation of abstract structures and progressions. Each family of numbers is a different *culture* of number that can be used to represent different objects in different ways. As I said, the current culture of numbers is dominated by the binary digit (bit), which is typically used as representation of a twofold physical state (e.g., on/off). Insofar as progressions of binary digits make up the language of universal electronic computing, the evolution of pensement at the level of numerical progressions points to an ever-changing technological and material condition of thinking, and to the possibility of connecting the interior of movement to a language that supports not only human intelligence but also machine intelligence. Thus, *Binary Flesh* highlights the idea that the numbers counted by the dancer might well have been counted by a digital computer. This leads me to my next question: How is movement internalized by the machine? How is the progressional sense of enumerated movement increasingly dominated by the representation of numbers as digits, due to the ubiquity of electronic and computerized forms of number reckoning? This is the subject of the final part of this book.

6

The Lucky dance

In a memorable scene in Samuel Beckett's tragicomedy *Waiting for Godot*, Pozzo asks Vladimir and Estragon whether they would like to see his servant Lucky think. Vladimir accepts the offer, but Estragon suggests that he himself would rather see Lucky dance. And so an argument ensues. The characters cannot agree on what would be more amusing, a solo dance or a monologue. At this point, the question arises: Do people dance or think first? Pozzo promptly answers: First comes dance—this is "the natural order" (Beckett 1990, 39). Lucky is then forced to dance. As it turns out, the order does not matter much in Lucky's case, for he is not much of a dancer. Although Pozzo acknowledges that Lucky used to dance the farandole, the fling, the brawl, the jig, the fandango, and even the hornpipe, he now only dances this dance, called "The Net," because "he thinks he is entangled in a net" (39). Nor is Lucky much of a thinker. Unfortunately, Lucky is not alone in failing to realize the connection between coordinated movement and coordinated thought. In fact, the entire play revolves around a failure to carry out basic physical actions, or basic moves, coupled with a failure to think.

Beckett's French original retains a terminological association that is worth digging up here. As I said, Pozzo orders Lucky to think. In the French version, Pozzo's line is: "Pense! Porc!" (Think, pig!). The juxtaposition between the French imperatives *pense* and *danse* is similar to that between the terms "pensement" and "movement," introduced in chapter 5, except that the characters in Beckett's play see the two categories as being divided. Because Lucky cannot express himself in a coordinated physical way, it does not come as a surprise that he cannot articulate mental thought either. Disconnected pensement is conducive, as Lucky himself seems to suggest in his famous monologue, to an acacademia—to a pointless logorrhea of disembodied thought. In Walter Asmus's 1989 film version of the play (supervised by Beckett himself four months before his death), this dance is interpreted as a problem of coordinated balance. Lucky, played by Roman Polanski, attempts to perform the dance while standing on one foot, with the other leg suspended in midair, while gesticulating wildly with both arms. Polanski conveys the sense of a body devoid of any physical intelligence: incapable of coordinating different body parts into a coherent structure of movement. The same applies to Lucky's monologue, which Polanski underpins with a string of subtle but evidently disarticulated arm and leg movements.

So what comes first: thought or movement? Pozzo's problem is provocative, raising expectations of an order of succession. In seeking to understand what comes first, Beckett's tramps are trying to establish a division of movement and pensement—but due to this division they cannot accomplish either. Failing to connect thought to embodiment leaves the characters in Beckett's play living in a state of continuous procrastination, waiting for a connection that can marry body and mind, or at least explain the connection between them.

In this final chapter of part II, I build on preceding discussions in order to address logic in terms of interconnective pathways between physical and mental movement. So, whereas previously I introduced the idea of a topological model of inner-outer relations and the internalization of movement through numerical progressions, here I wish to speak about the shaping of mental and physical thought via logical structures. It is not enough to recognize that physical movement has an inner domain as thought, nor to internalize movement through mental objects that progress in time (for instance, numerically). Rather, we must understand that the articulation of these objects into patterns depends on a capacity to link, to join—quite literally, to articulate. What defines the articulation of physical and mental thought is the capacity to link, to connect parts into a logical structure. Every progression discussed in the preceding chapter is underpinned by logic. For example, the logic of a simple arithmetic count can be additive, by a unit of 1: thus, 1, 2, 3, 4, 5, ... That logic determines the link between each number in this sequence. The logic of a Fibonacci series, which I mentioned earlier in relation to the work of Mario Merz, is also additive, but not by a fixed unit of 1. In a Fibonacci series, one must add every unit by its preceding value; hence, 1, 2, 3, 5, 8, 13, 21, 34, ...

The trouble is: logic does not only move forward in a single direction, in the way these numerical progressions do. There are many types of logic, moving in more ways than one. As we will see, the logic of movement need not be linear or unidirectional; nor does it need to be expressed numerically. Fibonacci logic can be expressed logarithmically, as a spiral, or rhythmically, as music or as architectural space, or indeed as a choreographic progression. Regardless of the medium of expression, there is an underlying inner logic to progression and to movement. Accordingly, what Lucky lacks is an inner sense of direction and connection. Failure to understand this logic, or to embody it, means that it does not matter what comes first—both movement and pensement are bound to fail, as they do in Lucky's case. By asking which one comes first, the tramps are putting themselves in a paradoxical impasse (chicken versus egg). The question, assuming there is no starting point, should be: What is the underlying logic that produces a movement structure out of pensement, and vice versa?

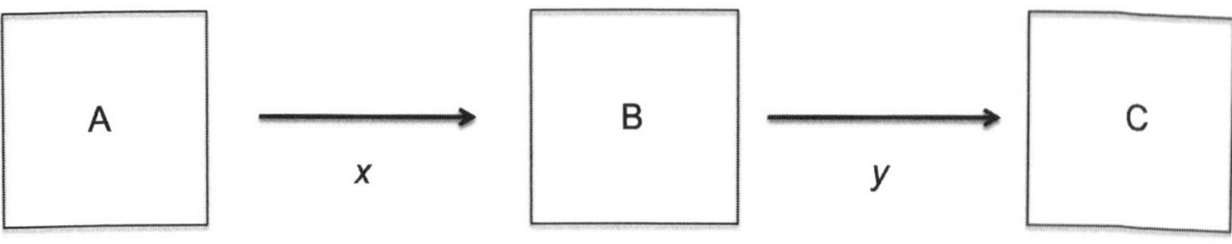

Three separate squares, A, B, and C, are connected by arrows named *x* and *y*. The diagram above illustrates a concept I touched on earlier, when discussing the language of categories. My intention now is to generalize these elements in order to speak—very broadly at first—of a sense of movement inside logic. Tim Cresswell writes that the basic signifier of mobility is getting from point A to point B: "Hence, A $\rightarrow$ B involves a displacement—the act of moving between locations." He continues, "These locations may be towns or cities, or they may be points a few centimeters apart" (2006, 2). Logically, the operation is the same. Cresswell laments that in social theory this line should be taken for granted every time movement is coded as travel, nomadism, routes, or lines of flight, concluding: "This line is a good starting point for such an exploration. I want to explore the content of the line that links A to B, to unpack it, to make sure it is not taken for granted" (2). My aim in this section is very much the same, except that I am not interested in unpacking this line in terms of a social theory of mobility, nor in terms of a social-theoretical understanding of movement. I wish to find within this line a sense of abstract kinesis. I will finish part II with a discussion of movement that is in fact purely abstract—the movement found inside pure thought.

Our line is found in a number of places other than category theory: in epistemic logic, in mathematical logic, in computer logic, in graph logic, in experiential logic. The basic premise of the line is very simple: to produce movement at a logical level, all that is needed are static forms and connective functions between them (position and transposition). Logic displays a sense of inner movement in which linear (or indeed nonlinear) directions connect a string of objects into a meaningful structure. Thus, logical movement always occurs in terms of a step-by-step procedure. When thinking logically, we are progressing along individual positions that make up the step-by-step spatiality of logic. When we express thought in words, we are continuously linking static objects: letters, words, statements, phrases, sentences. When we express thought in dance, we do the same: we connect poses, steps, movement words, and movement phrases. We also do the same when we stick together frames in a cinematic or animational structure, or when we carry out computational commands. Wherever there is rational thought, lines of logic are being drawn.

The line of logic is also conditioned by rules. In the same way that one can move physically in space in many different ways (walking, crawling, leaping), one can move in logical space in different ways. Among other rules, the line of logic is subject to the rules of commutativity and transitivity. Thus, if A = B and B = C, then B = C, so we have an axiom of transitivity. The basic operation, (A + B) $\Leftrightarrow$ (B + A), shows an example of commutative law. General logic is replete with symbols that convey different rules of connection (syntax) according to the laws of mathematical logic ($\supset$, $\Rightarrow$, $\leftrightarrow$, $\equiv$, $\Leftrightarrow$, $\rightarrow$, =). Logicians and linguists speak of "syntactical movement" to refer to problems of discontinuity in a logical or grammatical structure, not least because they recognize that even at this level of abstraction, to connect structures of language one must execute moves that are bound by rules. Thus, when considering movement inside thought, we must consider that movement is always formalized by the rules of reasoning.

Because my intention is to write not a theory of logic or mathematics but an integrated theory of human movement, what matters here is that the basic connection A → B, or A = B, or A ↔ B, and so on, provides different ways of moving mentally along objects A and B. If we flip the concept around, then one could argue that there is also logic inside physical movement. And it is in that direction that I wish to push this argument. In the same way that linguists speak of syntactical movement and mathematicians speak of mathematical morphisms as movements, so physical movement can be articulated by an embodied logic or an embodied syntax. Laban spoke of choreology precisely in these terms: of the logic of choreutic shapes. According to Laban, choreology refers to the study of "a grammar and syntax of the language of movement, dealing not only with the outer form of movement but also with its mental content" (1966, viii).

Perhaps the most formally prescriptive way of ordering a physical body is by arranging it like a chess piece on a formally prescribed board, similar to Schlemmer's notion of "space dance" (discussed in chapter 1). Anyone who has ever played chess will be familiar with the idea of a move, which can be indicated by an arrow in the instructional literature. The difference between the physical movement of a chess piece and a chess move will help illustrate my point. In the game of chess, each piece is allowed to change its position on a chessboard, defined by alphanumerical coordinates—hence, the algebraic notation of chess. The way a chess piece moves on the board obviously does not correspond in any way to the movements of actual queens or bishops. Assuming the game of chess is being played on a board rather than on a device, the chess piece has to be physically picked up and then moved to its desired position on the board. This involves a physical effort— typically, an arm-and-hand movement. It does not seem to matter *how* that physical movement is carried out; what matters is the *move*, not the movement. The move occurs in the mental map the player has of the game: the game is not happening physically, therefore, even though it is actualized in a physical space, with physical objects. This distinction between a move and movement is key to the difference and the association between physical and mental movement.

From this example, we may conclude that before we perform physical movements, we make moves. Not only does this mean that before physical movement comes a motivation, a thought process, a mental map of moves conceived by the subject. Before movement also comes a premotor move created at a neurological level, or a premotor plan created by the brain. Voluntary movement, or movement of the type A to B, is the product of a logical connection that is established neurologically and mentally even before it is performed by the body. Thus movement is also the intrinsic abstracting property of the human mind in imagining the physical pathway between places before it is experienced in a physical way. Barring the neurological production of premotor moves, I want to focus on movement behind the scenes, particularly in terms of the moves of logic. We return to the question of intentionality, which I raised at the very opening of this book. It is clear that moves must have a goal if they are to achieve something as purposeful movements. Llinás (2002) has argued that purposeless movement is wasteful, in that it does not communicate any meaningful intention. He adds: "The goal or object of movement must be well defined, and we may define it here as that which one intends to do in relation to that object or goal. Also an abstraction, intentionality is the premotor detail of the desired result of movement through which a particular emotional state is expressed: the choice of what to do before the doing of it" (2002, 227–228). This idea is key to understanding how moves start movements, and also how movements start new moves. It is key to understanding that in any language of movement, whether choreutics, ballet, gymnastics, athletics, or any other formal way of moving, the body does not execute any movement randomly or accidentally, unless chance is allowed to be part of the artistic and creative process. The body is moving according to moves planned internally, either in the slow reflective game plan of a chess player or in the more impulsively reflective plan of an athlete who visualizes the drive to run from A to B, or the football/soccer player who plans a penalty kick and then thumps the ball, hoping it will go from the penalty spot to the net.

Liaison forms, or how to plant Chomskian trees

In the same way that outermotion produces traceforms, so innermotion produces liaison forms. So, when one is articulating thought in a logically structured way, one is creating an articulated trajectory or pathway of logical moves. German mathematician Hermann Grassmann spoke of the "form-liaison" to express things that can come into being by thought through a double act involving position and transposition (cited in Châtelet 2000, 108). The outcome is a structure made up of ruptures, disconnections, quick snippets, and acts that posit and link (108). My next move will be to flip the term around and call this the "liaison form," to go with the traceform discussed earlier in this book. Thus, total movement is expressed in a double articulation, as traceforms and as liaison forms.

There are many examples of how liaison forms are traditionally represented dendritically, i.e., as treelike formations. These trees of logic occur in a number of language-specific and formal expressions that are typified by the step-by-step construction of syntax or even a grammar. Examples include mind-mapping, spider diagramming, decision trees, or—in the field of computational linguistics—abstract syntax trees and algorithms. In the field of epistemic logic, parse trees may be generated to represent the underlying logical structures in natural languages. Noam Chomsky (1957) developed the idea that sentences in natural language have two levels of representation—a deep structure and a surface structure. He argued that we could uncover the former within spoken or written language only by applying modern mathematical logic to grammatical theory. Chomsky evolved the idea into graphic representations of natural language—what I call liaison forms—by identifying the positions and transpositions that connect the parts of a tree at a deep-structural level.

This theory of transformational grammar provided a way to articulate syntax trees by using the logic of derivations. In Chomskian terms, a "derivation" is a sequence of grammar rule applications that transforms the start symbol into a string, proving that the string belongs to the grammar's language. In situations of discontinuity, Chomskian grammatology also uses the term "syntactical movement" to refer to ways in which syntax can address these discontinuities or displacements. In sum, since Chomsky could treat the construction of grammatical sentences as a system of *tree languages* or *tree automata*, his graphic representation of discourse reveals not only the step-by-step formal construction of word-based language, but also a representation of the internal movement of language involving the drawing and diagramming of grammatical moves.

I will not dwell on the formal account provided by Chomsky, because it is not immediately relevant to my consideration of liaison forms. The liaison form, as I have defined it above, is as broad a generalization as the concept of the traceform introduced earlier. To understand the notion of a liaison form in the context of this current discussion, one simply needs to recognize that the drawing of structures of inner logic to define how grammar is articulated and how its structures are transformed can be considered conceptually in terms of two basic intentions that are central to this book. First, I intend to draw language as a dendritic construct. Secondly, I intend to identify structures that are subject to transformation and movement (if only at the syntactical level).

In *Is the Man Who Is Tall Happy? An Animated Conversation with Noam Chomsky*, French film director Michel Gondry uses animation to explore some of the philosophical and general theoretical concepts emerging from Chomsky's thinking. At the heart of these talks is the emergence of language out of deep-set structural constructions. The premise of the animation, however, is the graphic representation of ideas as mental growth (movement), and the emergence of symbolic representation stemming from psychic continuity. Thus, the film neatly illustrates a point close to my own thesis: How is movement—internalized as thought—represented, drawn, or expressed in graphic form?

Chomsky asks: "How do we identify something as a [physical] tree? You plant a tree. It grows. You cut a branch off it and you put that branch in the ground. Suppose it grows and becomes exactly identical as the original tree. Is that new one the same tree? Why not?" (Gondry, 2013) The question "Why?" or "Why not?" is instrumental, according to Chomsky, in provoking thought, knowledge, and scientific discourse—in growing ideas through articulated questions and inquiry. For Chomsky, our concept of a physical tree has to do with a rather abstract concept of continuity: the tree is cut off, another grows, and in the gap that emerges between the original and the new stands a human capacity to fill in, to provide a seamless continuity, an ongoing mental stream. Meanwhile, to express this continuity, language emerges. And language is a very different kind of treelike system. It grows as we construct an infinite array of structured expressions, which in turn give an articulated representation to the continuum of psychic activity (innermotion).

Gondry's film is an animated stream of consciousness concerning trees of two very different kinds. The film is an exercise in parsing, or "treeing," as much as it is a reflection on physical trees and other objects found in the phenomenal world, which the human mind can imagine and represent. The film leads up to Chomsky's definition of a theory of language as a generative digital tree (digital in the sense that it has a discrete number of component elements branching off into discrete strings of articulation). Throughout the film, Gondry's animated drawings seem to illustrate a kind of "vital dendritism" underlying Chomsky's philosophy, in the sense that abstract dendritic patterns can be conceived to be the general representation of living (and moving) organisms and organizations at the deep-structural level. The point of animating Chomsky's thought process is to show in graphical terms that trees are ubiquitous structures found in natural life as well as in abstract life. There is a common patterning and an ordering logic to articulated thought, whether it is expressed in words or in algorithms.

Finally, the concept of the liaison form helps flesh out the idea that an infinite number of individual strings or branches can be followed through in the generative activity of thought. Gondry's hand-drawn animations reveal that drawing is always a process of capturing the fleetingness of thought. But in seeking to write thought down, or to draw it as animation, Gondry's film also warns that we cannot take language for granted as though it were a Meccano set, because one would then take the pieces that make up a thought for granted. Or as Châtelet put it: "it is not a matter of constructing space, but of letting oneself be bewitched by a rhythm: that which knots and weaves homogeneities gorged with tensions. Capture of the extension is an individuation in progression." Châtelet also commented: "To know, it is first necessary to be penetrated by the rhythm of learning. It is in this sense that the capture of the extension progressively makes the mind its own" (2000, 104). Movement is an open-ended and limitless reservoir of creative possibilities, hence its significance as an object of cultural representation and mediation. But to draw thought, as Gondry does in his film, it is not enough to have a language—one must invent the production of this language every time one speaks, because each time one speaks, one is devising a way of organizing the elements creatively, of drawing them and arranging them and generating new thought constructions.

The walking syllogism

Logic does not *stand* to reason, it *moves* to reason. Take the example of the Aristotelian syllogism: "All men are mortal. Socrates is a man. Therefore Socrates is mortal." The argument is made up of three *statements*. It is most fitting to speak of *statements* here, since these sentences are *static* components in the architecture of this argument. This three-part argument thus exemplifies the Aristotelian intention to reason from a given starting point (major premise), to a midpoint (minor premise), to a given endpoint (conclusion). It follows that, just like the arrows connecting the squares in my illustration a few pages back, there are links that connect these statements making up liaison forms. The argument can now be examined more closely as a drawing or diagram that carries the entire operation to a figurative level. What binds the first two sentences together is the term "man." What connects the second sentence to the third is the word "mortal." From this point of view, propositional logic could be said to be a linear movement of thought provoked by a common proposition. Aristotle's syllogistic model was expressed graphically in the so-called Porphyrian tree, developed by the Greek Neoplatonist logician Porphyry of Tyre. Porphyry expressed Aristotelian logic in terms of treelike diagrams of dichotomous divisions, indicating that a species is defined by a genus and a differentia, and that this logical process continues until it reaches the lowest species, which can no longer be further broken down.

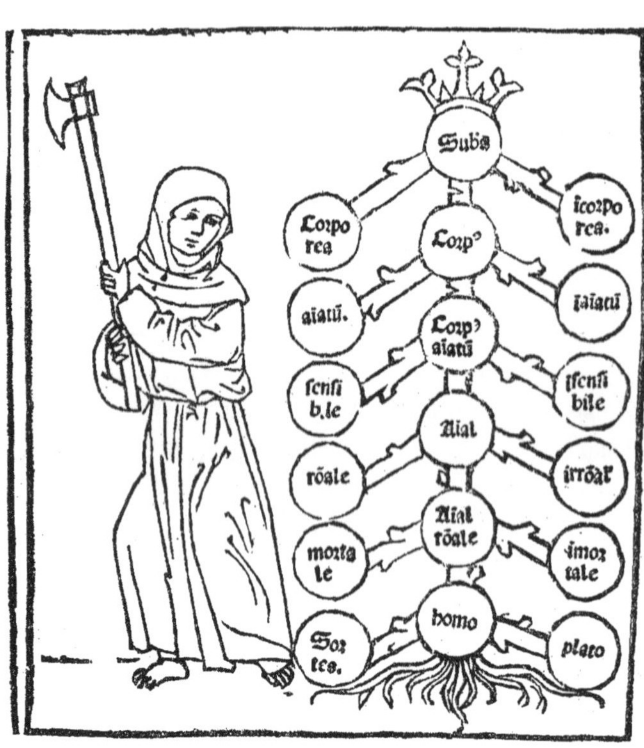

6.1
Destruction of the Porphyrian Tree (published
1503), after the work of Augustine of Ancona
(c. 1241–1328).

Châtelet described logicism as being "like a mathematics applied to the calculation of the liaisons between propositions and to the administration of proof" (2000, 8). But rather than speaking of logicism, which is confined to the domains of pure logic, mathematics, and computer logic, I will use the term "logomotion," a portmanteau that combines the words "logos" and "locomotion." This term will refer to the double life of the liaison form: i.e., a form that is found inside pure logic as well as in physicalized logic. The term can be cracked open with a question: To what extent is walking an expression of logic? To what extent is locomotion a means of structuring the space around us into interconnective pathways, or walkways? To what extent does the trajectory of the places and positions we visit over the course of a single day account for the spatial logic of that day? And is it not truly extraordinary to realize, asks Tim Ingold, quoting Balzac, "that ever since men have walked, no-one has ever asked why they walk, how they walk, whether they walk, whether they might walk better, what they achieve by walking, whether they might not have the means to analyze their walk: questions that bear on all the systems of philosophy, psychology and politics with which the world is preoccupied?" (2011, 33) But of course, this is not entirely true: the problem of walking is timeless, as is the question of how walking and thinking, or how movement and pensement, can become mutually inclusive. And it is a problem that has been addressed many times. After all, there is no walking without logic behind it, and there is no logic without a walk—there is no pure locomotion but only *logomotion*.

In the structure of logic defined and shaped by Aristotle, for instance, the implication is clearly teleological: logic is a movement committed to reaching an end. As noted earlier, Aristotle's syllogism can be broken down into major premise (A), minor premise (B), and conclusion (C). The line one walks in Aristotelian logic is straight and unidirectional, and it is made up of three points that define differentiated positions in logical space. But how is it that thought is sometimes followed by action and sometimes not; sometimes by movement, sometimes not? Aristotle posed this question precisely to argue for a relationship between action and thought, between motion and motive, between progressing physically and progressing in thought, between walk and talk. He argued that when one conceives the two premises of a logical argument (A and B), one immediately invites a conclusion (C). But in the case of walking, here the two premises result in an action. It is instructive to hear Aristotle in this regard:

> When you conceive that every man ought to walk, and you yourself are a man: immediately you walk; or if you conceive that on a particular occasion no man ought to walk, and you yourself are a man, you immediately remain at rest. In both instances action follows ... and the conclusion is an action. The action results from the beginning of the train of thought. (1961, 461)

Aristotle is trying to define the act of walking in terms of a syllogism: "All men walk. I am a man. Therefore I walk." But he is doing more than that. He is arguing that there is a connection between the syllogism as a mental structure and the syllogism as a physical action. In fact, Aristotle seems to be arguing that we walk because we deem this action good or possible—we deem it to be necessary as part of a fulfilled action plan, which is promoted by thought. According to this theorization, walking is an action that expresses an intention, or a necessity, at the level of thought. Yet one does not consider and dwell on the pure logic of walking; it would be ridiculous to think that when one walks one first needs to dwell on a minor premise, "I am a man," or a major premise, "All men have legs," or a conclusion, "Therefore I walk." Instead, walking is driven by intention or desire, and desire is a substitute for reflection, according to Aristotle.

Aristotle thus offers the insight that movement is an embodied and desire-driven logic. Even though one does not need reflection to move (reflection demands a stillness and a re-moval from kinesthetic life), the mover is carrying out a syllogism nonetheless. Walking is a physical syllogism from departure point, to midpoint, to arrival point. It is somewhat similar to the notion of a logic of movement encountered earlier in Laban's film. In this case, the logic of movement refers to an association between a step-by-step mental procedure and a step-by-step physical action.

As shown in figure 6.1 (a sixteenth-century print based on Augustine of Ancona's interpretation of Aristotelian logic), the Porphyrian tree can be cut down. Logic can be replanted so that it may grow as a different tree. In the context of this discussion, trees are cultural programs: each one is put in a piece of ground and grows differently, even if they are all the same species of tree. In tree logic, one does not have to move mentally only according to the linear walks prescribed by Aristotle. But what other kinds of tree logic can grow once the Porphyrian tree is felled? Modern logic can be non-Aristotelian, in that it can allow a different family of tree to grow, one where logic is not epistemic (logic of worded structures) but mathematical (logic of mathematical structures). Nowadays, trees of thought do not grow straight or in a linear fashion. In more modern types of logic, syntactical moves are sometimes performed between predicates rather than between propositions. If I were to say, "Socrates is a man. Cows are mortal. John is an architect," the movement within this architecture would be very different because there is no common proposition. The three statements are now disjointed, and the liaison form between them is not so immediately clear. A tenuous logic still remains, however, at the level of a different kind of liaison—a different quality of logical movement. In this odd kind of syllogism, all of the sentences possess four words and all sentences have one word in common: the verb *to be*. Thus, movements of logic persevere across various levels of expression—not only in cases of propositional or predicate logic, but even at the most formal and automated level, such as numerical liaisons or liaisons between propositions of computational logic.

Miming logic

The idea that a structure of thought can be realized in a nonreflexive way, and by extension, without using words but simply by walking, is one that Beckett came up with by way of a "geometric mime," a theatrical form he first experimented with in his piece *Act without Words II* (1956). Beckett (1990, 209) prescribed a rectangular platform at the back of the stage, violently lit in its entire length, with the rest of the stage in darkness, creating a frieze effect. Beckett's stage directions call for three items on the platform named A, B, and C. A and B are both sacks, each containing a man, and C is a stack of clothes. Throughout the short mime, these objects change into three given positions: CBA (stage left), CAB (stage center), and CBA again (stage right). The three positions are changed when a horizontal pole or goad enters stage left and prods the objects, prompting the men to come out of their sacks and carry out a number of seemingly disconnected actions.

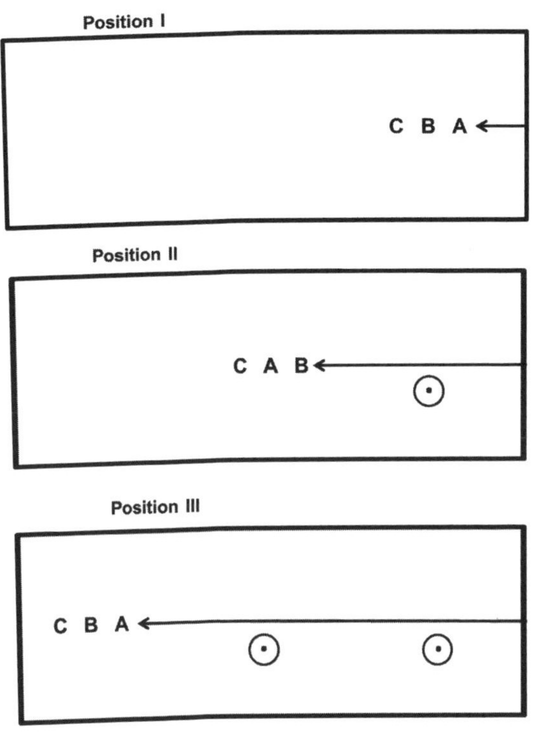

6.2
Samuel Beckett's stage diagram for
Act without Words II, adapted by the
author. See Beckett (1990), 208–211.

The piece is conceived very much as a theatrical representation of a failing logic. The three elements A, B, and C make up a syllogistic structure—beginning, middle, and end—as if to mock the Aristotelian logic of drama. These three parts are expressed quite simply as three different positions along the rectangular platform prescribed by Beckett. The agency of the pole is indicative of the arrow function in general logic: it connects one static position to another, and thus provides the sense of movement or progression of the piece. Despite this evident illustration of a structure and a logical sequence of events, and despite the blunt representation of logical movement via the intervention of the goad, the actions the two men carry out make no sense. Although they are highly contrastive, they are equally disconnected. A is slovenly and disorganized. He gobbles pills, prays, and dresses randomly. B, on the other hand, is well-dressed and neat. He brushes his teeth, he checks his watch—eleven times in total—and he consults a map and compass. Yet, as with A's actions, what B does has no logic to it. There is no beginning, no middle, and no end to the series of actions these two men perform. The movements are not mandated by a given input or output, and nothing is achieved in the end. Despite the blatant structural logic of this piece, despite this perfectly Aristotelian model of a drama, human logic is revealed to be an action that fails either way.

Beckett again entertained the idea of the geometric mime in 1963, when he started to write a piece for the actor Jack MacGowran. The discarded work, generally referred to as "J. M. Mime," was intended as a mime for two players (a son and a father or mother). The stage was plotted out as a square, the four corners of which (lettered A through D) were to be marked either by two boots and two hats or by four boots, recalling the boots and hat found onstage in *Waiting for Godot*. In 1981, Beckett revisited this concept in a short television play, first broadcast in Germany in 1982, entitled *Quad*. Beckett here explored a theme that is central to a number of his works for the theater and some of his novels: walking. More specifically, he explored rhythm (temporal and spatial), which is conveyed in this piece in relation to four distinct percussive sounds and four colors assigned to four anonymous and characterless walkers. Beckett has the four figures appear one after another, scurrying along the sides and across the diagonals of the square, shuffling in strict rhythm to complete a progression determined numerically by the author. First, according to Beckett's instructions, Player 1 enters at point A in the quadrilateral (see figure 6.3). His course is scripted as a movement along lines AC, CB, BA, AD, DB, BC, CD, DA. Once Player 1 has completed this course, he is joined by Player 3, who enters at point B. This is followed by Players 4 and 2, entering at different points.

In keeping with Beckett's instructions, each player starts and finishes his course at a given point in the square, and each one has a different point to which he or she must move, which means that at no stage in the dance/mime do the players share the same point in the square. Once all four players have completed their course, they begin to exit one by one, thus ending the first series. In total, the play consists of four ongoing series, each started by a different player, and following a different exiting order. As Deleuze explains the play, "the form of the refrain is the series, which is no longer concerned here with objects to be combined, but solely with objectless journey" (1995, 13). Instead of conceiving the drama in terms of the psychological and emotional tensions elicited by a conflict between two or more characters, Beckett is concerned here with formal conflict: i.e., the conflict evoked by the formal tension between the center of a square and its perimeter, or the diagonal versus perimetric line. Once again, despite the detailed numerical logic of the piece, the actual journey itself is pointless. The structure executed by these walking figures communicates nothing, save an empty and meaningless logic.

Likewise, instead of thinking about the progression of the piece in terms of a conventional rise and decline of dramatic action, the mime's logic is determined by the numerical sequence given by the geometric object in question (the square). Deleuze saw this space as any-space-whatever that is populated and well-trodden. Deleuze's reading would suggest that the setting of *Quad* is a recognizable space because it can be known via the act of walking. And yet, paradoxically, Beckett's *Quad* opposes itself, at least in Deleuze's reading, to all our pseudoqualified places, for Deleuze says the space in the play defines itself as "neither here nor there, where all the footsteps ever fell can never fare nearer to anywhere nor from anywhere further away" (1995, 10). Deleuze's reading of Beckett's *Quad* as having a two-way logic explains why the characters in this piece walk and walk and yet get nowhere. This problem of a logic or a walk that gets us nowhere points to a Beckett trademark: the subject is incapable of knowing itself or the space it inhabits because it fails to think itself, or to coordinate a logic for itself. The piece questions the ability of logic to make sense and to communicate, in the manner proposed by Aristotle. For all its exact structure, for all its perfect numerical arrangement in time, the play's logic still does not get us any closer to a communicable meaning, or a satisfactory outcome.

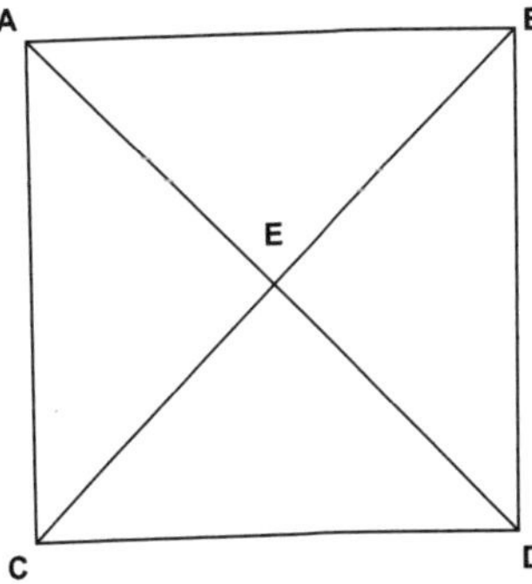

6.3
Samuel Beckett's stage diagram for
Quad I (1981), adapted by the author.
See Beckett (1990).

Beckett's piece also focuses on the problem of the center. As Beckett described the conflict of the piece: "Negotiation of E [the center point] without rupture of rhythm when three or four players cross paths at this point. Or if ruptures accepted, how best exploit?" (1990, 453) The conflict for the four hooded figures in *Quad* is to avoid collision and to negotiate the restricted space within which they operate as a unified whole. As such, the four players are as important as the center of the square, which represents the potential of encounter. Beckett's initial conception, which refers back to the "J. M. Mime" conceived almost twenty years earlier, was to have a pair of characters walking along quadrants in all possible paths starting and returning to this point of origin (called 0 in the earlier version). Whereas in the earlier version the center is a place of reconciliation, in the later version it is a point at infinity or at nothingness. Beckett's performed diagram thus produces no meaningful outcome, save to avoid collision in the middle.

114

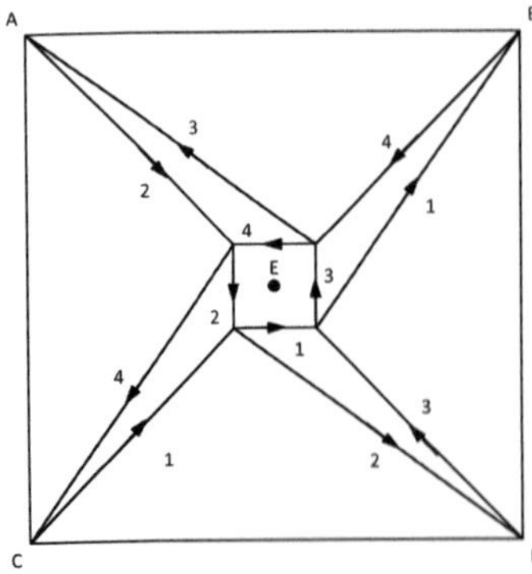

6.4
Samuel Beckett's diagram for walking mimes
to avoid collision in *Quad I* (1981), adapted
by the author. See Beckett (1990), 454.

Deleuze calls this problematic center the "potentiality of the square," avoidance of which leads to an exhaustion of space, a "withdrawal from its potentiality by making any form of coming-to-gether impossible" (1992, 77). In avoiding the center, the hooded figures also avoid physical or verbal contact. Because the center is potential, because it lies ontologically in a different plane from the actuality of the physical body in motion, the figures have no other option but to circumnavigate the point of communication (E). These figures are products of logic and language who cannot reach the formless center that is our point of true contact (our communion through pure thought). Thus, the four hooded figures remain mute pacers negotiating the course of incommunicable existence and pointless walking. If no communication takes place, then what does?

The Beckett walk

Steve Connor (2000) is one of many commentators who have noted an affinity between the works of Samuel Beckett and those of American conceptual artist Bruce Nauman. Both artists find the act of walking compulsive, and thus pay careful attention to how awkward and how prone to failure perambulatory activity can be. Clumsiness, according to Connor, is the infiltration of falling (and failing) in human action. The clumsy perambulators convey a sense of failing in a way that is almost redeeming, for in striving and not completing their characters' actions, the two artists seem to connect with a frailty in human nature that is also endearing and comical, like Chaplin's walk or Monty Python's Ministry of Silly Walks. Likewise, Nauman and Beckett represent the natural human failure to communicate by representing the awkwardness of walking or the awkwardness of physical (and by extension, mental) thinking.

Nauman's idea for a series of film performances addressing the theme of walking stems not only from reading Beckett but also from his own experience of spending hours pacing back and forth across his studio floor. Like other pieces in Nauman's repertoire such as *From Hand to Mouth* (1967), which is a wax imprint showing a movement trajectory making up a curious organology, the moves performed in Nauman's walking videos can be considered activities of a strange pedestrian logic. By pacing around his studio space, Nauman might have been hoping that locomotional activity would trigger a eureka moment. And so he decided to film just that—the pacing.

Nauman produced four black-and-white films during the winter of 1967–1968 showing walking activities carried out in his studio. The experiment extended to a number of other performance films he made in 1968–1969 using 16 mm video, which continued to address the relationship between the artist, the studio space, and the way these become entangled in the act of thinking (pacing). The relationship also points to an impossibility, an encounter with an insurmountable wall or boundary, and a failure to reach the meeting or center point, the eureka moment. Thus, the films address the process of getting to a work of art, or getting to the concept behind a work of art, rather than the actual artwork or the concept itself.

Nauman's video performances illustrate a process that fails, and thus never materializes as anything other than a pointless process. There is a humorous silliness and faultiness to these walks, a stupidity in the repetition, which prevents them from fulfilling the *telos* or end which Aristotle attributed to walking logic. Like Beckett's *Quad*, these quadrangular walks do not reach a conclusion. Rather, we see the exhaustive prolongation of the process, which becomes a surrogate or negative conclusion. In the end, the process becomes the end result, and so one might argue that the problem of not being inspired to think can be overcome by the paradox of a movement that goes nowhere.

Nauman's *Walking in an Exaggerated Manner around the Perimeter of a Square* (1967–1968) has much in common with Beckett's *Quad* (1981). Both filmed pieces, these works have as their boundary not only the unrealizable concept but also the video frame, which makes a decisive distinction between what lies within the shot and what lies outside. The intermittent disappearance of Nauman from the frame in *Walking in an Exaggerated Manner* creates an out-of-field space similar to point E in *Quad*, which is never occupied by the hooded performers. What happens with Nauman when he walks out of shot? The impossibility of walking across the first boundary (Nauman's uninspired and uncreative state) is further problematized by information that is left out of the video frame. The logic of vision and the logic of spatial locomotion are almost independent from one another; they do not speak or relate, thus provoking a loss of visual information, a loss of meaning.

Perhaps the most Beckett-like of Nauman's performance films from this period is his *Slow Angle Walk (Beckett Walk)* of 1968. The piece was inspired by Beckett's novel *Watt* (1953), in which the eponymous hero is described as having an awkward gait. In *Slow Angle Walk*, Nauman videotaped himself walking slowly and with awkward precision over a line marked out on the studio floor. This video performance enacts a description of Watt's attempt at "walking eastward":

> Watt's way of advancing due east, for example, was to turn his bust as far as possible towards the north and at the same time to fling out his right leg as far as possible towards the south, and then to turn his bust as far as possible towards the south, and at the same time fling out his left leg as far as possible to north, and then again to turn his bust as far as possible towards the south ... and so on, over and over again, many many times, until he reached his destination, and could sit down. (1959a, 30)

Taking his cue from Beckett to make a statement about the failures of walking logic, Nauman performs the Beckett walk by making a series of complicated and overcooked leg movements. First, he raises one leg while standing on another, similar to Polanski's Lucky dance. He then makes a quarter turn on his heel, then completes the step. Nauman filmed the whole procedure from different angles, so that in the end the audience does not get to see him walking in any predefined way or in any clearly defined direction. In watching Nauman's video piece, I am at once reminded of Merce Cunningham's instructions for a chance dance: "rather than thinking in one direction, i.e. to an audience in a proscenium frame, direction could be four-sided and upside down" (1968, n.p.). If the direction of this walking logic is not forward, backward, or one-sided, then the thought process is moving in unknown directions. Here is a thought process that is not governed by the unidirectional reflexive process that governs Aristotle's syllogism.

The Beckett walks, whether they refer specifically to Molloy's circling, Murphy's rocking, or Watt's spavined gait, all reveal the same failure to walk toward a resolution. In Beckett's *Molloy* (1959), the eponymous hero spends his time at the beach engaged in bizarre pastimes. For instance, Molloy has devised a system to move four stones along four pockets, with one placed in his mouth so he can suck on it. Molloy goes on to rotate the stones in many different combinations of moves to ensure the stone in his mouth is always a different one. Beckett's comment on this ridiculous calculus—literally, in the sense that Molloy is counting stones—is another example of the performance of alogos, which I have elsewhere discussed in terms of a "theatre of the surd" (Salazar Sutil 2010). For Beckett, what matters is not the proper functioning of language, but its malfunction. As such, the Beckett walks emphasize that logic and language are human constructions, and are prone to failure in their attempt to represent both mental and physical thought.

The liaison form underlying the thinking patterns of Beckett's walk-talkers is more like a vicious circle than an arrow. Rather than having a liaison form that connects one object to another—for instance, a subject to its predicate—alogical movements provoke a self-referential, self-pleasurable, self-directive movement, which means nothing is communicated or moved beyond the self. So, as opposed to a logical connective such as A → B, we end up with the foreclosed operation A ↺. If we move alogically, according to this argument, then we return to the same starting point after every start. In other words, alogical movement has no progression, no formation of sequential trajectories. There is no dance, but only "paradance."[1] Unsurprisingly, then, I must finish by returning to the place where I started. But this vicious circle does not merely bring us back to where we started; it brings us back to the same point I have made throughout: movement is an endless possibility of starting points and endpoints. Nauman's videos and Beckett's characters ultimately show not a failure of thought but a way of thinking through failure. Failure to find is also part of that quest to express a personal intention through movement. But the question is how to start. Unlike the teleology of Aristotle, or the goal-directed thinking and moving of Llinás, I would like to propose that the movement of thought is significant *because it starts*, regardless of where or how it starts or whether or not it finishes. Following his failed dance, Lucky, in Beckett's *Waiting for Godot*, is forced to think (Pozzo commands, "Think, Pig!"). Similarly, in his 1993 video *Think*, Nauman shouts at us, upside-down: "*Think!*" But how? How do we trigger thought? By walking, as Nauman suggests in his walking videos? By counting? By drawing diagrams? By jotting down nice little spider diagrams? By making a list of steps? How does pensement start to move? How does creative thinking start? Returning to Cresswell (2006), it is worth noting that one cannot take for granted the line of logic A → B, because this progression has to be invented every time one thinks. There is no starting place or starting line for thought: it can start outside thought (in external movement), or inside, or in between. The problem is that, like Lucky, Beckett's walk-talkers are waiting for something or someone else to make them think and dance. This idea is encapsulated neatly in one of Nauman's works, from 1994—a penciled message written on paper that reads: "MAKE ME THINK ME." And so the problem is when thought cannot start on its own. The problem is when the mind is no longer self-motorized, and when physical thinking becomes unsouled, uncreative, and externally motorized.

MOTION NOTATION

MOTION NOTATION

7

Notating movement

The second half of this book is an investigation of the process of inscribing movement, of laying it down on paper or on screen; of the way integrated movement can be objectified in writing or some other inscriptive medium. I will address this question in two ways: via the medium of movement notation, and later, in part IV, via the medium of data-processing technologies: i.e., motion capture and electronic data transfer protocols. In addressing both motion notation and capture, I will be exploring two very different material histories of the representation and inscription of human movement. I will also be looking at two very different ways of generating a literacy (or "digiteracy") of human movement. In the case of motion capture, human movement can be recorded as computational datasets extracted directly from tridimensional physical samples. Movement notation, on the other hand, is the process of recording and representing human movement via written symbols, which impose various calligraphic and orthographic rules of inscription. While one technology records movement as physical information directly, the other requires a further layer of symbolization, which may or may not be extracted live from an observed sample.

At least since the earliest recorded evidence of a dance notation system, which is a fifteenth-century document known as the "Catalan Manuscript" from Cervera, Spain, purportedly used to record Catalan court dance of the period, the most basic and ubiquitous way of recording dance has been dance/movement notation.[1] As movement notation historian Ann Hutchinson Guest has shown, there is no single movement notation system or modality of notation that can be said to have acquired universal use since the Cervera manuscript first came into circulation. Many movement notation systems have been put forward over the centuries, but none has acquired the degree of standardization that musical notation did within a neighboring artistic discipline.

According to computer scientist and movement theorist Alberto Camurri and colleagues, movement and dance notation attempts to "express in symbols the holistic nature of movement, while trying to tackle the observation of movement in a scientific, unambiguous way" (Camurri et al. 1986, 86). This argument stresses the obvious: movement notation is not straightforward, not least given the complexity of human movement. Camurri et al. argue that the problem of giving symbols to movement has not been solved by any single movement or dance notation in existence, given the inherent deficiencies of manual inscription and the arbitrary coding of a motor process involved in notation. Having said this, these authors hold that the advent of the computer era can change the picture, not least because the digital computer can provide a multidimensional representation and a high-level semantic. How can notation media compete with computational means of capturing movement as physical and mental activity? The key distinction between motion capture and notation, from the perspective of represented language, is that while the datasets of motion capture are also coded, and the computer also demands a notation system of its own (a programming script), motion capture datasets are not expressed in terms of arbitrary symbols. Computer code represents physical data directly captured from living movement. Notation is by definition an indirect medium, insofar as it focuses our attention not on the movement but on the symbols that *mean* movement. Notation is a medium that features an extra layer of mediation, given the intervention of symbolic representation, which imposes a linguistic meaning, an extrinsic layer of semantic interpretation, on the process of communicating scripted motion.

I will argue that the history of movement notation—of alphabetic ways of writing movement—has met a dead end with the rise of digital media technology. We are now living a different history and a different materiality of recorded and represented movement. Compared with the explosion of motion recording technologies available today—with the application of consumer products like Microsoft Kinect to motion research, for instance (more on this to come)—movement notation appears an isolated and conservative medium. Whereas mobile and smart technologies have had a global effect on people's understanding of mobility and movement, leading to a deep and democratic transformation of the way we record and represent movement (more on this also in part IV), an ideological position has penetrated knowledge of movement notation leading to rather dogmatic and, in my opinion, segregating attitudes among experts in the main notation systems (e.g., Labanotation, Benesh, and Eshkol-Wachman).

Having said this, contemporary movement notation does afford a literature of movement, which motion capture does not. It affords the means of recording movement in fine-grained detail, not only a given performance (in the way a video recording might) but also the actual composition of a movement idea. But as opposed to linguistic and computer literacy, which in principle are universalized by school curricula, very few people learn to notate movement at school or university. The acquisition of notation literacy has become increasingly bureaucratic, with official bodies imparting the qualification and certification of notation skills. Compared to the rapid growth of code literacy and the ready access e-learners have to it online, as well as the open-source availability of programming languages, notation seems like a monastic system. It is somewhat contradictory that knowledge of something as universal as the experience of human movement should be confined, as it were, to ivory towers of movement notation research. It is in this respect that computational technology affords a more inclusive, unrestricted, and nonprescriptive understanding of written movement.

Movement notation bureaucracy, I would argue, can create a sense of exclusivity surrounding the knowledge of movement, in the sense that those who understand movement according to their prescribed canon (say as determined by Labanistas) can become isolated from those who do not. By comparison, computational approaches to movement analysis and movement inscription have had a more inclusive, widespread, and practical effect. Movement notation is not a lingua franca: it is a highly politicized arena in which different apparatuses vie with each other to provide the best or most complete material record and material literature of movement. In subscribing to the use of a given movement notation system, one is agreeing to accept the rules of the system a priori, which are not universal in the way music notation arguably might be. Notating movement not only redirects the focus of knowledge away from the I-who-moves to the I-who-writes or reads; it also points to an orthodoxy, to a way of writing and reading according to rules, and to political organisms that officiate over these rules, to different material histories of representation, to different national and international interests dictating the way movement notation is taught and its academic programs are managed. Thus, someone who can use the language of Labananalysis might take the official title of certified movement analyst (CMA) once they have passed the necessary programs available from one of many dedicated bodies (including the Laban/Bartenieff Institute of Movement Studies in New York, Trinity Laban in London, and Centro Laban-Rio). A division between the New York-based Dance Notation Bureau (DNB) and the International Council of Kinetography Laban (ICKL) represents a further dislocation of Laban's original notation systems into two very different apparatuses vying to promote individual schools of notation. Each of them uses a different name for Rudolf Laban's movement notation, DNB calling it Labanotation while ICKL calls it Kinetography Laban. These divisions are of course not unique to the notated knowledge of movement; a similar fate may befall any knowledge based on a literary and ideological tradition that can be symbolized and interpreted in more ways than one.

Before I turn my attention to the inevitable technologizing of notation media, I would like to flesh out three basic tenets of a precomputational understanding of movement notation: the arbitrary determination of symbol and meaning (with reference to Eleanor Metheny's theory of the kinesymbol), the extraction of the symbol from a physical context to scripted representation (with reference to footprint movement notation), and the representation of specific elements of movement within a well-established system of contemporary movement notation (with reference to Labanotation/Kinetography Laban).

Kinesymbolism

Rota Mundi, or the universal wheel, is a near-universal symbol of movement and change, in the same way as the universal sphere discussed in part I. What I find most significant about this wheel is that it can symbolize motion of a biological kind (circular or recurring cycles in nature) as well as of a machinic kind (a technology of movement and change). This example is useful when trying to understand what effects symbolization may have in the representation of human movement. The symbol of the wheel relies on the kind of one-to-one correspondence linguists like to trace between signifiers and signifieds. Indeed, the wheel is a carrier of meaning from symbol to interpretation. The sphere, as I discussed it in chapter 1, does not mean anything. After all, what does

Laban's kinesphere mean? What does the icosahedron model of the kinesphere mean? Whereas the wheel is a figure of speech, the sphere is a figure in itself, which would suggest that the latter does not exist in the domain of linguistic language. As soon as we enter the orbit of words and signifiers that mean something, or as soon as the symbol becomes literary and linguistic, we create an arbitrary division between movement and meaning, between representation and interpretation. This begs the question: Why does movement have to signify something? Why does movement have to be subsumed within the confined domain of worded and symbol-dependent meaning, as though it was a word or a figure of speech? Why does the language of movement have to be a linguistic language? What produces meaning in this case is not necessarily the movement, but the semiotic codification of auxiliary gestures and words attributed to a movement, which is established by the power of convention. Unlike the free gestures of unworded languages (e.g., mathematics, programming, formal choreography), hand and body gestures that are auxiliary to verbal communication reduce the semantic potential of gestural movement to a proxy speech, a linguistic crutch that supports and assists in the relaying of worded communication. The gestures used in verbal communication or body language are subservient gestures—slave gestures. To sum up, meaning does not derive from movement nor from free gesture, but from the representation and interpretation of spoken or written symbols.

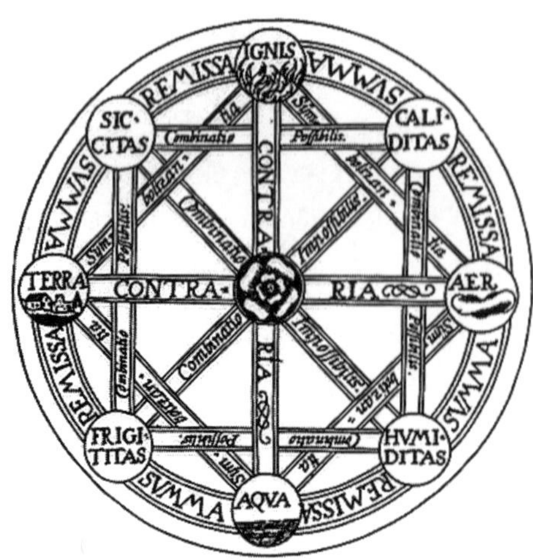

7.1
Rota Mundi or the Universal Wheel,
Leibniz's frontispiece diagram for
Ars combinatoria (1666).

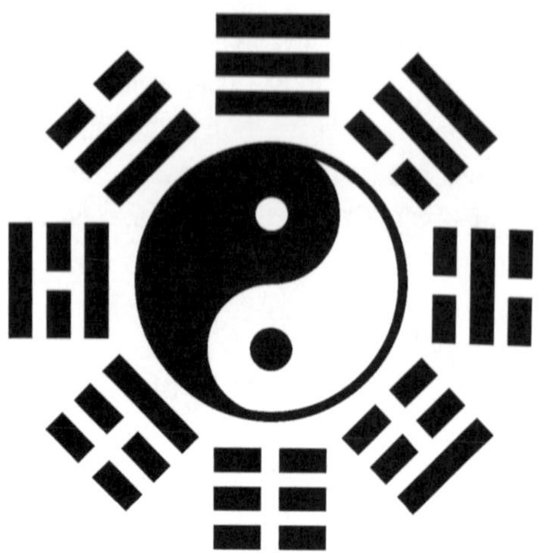

7.2
I Ching wheel showing the taijitsu
diagram and hexagrams.
Graphic design by the author.

And herein lies the confusion, caused no doubt by the literary symbol's provocation of meaning. Notation mediates between lived-in movement and represented movement via literary symbols that signify and give meaning to the written record. The problem is that while meaning ought to be assigned to the linguistic symbol, it is sometimes assigned to movement as well. One can be mistaken, then, for thinking that movement has a meaning, that it signifies something else. There might be a direct relationship between auxiliary gestures (say a pointing finger) and its semantic interpretation (say the translation of the action into words). But as I pointed out in my introduction, I will not treat the language of movement using this linguistic paradigm. There is no need for semiotic interpretations of movement here, since my concern is with the value of physical movement as a function or extension of pure, unworded thought. This is why, in my opinion, movement languages are comparable to programming languages, to mathematics or to logic. The trouble with movement notation media, as I see it, is that it often does not recognize this independence of movement from linguistic languages. On the contrary, a Laban-based model like the Language of Dance or motif notation, as put forward by Ann Hutchinson Guest, subordinates movement to the power of linguistic language (more on this to come).

Bodily movements used in the context of sign language are also meaning-coded, inasmuch as the language of signing is intended to provide an alternative, an auxiliary, or a parallel to speech—for instance in the case of deaf-community sign languages, home sign, or video remote interpreting. By the language of movement, however, I do not mean body language or sign language, but rather formal structures of physicalized thought. And this poses a fundamental problem applicable to any system of movement representation: how can you add interpretation, meaning, and semiotic arbitration, which are extrinsic processes removed from physical/mental experience, and which belong to social convention, in order to communicate physical life? There is one way of bypassing the problem, which is to redefine these notions so that "meaning" does not refer to symbolic, speech-dependent, and linguistic language.

Eleanor Metheny and Lois Ellfeldt's philosophical theory of physical education seems the most appropriate solution, insofar as these thinkers deal with the issue of meaning in movement while avoiding a linguistic regime. The exclusion of linguistic analysis implies no judgment but simply a recognition that the understanding of physical experience must reside in kinesthetic life, not in the abstraction of natural language and linguistics. Metheny's work (1968, 1975) concerns a philosophy of physical education focused on how concept-ideas can be derived not only from word-based discourse but also from sensory experience and movement-based discourse. In other words, this author argued that sense experience can be conceptualized—much as abstract ideas can. For Metheny (1968), a movement can mean something because it is performed physically and because it achieves a given communicational or performative value—its significance follows from this determination. Thus, bypassing a linguistic theory of symbols, Metheny and Ellfeldt speak of the "kinesymbol." Conceptualization of how to make meaningful movements depends on the performance of movement, not the symbolic inscription of the movement on a piece of paper. For this reason, the symbols Metheny had in mind cannot be worded, nor can they be represented in a domain outside or entirely removed from the body. When a golfer swings a club, or a ballerina conducts a ballet step, the body feels these structures and then abstracts these situated actions into body-symbolic expressions that convey a meaning. This meaning is situated in physical action, not in discursive or worded interpretation—it is a meaning that can only be interpreted by performing the activity of golfing or dancing.

Metheny's thesis is grounded on a theoretical distinction between what she calls the "kinestruct" and the "kinescept." Kinestruction, according to this thesis, refers to somatic forms or structures produced by the physical body in movement. Kinesception, meanwhile, refers to sensory feelings created by a kinesthetic perception of these structures. For instance, in the language of classical ballet, an arabesque could be defined as a spatial kinestruction, in the sense that the structure is realized by a body-mass arranged in this archetypal balletic position. *Pas de bourrée* is an example of a temporal kinestruction: the movement is structured into three times, or three short steps that typically provide transition to another movement. The issuance of these spatial and temporal structures also produces a *feel* for the movement, or kinesception: in addition to achieving the archetypal structure, the ballerina can sense how this structure feels from within, without actually seeing the position or temporal structure in a mirror or video footage. Finally, Metheny argues that insofar as it is a natural and unique faculty of human beings to reason through symbols, so movement is not only habitual but also conceptual. Thus, when we conceptualize through movement, we do not reflexively articulate concept-ideas, nor do we express these concepts in words. The ballerina is not necessarily communicating anything via words in order to acquire a sensory feeling of that symbol that is the arabesque. Like Aristotle's logic of walking, the kinesthetic concept is realized directly by the body via kinesthetic action. We are thinking, in effect, without using reflexive or word-discursive strategies of communication. According to Susanne K. Langer, this symbolic activity "never breaks faith with logic in the strictest sense: wherever a symbol operates, there is a meaning ... no symbol is exempt from the office of logical formulation" (quoted in Metheny 1975, 4). In other words, movement language is liable to a kind of internal logic, and to the movement contained in thought (as discussed in the preceding chapter). The significance of a kinesymbol depends on the natural connections afforded by the human body and by situated movement within specific sporting and dancing contexts. Neither verbal, visual, nor auditory, the kinesymbol is a formulation of experience perceived kinesthetically.

Following on from Metheny's theorization, I propose to consider the notation of movement as a break away from this embodied level of symbolization. Thus, while kinesymbolism is nonverbal, nondiscursive, and nonliterary, it is still meaningful, and it is still a knowledge or conceptualization of movement. However, the term "meaning" has now been reprogrammed. As I said before, the only way we can understand the semantics of movement is if we redefine the notion of meaning in movement. For Metheny (1975), a golf swing does not provoke meaning in the same way that the word "swing" provokes meaning. And here is the crux of the matter: whereas the former model extracts meaning directly from physical activity, the latter extracts meaning from the word, which is an extra layer of mediation, removed from physical life.

Bearing this in mind, movement notation could be said to provide, generally speaking, a scripted and literary axiology that can record the golfer swinging a club, or a dancer feeling a structure of ballet, from the disembodied and third-person perspective of the notator. Even if the dancer and the notator are the same person, the same ballerina, the moment the ballerina writes her movements, as opposed to simply moving, she is shifting from a first- to a third-person perspective and thus taking a completely different "persona," which is reflexive and removed from her own physical movement. The problem, as I noted above, is that whereas the kinesymbol is expressed directly by the sensing body, and whereas the concept emerges sense-schematically, when we try to represent these actions in writing, the disembodiment of writing can forget the kinesymbol, or rather, can fail to record the kinesymbol, by giving prevalence to arbitrary and abstract symbols instead. If, as I have already shown, human movement is a complex interplay of mental and physical determinations, then movement notation could be said to side with a mental consideration of movement, a detached intellection that is much closer to literary writing. In the following pages, I will be paying close attention to the susceptibility of movement notation to forgetting its determination in somatic and kinesthetic situations, and its liability to succumb to a linguistic approach.

The impression left by footprints

In 1962 American pop artist Andy Warhol produced a series of works entitled *Dance Diagrams*, showing lines and numbers connecting color-coded footsteps (white for left foot, black for right). Warhol's diagrams show conventional steps in a number of dance styles including tango and foxtrot. The unit used to represent movement in these diagrams is, of course, symbolic. However, everyone knows what the footprint symbol means—it is not an arbitrary but a natural symbol. It does not need to be interpreted, only to be reiterated. The fact that these diagrams could be serialized, printed onto a floor, a canvas, a poster, or any other surface, reinforces Warhol's vision of the artistic value of everyday objects, activities, and experiences—the possibility of depicting cultural expressions like pop dance as gallery artwork. The work also shows how an enduring system of representation of movement such as footprint notation, which within the ambit of dance history can be traced back to the sixteenth century at least, will almost certainly survive the test of time. When we walk, our feet leave footprints behind, as opposed to words or glyphs. Speaking in relation to his piece *Traces* (1969), in which a sequence of seagull footprints were carved onto the *inner* wall of a building in

San Benedetto del Tronto from floor to window, Italian artist Mario Merz pointed out that this imprint signifies a "passage of the environment onto itself." Like Warhol's *Dance Diagrams*, Merz's footprints are a found "writing" that is part and parcel of any natural environment (1989, 107). There is a sense of immediacy to these works, in the sense that footprints and footsteps (the sound of falling feet) can be followed by anyone who can walk over them, or anyone who happens to hear them. Anyone who has two feet and can walk—or rather, anyone who can create a kinestructural idea of the movement in their head—is able to follow Warhol's instructions (hence their popular appeal). Movement does not rely on any other symbolic layer or encumbrance. Warhol's dance steps are an invitation to move. A printed footstep is an invitation to walk over someone else's movement. Thus, the logic of writing and of language, which is iteration, is realized by the most natural of printing and inscriptive media: the printed feet.

When the earliest human footprints found outside Africa were discovered in 2014 in a mud estuary in Happisburgh, 17 miles northeast of Norwich, England, scientists set out to *read* the prints, as though they were in fact written symbols. They were found to be 800,000-year-old footprints belonging to a small group, perhaps a family of a long-extinct hominid species known as *Homo antecessor*. 3D mapping of the footprints provided scientists with considerable amounts of data. For instance, archaeologists could ascertain the weight of the individuals, their size, the footwear they used. What this archaeological find points to is the inevitable link between the accidental footprint and its natural symbolic value. As a signifier laden with information, the footprint becomes much more than a telltale sign reading "someone was here." Indeed, the footprint can be considered one of the most basic forms of recorded movement. Furthermore, footprints are one of the earliest forms, if not the earliest, of kinesymbolic writing, which is meaningful in itself.

Tim Ingold and Jo Lee Vergunst hold that footprints are part of the same action as thinking or memorializing a space, adding: "knowledge and footprints are not opposed as mental to material. The relation between them is rather tantamount to one between bodily movement and its impression" (2008, 7). As such, and as the Happisburgh prints show, footprints leave information about a spatial and even social context, which can be partially reconstructed by deciphering the printed movement record. From this perspective, the Happisburgh prints can be considered a kind of odography—a natural writing with the feet. Their interpretation is applied to the reconstruction of pre-human movement as part of a kind of archaeology of movement. Not unlike Étienne-Jules Marey's odography, this form of writing involves capturing a physical action—the footfall—in the form of a material record. What the footsteps of *Homo antecessor* in Happisburgh evoke for me is an ancestral way of recording our kinetic experience. Footprinting is a way of showing the passing of movement and the friction of living movement against the materiality of a floor, of a physical domain against which the virtuality of movement leaves its enduring impression. Crucially, these natural signatures can be utilized as cultural systems of representation, and not only in simple dance steps like the ones recorded in Warhol's artwork. Underlying the Australian Aboriginal dream-tracks made famous by Bruce Chatwin in his book *Songlines* (1987) are unique systems of representation based on the tracking of ancestral footprints connecting a country or landscape into a cultural network of great complexity. As Chatwin pointed out, an Australian aborigine can walk into this system of representation and in so doing can "tread on the footprints of Ancestors" like scientists following those of *H. antecessor*.[2] As Merz noted of his seagull footprints, this form of representation allows the environment to fold on itself and to be known within the domain of representation and impression, through the action-provoking power of kinesymbols. As Ingold and Vergunst put it: "footprints are formed by walking within the world, rather than tramping upon its exterior surface. Prints are not stamps but impressions." They conclude: "This is why treading in predecessors' footprints, so that they mingle with one's own, is enough to establish a co-presence. Footprints are traces of memory" (2008, 7).

In a historical and literary context, the use of footprint recording is evidenced in a number of early forms of dance notation. *Discursos sobre el arte del dançado*, a dance treatise produced by Juan de Esquivel Navarro and first published in Seville in 1642, contains a Warhol-like illustration intended to show the difference between two kinds of dance step (*reverencia*). It is possible that Navarro's notation system was borrowed from French fencing manuals, in which footprint notation had been used as early as 1523 (Guest 1998). Where exactly the idea came from ultimately makes no difference. What matters is the fact that a footstep is a naturally occurring kinesymbol, and that it is not encumbered by layers of linguistic meaning and interpretation. Thus, Navarro does not need to explain what a footprint means. However, Navarro's manuscript does not only record physical footprints, in the way the Happisburgh prints did. Navarro's dance notation system takes the kinesymbol one step further, toward a purely symbolic value. Other orthographic symbols are needed in addition to footprints. Thus, in 1661, while director of the Académie Royale de Danse, the choreographer and dance master Pierre Beauchamp was commissioned by Louis XIV's court to devise a dance notation system, which Beauchamp produced by way of a refined formulation of Navarro's treatise. Known as Beauchamp-Feuillet dance notation, this system became the standard and most widely available medium for the recording of European court dance in the second half of the seventeenth century and the first decades of the eighteenth. What Beauchamp and later Raoul Auger Feuillet did was to assign footstep symbols to individual footsteps within the dance step and have these printed on either side of a track line. A variety of subsidiary marks would indicate sinking, rising, sliding, turning, and other features of the dance step, carefully placed at the point in the step where they were supposed to take place.

These dance notation systems take a step beyond natural odography, in order to introduce orthographic symbolism and arbitrary meaning. The orthographic markings on a Beauchamp-Feuillet score have to be learned before one can obtain an interpretation of the dance script. Unlike the direct expression of movement forms found in natural footprints, this type of dance notation marks a significant move away from an environmental form of writing—a writing of impressions printed onto the landscape—to a purely symbolic record, and to a modern, indoor literary understanding of movement as an authorial score. Clearly, there is a fundamental distinction between these two recorded histories of movement. Whereas the footprint record means nothing in the linguistic sense, the footprint notation *means* something. The symbols in the Beauchamp-Feuillet score mean different things: rising, sliding, sinking, and so on. Furthermore, the notation score carries the "meaning" of a dance, as conceived by an author of the dance, or an author of the dance notation record.

To recover the source or original movement, which the Beauchamp-Feuillet notator is trying to record, one has to reconstruct the meaning of the symbols. What does the notator mean when he or she writes this symbol in this way? The focus is directed away from the dancer/mover, onto the writer of the movement. As I said earlier, even if these two were the same person, they are not the same agent. The activity of reading the script slows down the process of moving. It demands, as I said, a moment of re-moved reflection, which encumbers the whole mediation process and turns mediation into a static and possibly disembodied experience. In sum, the fundamental purpose of the notation medium is to capture movement in the strictest sense—to bring experienced movement to a recorded standstill. Thus, this type of script is not necessarily intended to incite new movement, but to reconstruct, to reiterate, to repeat an author's movement.

Who are the "authors" of the Happisburgh prints? We know their size, possibly even their weight, but do we know their names? We know the names of the choreographers and dancers who produced manuscripts using Beauchamp-Feuillet notation. Symbolic dance notation does not only transform the culture of movement inscription by removing the movement from its natural landscape: it takes the movement away from the anonymity and commonality of people within that landscape to a private sphere, to a private space of interpretation (the dance studio or theater space), and to a sense of private ownership, to an author who writes. The symbolic notation medium turns movement into an object of proprietorship: as soon as one can write movement down, one can own it, one can claim rights over it, and thus place a completely arbitrary value (even a price) on the sharing of a movement script. The shift from natural to symbolic and socially convened forms of representation thus highlights a politics of ownership within kinetic experience, from public to private, from natural dance to dance as an art practice and an industry.

For a tracker who follows footprints and other impressions written on a landscape, the whole natural environment may be filled with meaningful records that transfer knowledge concerning an individual or entity being tracked (living or dead), whether the tracker is an Australian Aborigine or a scientist reading 800,000-year-old footprints. In the indoor and individualized orbit of seventeenth-century French court culture, signs are no longer embedded into an environmental space but onto a manuscript, a customized medium, which becomes a powerful vehicle for the transmission of an authorial knowledge of human movement.

Thus, the authorial character of footprint notation becomes the appropriate means of writing down works of choreography that are owned by a given master dancer or choreographer. Its extensive use within the cultural context of court dance is worthy of note: Beauchamp-Feuillet notation finds itself at home in the recording of an authorship or ownership of movement. Unsurprisingly, movement notation has endured as a representational medium used to score authored choreographic works. In computer-aided motion design and composition, however, the concept of the author of a movement composition and the ownership of a movement becomes less clear. The computerization and networked mediation of recorded movement open up possibilities of a history in which total movement has no owners or authors and no authorly textuality; the possibility of inventing a new landscape, a new country of common walks and open networks, in whose tracks a mobile system of knowledge is being anonymously performed.

Movement staves

According to Laban (1977), movement notation is the objective representation of human movement, such that movement may be recorded, preserved, archived, and thus communicated as a literary form. Laban's contributions in the development of a novel system of movement notation were also inspired by the desire to conventionalize and indeed standardize the representation of movement literature. Two features of his evolving system of movement notation can serve as linchpins for further analysis. First, Laban drew on the system of musical notation in order to propose a "stave" model of movement representation. Whereas in Western musical notation the stave is represented conventionally as a set of five horizontal lines and four spaces, determining the reading orientation of music from left to right (the same as Western canons in word writing), Labanotation/Kinetography Laban features three stave lines and a number of dotted lines indicating parts of the body, which are placed vertically. This means that the reading orientation of a Laban score is from bottom to top.

The adoption of a stave model of movement notation not only affords Labanotation/Kinetography Laban with the means of standardizing the practice of movement literature, it also equips the system with the means of matching the measures of a movement composition with the measures of the music, via the tick marks used to indicate the beats. Thus while symbols inserted within the vertical lines in Laban's stave indicate bodily information, horizontal lines indicate time. Tick marks, on the other hand, indicate alignment with music. The writing of movement according to a stave model is not without consequence, nor indeed is Laban's choice of standardization via musical notation unimportant as far as this critical examination of notation media is concerned. Laban was drawing on a symbolic apparatus that is the standard means of musical representation, not least because he intended his own system of movement notation to be adopted as a universal form, much as stave notation is in the canons of Western music.

The function of the stave in standardizing representation is also a key consideration in Jacques Lacan's theory of language, which I touched on in an earlier chapter. There are further instructive resonances between Laban and Lacan in this regard. Lacan argued that it is through the mark of arbitrariness characteristic of the letter that the extraordinary contingency of thought (or the subconscious) could be explained. On this basis, he argued that speech occurs on different staves, much as in a musical score, and that in representing speech and discourse via the arbitrary standard of this stave one can gain a sense of how thought is ultimately explained, or communicated. Not only did Lacan contend that all discourse is aligned along the several staves of a musical score; he went on to argue that analysis consists "in playing on the multiple staves of the score that speech constitutes in the registers of language" (2006, 241). By implication, in the same way that music or indeed Laban's idea of movement cannot be taken into account except by this standard representation of the staved score, speech and discourse cannot be fully grasped or analyzed unless written thought is laid out in horizontal lines that make up alphabetic writing. Unlike the lines of a musical or movement stave, the language stave is made up of lines of letters and words. Indeed, like the marks that cut through a musical stave, or a Labanotation/Kinetography Laban stave, Lacan's staves of language produce signification at its cuts, or in those marks that divide the stave into segments. In Lacan's words:

> This stave upon which every unit, every significance or sentence should be inscribed—undoubtedly at its cuts—shows how, at the two extremities of the sequence of these measures, this cut comes to circumscribe, striate, section the stave. Let us say that there is here, in this regard, more than one way of questioning oneself. (1964–1965, 17)

One could speak of the principle of the stave, according to which language by a rule of thumb is expressed in parallel lines that show discourse along different tiers (e.g., different musical notes, different body parts, different layers of speech), as well as different cuts showing how the progression of language is inevitably discrete and broken in time. The spatiality and temporality of staved language is broken into letters or words, into notes or beats, into body parts or movement beats. Language is always a breakdown of thought. This principle of the stave is at the heart of Laban's ambitions to standardize a system of movement notation and his aspirations for the formalization of the representation of human movement as scripted language. Indeed, the stave principle is also featured in Benesh movement notation, where ledger lines are also used to represent extensions above and below the body. In seeking to stave off the writing of multidimensional movement, Laban seems to be echoing Lacan's theory of language as a linear chain of signification, a linear logic of component parts that make up, in Laban's case, a syntax and a grammar of movement. Labanotation scholar Ann Hutchinson Guest draws on Laban's notion of a movement grammar and syntax in order to position movement language alongside linguistic discourse—much in the same way as Lacan places musical language alongside word-based discourse. In [Hutchinson] Guest's analysis, we find the principle of the stave justified in terms of the way movement involves a language of kinetic gestures that make up basic "parts of speech." Thus, according to this author, "there is a clearly constructed grammar which defines the relationship of the movement 'words' to each other and their given function in the movement 'sentence.'" She adds: "the basic elements in this language of movement fall in the categories of nouns, verbs, and adverbs" (1977, 14). As I mentioned earlier, the danger of this linguistic ideology is to see all languages, including movement languages, as subordinate to speech. Thus, Laban and [Hutchinson] Guest seek linearization of movement in order to subscribe to the linearization of spoken language. In succumbing to a linguistic approach to the writing of movement, these theories are caught up in a basic and yet flawed assumption: that language unfolds like a set of parallel lines, always unidirectionally, and always in such a way that it can be equated and indeed subsumed within the linguistic paradigm. As I will show toward the end of this chapter, the stave notation paradigm is undermined by other forms of writing movement which are neither linear, nor alphabetic, nor indeed associated with speech.

Troubling the symbol

Before I turn my attention to a critique of stave notation, I will consider one other rather problematic element of Labanotation/Kinetography Laban. I am referring to the arbitrary symbols that are necessarily placed within the stave to indicate different units of a language of movement, as conceived by Laban. Laban drew not only on a modern historical tradition of movement notation but on the ancient symbolization of movement. Laban's intention was to find what he called "primary action signs" (Laban 1977, xiv): symbols shared by different cultures which could be used to represent movement universally. Laban wrote that examples of these primary action signs could be found in the mantic symbols invented by Tibetan monks, or in Babylonian cuneiform characters as well as Egyptian and Chinese scripts. He also pointed out that systems like Beauchamp-Feuillet notation provide basic principles that are universally valid and are simple and rational, the only problem being that these particular symbols are restricted to the cultural practices of court dance. Thus, the trouble for Laban lay not in the principle of an orthographic and symbol-dependent system but in the cultural transformation of movement in a modern context: he wanted a system that could provide the level of standardization that Beauchamp-Feuillet notation provided in the context of seventeenth-century court dance, but in the context of a modern culture of movement defined by industrial activity, the rise in physical and movement education, and the growth of a psychologically inflected understanding of movement (xv). Laban was touching on the idea of a universal form of script, which could be used to represent objectively the modernity of human movement.

Laban also wanted a universal script form that could give material expression to his universal language of harmonic space, or choreutics. Thus, Labanotation/Kinetography Laban is a system that transcribes the formalized space models used in choreutics to a collection of symbols that indicate tridimensional points in movement space. I will argue that the process of transcribing movement from choreutic space to a kinetographic stave highlights a fundamental problem, given the arbitrary nature of symbols and the stave model of linguistic representation.

How can movement be represented faithfully and fully in the domain of script? How can a flat page or screen contain tridimensional movement? We have already discussed how Laban formalized choreutic space according to geometric solids. In figure 7.3, we can see how—based on the cubic determination of the kinesphere—Laban could identify specific spatial elements (e.g., the vertices of the cube) to help define some of the basic symbolic units of kinetographic script. In other words, Labanotation/Kinetography Laban is a transcriptive operation. It starts with the formal understanding of geometric space in terms of a diagram of the choreutic model (in this case the cube). From this determination, specific elements are ejected onto the domain of script as individual symbols spaced out within a stave. If you look closely at the figure, you will note that on the left side the symbols are still embedded within the diagrammatic representation of cubic space. On the right, they have been liberated from this diagram and have been floated onto the domain of symbolic inscription, landing on a stave in order to be reassembled as elements within a movement script. This cut-and-paste procedure evidently involves turning a representation of 3D space into a flat analogy within the plane of written representation, i.e., the kinetographic score.

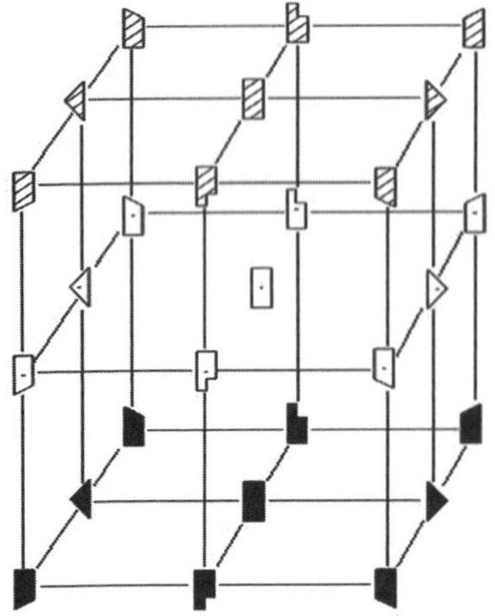

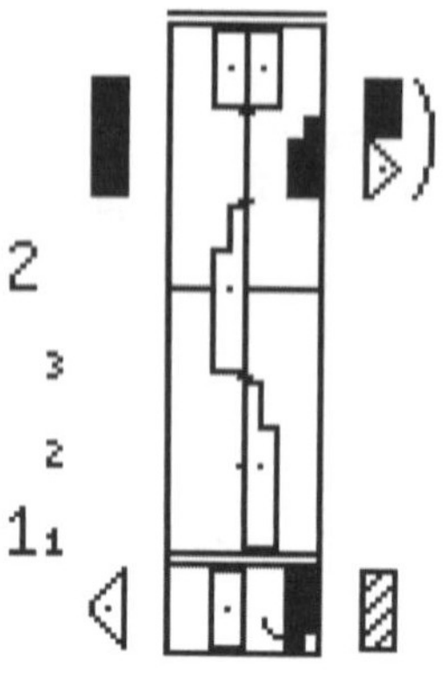

7.3
Representation of Laban's direction symbols in
choreutic diagram form (left) and stave notation
form (Labanotation/Kinetography Laban) (right).

While the symbol is preserved in this operation, thus extracting key spatial information, the qualitative properties of space are not transferred onto the script, nor is the qualitative temporal determination of movement. A great many determinations are lost in this jump from lived movement to represented movement. What the cubic description of the kinesphere affords, as far as Laban's kinetographic record is concerned, are twenty-eight "Direction Symbols" that can be written down to describe arbitrary points in 3D space. Of course, Laban must ensure that each direction symbol is expressed in a contrastive fashion so that each represents a discrete unit in his script system. Since he settled on eight different formal directions in space, he required eight symbols. And because he split space into three different levels (high, middle, low), he required three modifications in the shading of these eight symbols. But are these symbols and modifications enough to understand the entire space available within a cube, or the kinesymbolic concept of cubic movement in lived-in space?

So far, this entire system rests on a three-step process toward abstraction: from lived-in space, to a diagrammatic description of geometric space, to a respacing of symbols within the domain of script (stave notation). This three-step process guarantees the transcription of the symbol from a 3D diagram to a 2D script in such a way that the symbol does not lose its association with an original lived-in movement and a stereotypical movement space. However, when we read these symbols on a stave, rather than as units within a diagram, or indeed rather than kinesymbols obtained directly from physical life, they lose their concrete existence within movement space and become arbitrary symbols. As such, Laban's notation system cannot bypass the problem with any stave model of movement inscription: once we lose the lived-in sense of the kinesymbolism, we lose a basic connection with the space where we actually move. We no longer experience the symbol by physically moving inside the cube (in a physical or imaginary sense). We no longer have access to the movement, but only to the reading and writing of movement. Once again, the agency shifts from the choreutic mover to the notator. And while these two might be the same person, I must insist, the moment this person shifts from moving to writing, a fundamental change of agency occurs, since notation is a medium so abstracted from the actual movement that it provokes an intellectual understanding of movement, a third-person perspective that is cut off from its physical determination. This is not in itself a problem, since an understanding of total movement demands, as I pointed out earlier, an external representation of internal phenomena. Except that as a medium, stave notation slows down the transference from physical to mental, creating a disjointed and cut-off connection in which intellection becomes divided and excluded, often provoking a Cartesian split between two differentiated agents: the one who moves and the ones who writes.

Automating notation

Is there such a thing as a notation converter tool that can translate movement notation into animation? Can an artificial movement notation machine script notation? In short, can notation be automated? The short answer to this question is yes, at least in principle. As we will see, the desire to marry notation and automation also highlights a fundamentally uncongenial relationship. According to computer scientist and software engineer Tom Calvert, the need to automate notation stems from the fact that although notation is fundamental to dance reconstruction and dance research, few dancers or choreographers can read it and even fewer are capable of producing scores. Calvert's assumption is that in the ambit of movement reconstruction and research the dancer/choreographer will always require a medium to script movement, and that if he or she does not know how to notate, a machine notator might provide the answer.

No doubt the first step toward an integration of automated technology and movement notation would be a digitalized version of a notation system. One thing computer technology can do, within the context of movement notation media, is help notators edit and process their movement scripts via a digital platform—what Wilke et al. called the "word processor" paradigm for human movement notation (2005).[3] But how can movement word processors gain comprehensive implementation, if they stem from a history of movement representation that is in many ways in conflict with the culture of movement representation found in digital platforms? Knowledge of how to compose and notate movement is more broadly acquired via the understanding of AutoCAD technology, Microsoft Kinect technology, and other comprehensive systems. And I have not even mentioned motion capture. Indeed, quite unlike motion capture, which as we will presently see is a medium that finds its way easily into comprehensive applications in a wide array of disciplines and industries, digital notation remains an academic concern. Why so? In my opinion, it is because of its authorly, exclusivist, and even elitist understanding of movement literacy.

What word processor tools cannot do (among other things) is automate the notation process, so that the computer can read a live movement and turn it automatically into notation. Nor can the system turn an existing movement notation score into an animation. The impetus to create a system capable of achieving this can be traced back to the early seventies, particularly to A. Michael Noll's vision of computerized choreography and Merce Cunningham's collaborations with Tom Calvert and his team at Simon Fraser University. Parallel projects were subsequently drawn up to realize systems that would be able to assist in the creation and editing of dance notation scores, with a specific focus on dance and choreography. For instance, Calvert and his team developed a variety of human animation techniques that would lead, in 1995, to the creation of LifeForms (later DanceForms), an animation tool for choreographers. The impetus to technologize dance notation culminated with the development of LabanDancer, developed by Ilene Fox, Rhonda Ryman, Tom Calvert, and Lars Wilke in 2004.[4] The intention behind this technology, according to Wilke et al., was that it would be able to handle the great majority of movement situations available in Labanotation correctly and that it would recognize the context for the movement (2005, 202). In practice, the system would be able to read LabanWriter files (.lw4) and create animation out of them automatically. The development

of the LabanDancer prototype remains on hold, according to Calvert, for "financial and intellectual reasons" (Calvert n.d.). As Calvert himself suggests, LabanDancer poses more problems than it
seeks to address. For instance, "can 3D animation replace notation for archival purposes?" Or, "how
can a computer-aided system create an unambiguous, unique representation of human movement?"
During a workshop on movement, dance, and notation methods held at Ohio State University in 2004,
this missing link between LabanWriter and LabanDancer (or between notation and animation) was
referred to as an "interlingua," which according to Calvert has become the top priority for the field.
This crossover between notation and animation also raises questions regarding the need to further
augment the possibilities of movement notation within technological domains, so as to be able to
utilize the literacy and knowledge amassed by notation media within new display environments, or
within remote forms of collaboration and movement practice, or even within web-based environments or virtual worlds, for instance by using notation expertise to score movement compositions in
online virtual worlds like Second Life.

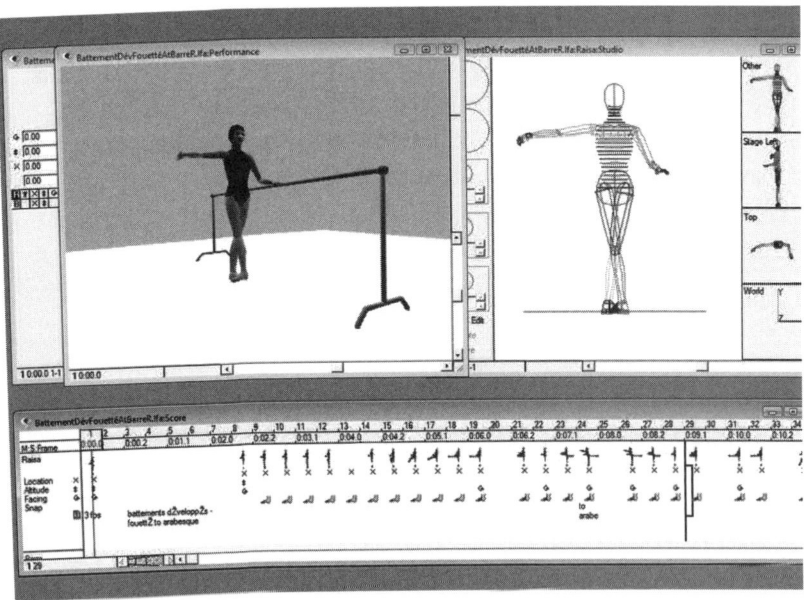

7.4
Still from DanceForms software, developed by
Tom Calvert et al. © Credo Interactive (courtesy of
Tom Calvert).

But despite these attempts to reconcile the media of movement notation and movement animation, there is an ideological bias attached to movement notation that goes all the way back to the authorial systems of regal balletic notation developed by Beauchamp and Feuillet. In seeking to create a bridge, the expert community does not fully address the fundamental tensions between the authorial history of notated movement and the largely anonymous history of computer-coded movement, or between the iterative and convergent character of notation and the creative and divergent character of computer-aided motion composition. The trouble with this synthesis is that the historical materiality of written notation and that of automated and computer-aided motion are radically different and incompatible in many ways. Thus, the demand for notation among the creative movement industries will be—generally speaking—confined to more conservative sectors like ballet or certain arms of academic research, where the desire to preserve traditional forms may be stronger than the desire to innovate technologically. The point is that the synthesis of notation and automation highlights the imperfect affinity between two communities.

The stalling of LabanDancer and the interlingua project further reinforces this gap. The LabanDancer experiment shows that one history of representation (notation) does not flow into the other (computer animation) quite so easily or arbitrarily. The difficulty of finding unambiguous ways of representing movement, of revealing how it is materialized, in what context, to what effect, in what conditions, and in whose terms, all point to the need for these systems of representation to be continuously catching up with the times in order to provide ad hoc solutions. In the same way that Laban's system to represent movement took into consideration the industrialization of labor, the mechanization of life, and the development of a movement education system and a psychology of movement, current research seeks to find ways of representing movement that reflect the digital era and the way human beings are moving in its context.

Post-stave notation

Within the context of experimental graphic notation in music, postnotational experiments can be traced back to the works of a number of avant-garde practitioners, including Morton Feldman's *Projections* (1950–1951), and of course the experimental notation pioneered by members of the Fluxus movement, especially Al Hansen, David Tudor, and John Cage. Graphic forms of notation brought these experimental music practitioners into a collaborative dialogue with visual and movement artists, in an attempt to devise graphic or indeed intermedial scores instead of traditional stave notations. One of the goals of this movement was to allow performers to play music more freely and in a way that was more open to chance. The move away from notation and into graphic scores provided Cage in particular the opportunity to move away from a prescribed and authorial interpretation and performance of a musical composition. The function of notating music and dance thus became an artistic process in itself, rather than a standard recording method. From this perspective, the Fluxus experiments represent a radical paradigm shift—a turn away from notation as the authoritative medium for the standardizing record of music (or indeed dance). Multilayered plexigrams, for instance, allowed Cage to play with transparent sheets on which images could be screened, producing not only graphic forms of musical ideography but animated forms of notation as well. In fact, these objects were intended not only as scores for musical performance but as works of art in themselves—an idea that extended from the musical score to the working diagram to a newly conceived vanguardist art object. Here is an idea that is central to Warhol's *Dance Diagrams* of the early sixties. Likewise, the impact of Fluxus on the movement arts, particularly as Cage and Tudor worked in proximity to Merce Cunningham, further expanded the possibilities of graphic and ideographic forms of writing dance movement using unconventional and personalized forms of choreographic writing.

Cunningham's commitment to an experimental form of dance scoring is of enormous consequence to this discussion, given his influence on a host of experimental dance and movement practitioners as well as graphic artists, particularly during the sixties and seventies. The possibilities of developing graphic notation in dance and movement practice further questions the authoritative history of movement and dance notation going back to the balletic tradition of dance scoring. Reacting against the prescriptive culture of representation found in traditional stave notation, especially Labanotation/Kinetography Laban, graphic movement notation offers a different view of movement literacy that is open to new forms of mediation and new technological processes of representation. Thus, Cunningham was open to experimentation with video forms of recorded dance—especially in his collaborations with pioneer video artist Nam June Paik—as well as to automated forms of movement notation using Calvert's LifeForms software. These crossovers also led Cunningham to the use of motion capture technology for real-time animation of graphic notation and choreographic writing, as featured in works like *Hand-Drawn Spaces* (1998)—the first of a series of collaborations between Cunningham and OpenEnded group.

Hand-Drawn Spaces is a virtual dance installation that uses corporeal movement data extracted via motion capture technology to compose intricate choreographic movements designed by Cunningham. Crucially, the drawing of movement via motion capture technology invites a radically different modality of representation, one no longer divorced from a source body and no longer caught in a static representation of movement as pure symbol. Like Cage's plexigrams, motion capture technology proposes a dynamic way of writing movement in motion. In sum, the turn toward a graphic notation points to a changing paradigm in the culture of representation and mediation, one in which writing is not static but in fact moves, in which the markings of a recorded movement score are no longer fixed symbols on staves but animated ideographs that express movement qua movement. In the context of this novel application of motion capture, Paul Kaiser of OpenEnded Group wrote:

We are after a new art form, which seems about to emerge from this odd confluence of the dance, visual art, and computer worlds. I imagine that in this new form, performance and recording and notation—three strands of the performing arts that have always been separate—will be fused. So that you can have the notation shaping the performance, the performance shaping the recording, the recording shaping the notation, and so on. Perhaps this new process, which builds on itself, can bootstrap a new way of making art. (Forsythe and Kaiser 1999, 70)

Building on their collaborations with Cunningham, Trisha Brown, William Forsythe, and other well-known experimental choreographers, OpenEnded Group have more recently put forward a dynamic electronic platform for the representation of movement information and the graphic notation of movement. Choreographic Language Agent (CLA) is a project developed by the OpenEnded Group using Field, an open-source and hybrid software developed by Marc Downie combining visuals and code within rapidly and experimentally assembled algorithmic systems. CLA works by interpreting a sentence written in a language known to this tool. For instance, the system interprets words, point topologies, or diagrams fed by the choreographer or movement composer into the system. OpenEnded Group's webpage describes the platform as "pseudo-linguistic operations on the language level." This means that the tool can take an input and then generate a new sequence through superimpositions and modulations of the original input, thus turning static elements into a kind of animated notation. From this perspective, the move away from static forms of movement notation is likewise a turn toward more graphic and ideographic forms of dynamic notation.

It is clear from the above that CLA's intention is not only to *record* movement, in the way conventional movement notation does, but also to help *compose* movement creatively. This is no longer an iterative model whose main ambition is to repeat, recreate, and research movement: CLA is a machine that can create movement kinetopoietically. What comes out of the machine is not an authorly textuality, like a dance notation score, but a generative agent that helps coideate movement. This poststave notational paradigm proposed by OpenEnded Group also stems from an understanding of the composition of movement in the visual and movement arts as an inherently collaborative and multiauthored process. More generally, CLA indexes a more profound paradigm shift in the mediation and representation of movement literature, characterized by distributed or networked ways of writing and composing movement. CLA is intended to support an active and creative exchange between choreographers and visual artists, so that the material inscription and instruction of dance need not be confined to a single individual, nor indeed a single disciplinary focus. Accordingly, CLA posits a more flexible and process-led creative exchange that points simultaneously in two ways: either toward conventional versions of movement language, or else toward choreographic grammars of dance that are unique to a given choreographer. As a result, this agent proposes a form of representation that is not standardized, in the way stave notation is, but personalized—in the sense that each grammar is unique to the artist or team of artists using the software tool.

PART III: MOTION NOTATION

One choreographer who has explored the uses of CLA in the writing and composition of choreography is Wayne McGregor, whose investigations into animation graphic notation using CLA led to the composition of the 2011 piece *Undance*, with Random Dance Company. McGregor's intention is for CLA to provide research methods that fulfill the promise of an intelligent software agent capable of generating unique solutions to unique choreographic problems. For a start, CLA augments the dance maker's own creative decision-making processes by facilitating an autonomous choreographic agency that can help blend physical and mental processes, a synthesis that according to McGregor constitutes the core of dance and dance making.

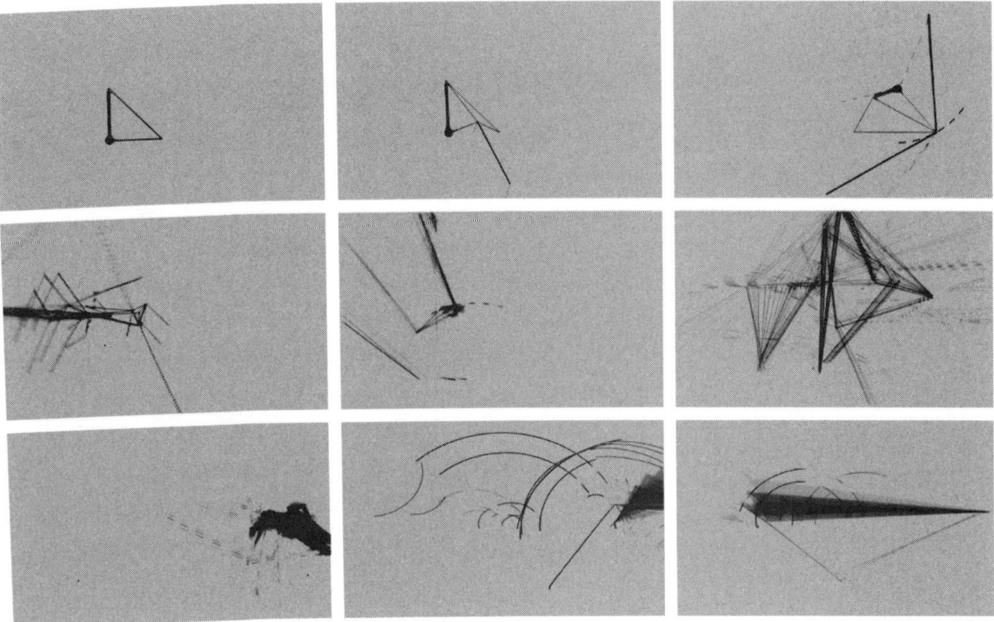

7.5
"Triangle creature," Field software visualizations
featured in *How long does the subject linger
at the edge of the volume* (2005), choreographed
by Trisha Brown. Images by Marc Downie (courtesy
of OpenEnded Group).

In seeking to advance a technological medium that can fold innermotion and outermotion, mentality and motility, CLA ultimately highlights a synthetic approach to movement writing and composition characterized by a distribution of the agency behind writing, which is not only prompted by collaborative, intermedial and interdisciplinary work. The technologization of that agency also provokes a unique sense of whose intelligence is being expressed and written out. The choreographic language agent alluded to in this project's title is neither a choreographer nor a visual artist but rather a composite or hybrid agent, a cybernetic agency shared by human and machine intelligences. CLA therefore attempts to fulfill the promise of automated agency, which, according to OpenEnded Group, can generate variations of sentences by mutation, selection, and parameterization. The computer is intended to transform the input operations not only by animating them but also by processing them in nonlinear ways, and modulating them via self-generative and artificially intelligent computational processes.

8

Kinetic alphabeticism

One thing word-based languages afford, according to Antonio Camurri and colleagues (1986), is a dictionary of movement-related terms. Camurri et al. have proposed two ways of putting together what they call a "movement dictionary." First, one can create a *general* movement dictionary, identifying individual everyday movements and compiling an alphabetic list or A–Z of words that describe these movements. Media artist Paul Kaiser (2013) describes a similar idea: a pedagogical tool that can be used to think up motor words. In Kaiser's motor lexicon exercise, students are asked to move from a given point A to a given point B in any manner they wish, while the rest of the class identifies the word the student is pantomiming. Thus a list of word entries is produced describing different ways of moving. Kaiser provides the following example of such a list:

A		?		B
pirouette	waltz	stride	march	prance
creep	leapfrog	sneak	boogie	dance
slither	trot	stagger	amble	prowl
gallop	tiptoe	skip	crawl	stomp
enter	twirl	strut	run	slip
tear	twist	snake	steal	cartwheel
limp	goosestep	slide	stumble	promenade
hop	walk	streak	parade	race

According to Kaiser, the point of this motor lexicon exercise is to show students that "they have many more words in their heads than they know of" (Kaiser 2013). Like the A to B model I discussed in chapter 6, this exercise illustrates that our kinetic memories have a robust storage capacity that we are perhaps unaware of. As different movements can be used to bring the space between A and B to life, so different words emerge, creating a lexicon. The reservoir of words that emerges from this experiment is considerably vaster than what many people might expect. As I have pointed out, one should never take for granted what happens in between A and B.

The second model of a movement dictionary proposed by Camurri et al. involves the compilation of a *special* movement dictionary, derived from specialist terminology. In this case, specialist motor knowledge is typically coded into terms that may be considered, at least according to these authors, a component unit or subprogram in a motor language (1986, 104). Take, for instance, terminology derived from the French ballet tradition. Ballet demands an awareness of specialist terms that describe positions and moves that are unique to this embodied language of movement (e.g., *jeté, plié, assemblé, fondu, épaulement*). Camurri et al. then propose a framework for a computational approach to movement notation, which can lead to a terminological compendium of moves in a computerized environment, or moves that are germane to a computational approach to motor analysis.

In response to this technology-specific A–Z of movement, Marino et al. proposed a rather awkwardly termed model for the computation of notation known as NEM language, a programming environment designed to provide a procedural and nonhierarchical representation of motor knowledge. The acronym stems from New Men, or New Computational Models of Men (Marino et al. 1986, 131), yet another nod to the oddly gendered attitude to the ordering of movement representation—an idea that I have already touched on in relation to phallocentric beliefs stemming from Vitruvian Man models of geometric bodily canons. What concerns me now is not so much the question of gendering, but how systems of representation that have been under a certain cultural hegemonic influence can begin to be liberated of their inherited cultural prejudices by the agency of computer-aided representation.

In what follows, I will discuss the hegemony of an alphabetic tradition of movement knowledge—which is often associated with a balletic tradition in the movement arts, as well as a rhetorical tradition in the art of gestural oratory. Subsequently, I will propose a model that undermines this hegemony by offering a postalphabetic understanding of movement representation. Before I turn my attention to postalphabetic ways of writing movement, however, it is important to examine in more detail what the construction of motor knowledge via alphabetic and linguistic models ultimately involves. It is important to have a clear understanding of what alphabeticism does to the knowledge of movement: what it can and what it cannot afford to do.

Motor lexicon exercises and motor dictionaries such as the ones mentioned above are underpinned by a linguistic approach to motor knowledge. To be able to represent movement in writing, and to be able to order movement according to a system of classification and collation, the linguistic regime—and alphabeticism in particular—provides one of the most basic systems. Insofar as the process starts at A and finishes at B (or in this case at Z), alphabeticism is a finite and linear system by definition. Motion lexicons and motion dictionaries can be grounded on the alphabetic premise that movement is composed of finite units (words), and a finite number of units that make up a limited reservoir of movements (a dictionary). The underlying thinking here is that infinite movement can be framed within a finite system. Like the intention to represent 3D movement within a 2D stave model of representation, alphabeticism poses an inherent problem.

Camurri et al. point out that because there are multiple ways of representing the same motor phenomenon, representation places demands on memory. Embodied knowledge, according to these authors, is an obvious drawback, "because it leaves out an enormous amount of knowledge that remains unavailable for the community of users." They conclude: "this is enough motivation to try to devise methods which can capture the essential aspects of movement in a symbolic, explicit way" (1986, 87). And so, like the footprints at Happisburgh or the stave notation systems discussed above, the alphabetizing of movement is intended to provide a means of memorizing or recalling stored movement information. However, the need for movement information to be stored, archived, classified, ordered, and cataloged, the need to organize the vast and ephemeral knowledge of movement into an ordering system, does not necessarily justify the imposition of an alphabetic model. In the same way that the gendering of motor knowledge is a cultural convention, so is its alphabetization. I shall state again what I have said from the outset: the language of movement is not a linguistics of movement.

Gesture alphabets

The distinction between alphabetic and postalphabetic understandings of movement is one that cuts through the different representations of movement, whether as abstract symbols or as physical data. Whereas media technologies that notate or hand-write movement are more liable to simplified lists of movement symbols, the computerization of movement has led to the production of data systems that have lost their alphabetic simplicity and their linearity in order to create multiordered systems of collation. Assuming my reader is familiar with the idea of a letter alphabet, it is perhaps worth taking a moment to expand on the idea of a movement alphabet. Before I do so, I will touch briefly on the construction of gesture alphabets.

Whereas a letter alphabet will be based on the general principle that a letter represents phonemes or basic significant sounds of the spoken language, gesture alphabets are based on the idea that human gestural communication is underpinned by a limited array of hand and facial gestures. Most letter alphabets are entirely determined by linearization: the letters themselves are made up of lines; the assemblage of letters make up linear words, which in turn form linear sentences. Gestures, however, are tridimensional and nonlinear. Having said this, the basic function of the alphabet— whether phonemic, gestural, or kinetic—remains the same. Alphabets are associated with a standard ordering of a finite number of units of language. From A to Z lies a single line. So how can we organize gestures in this way if they are tridimensional and nonlinear?

Back in Roman antiquity, the first-century rhetorician Quintilian produced a twelve-volume textbook entitled *Institutio oratoria* laying the foundations of rhetorical studies, devoted to the understanding of gesturally inflected speech and proper delivery in oratory. The work remained a standard up until the nineteenth century, when a number of theorists revisited Quintilian's treatise in order to propose a field of study known as *chirologia* (the study of the natural language of the hand) and *chironomia* (the study of manual rhetoric). The invention of these fields of study can be credited to the work of English philosopher John Bulwer in the mid-seventeenth century. Bulwer undertook to develop a science devoted to the study of a natural hieroglyphics or a writing in the air, a notion apparently first advanced by Francis Bacon in the early seventeenth century.[1] This new system would include a complete understanding of the use of hand gestures as a means of fingerspelling and the formal description of a finger sign alphabet. The work was taken up by English preacher and declamation teacher Reverend Gilbert Austin, in whose treatise *Chironomia* (1806) elementary hand and arm gestures are mapped onto a chironomic sphere, for subsequent transcription into a system of gestural notation. According to this author, the human figure can be placed within a sphere whose center coincides with the center of the breast, and whose diameter is drawn by the endpoint of an outstretched arm (i.e., the tip of a finger), perpendicular to a radius drawn from the shoulder—much like Laban's kinesphere.

Austin argued that when seeking to express gestural movement in writing, it is necessary to work from figures that can express gestural actions and transitions between these actions. Once again we have the basic logic of position and transposition. Austin's ambition was to produce a language of symbols that could represent with facility every action of an orator throughout a speech, or every gesture of an actor throughout a dramatic performance, and to record them for posterity, especially for the purpose of repetition and practice. In fact the system would be applicable to any modality of public speaking (e.g., reading, recitation, declamation, oratory, or acting). The system proposed by Austin draws on the linguistic idea that there is a limited number of auxiliary gestures, and that each gesture can be dealt with as a unit of a gestural language. Thus, by completely ignoring the continuity and infinity of gestural movements available to nonworded languages, Austin argued that similarity and relation among speech-dependent gestures make possible a regular classification and nomenclature. In addition, this author proposed to categorize movement in relation to the most distinguished parts of the body, which produce the principal gestures and which are supposedly seven: (1) the head, (2) the shoulders, (3) the trunk or body, (4) the arms, (5) the hands and fingers, (6) the lower limbs and knees, and (7) the feet.

The system managed to restrict the magnitude and freedom of gestural movement. For instance, Austin proposed to have arm gestures bound not only by the natural angles in which a human arm can rotate, but also by arbitrary angles intended to break down the spatial spectrum of any given arm movement. Thus, Austin proposed that the scope of an arm movement could be restricted between two polar positions in the chironomic sphere. According to Austin, in the case of vertical arm movements, gestures are bound by endpoints in an arc between the zenithal and arm-resting positions (equaling 180 degrees). He further proposed to divide this arc into four gestural subregions, each of which took up 45 degrees of rotation. Having broken down the space of gestural movement into measured and discontinuous zones, Austin assigned letter symbols to key gestural positions, and star or dot symbols to transitions between positions. The assignment of letters to gestural movements is quite straightforward: right leg is notated as R, left leg is notated as L, front right is notated as FR, and so on. Similarly with step movements: advancing becomes (*a*), retiring (*r*), traversing (*tr*), starting (*st*), stamping (*sp*), and so on. Because in addition to spatial positioning the system also includes the attitudinal qualities of gestural movement, Austin had *akimbo* written as (*k*) and *reposed* as (*rp*). He noted that, because the names of many of the gestures begin with the same letter, it became necessary to choose some other letter in the word to avoid confusion; thus *x* is used for *extended*, *l* for *collected*, and so on.

Although Austin's ambition was to record gestural communication with clarity and precision, detailed examination of his notation shows that no such clarity and precision is obtained from it, not least because the system assumes that gestures are supplementary to words, and that words can be used to account for the full communicational extent of a gesture. In actuality, there is a great deal of information in gesture that is not contained or preserved in words; nor is the full scope of gesture confined to supporting the communication of words. The decision to have letters notate gestures also presupposes that alphabeticism, with its predisposition to linearization, is enough to describe the tri-dimensionality of gesture. The tendency to approach gesture with a linguistic bias is glaringly obvious.

Although I have tried to read Austin's movement notation, I cannot fully retrieve the gestures he has notated—nor can I actually read the quality, the identity, the feel of the early nineteenth-century public speakers captured in Austin's alphabetic records. I can decode his score, but I cannot bring back to life the embodied identities of a Mr. Kemble (actor), a Mrs. Siddons (actress), or a Reverend James Fordyce (a fellow preacher), and the numerous other actors, orators, politicians, and rhetoricians whose gestures Austin notated in this work. Though he afforded the practitioner an elementary record and an objective memory of gestural activity, the fine-grained details of gesture, and the living bodies behind them, are no longer there. As Giorgio Agamben pointed out: "by the end of the nineteenth century, the gestures of the Western bourgeoisie were irretrievably lost" (1993, 149). The period's concerted effort to make good this loss, so Agamben contends, is perceivable in the exaggerated articulations of silent film and the mad leaps of modern dance. The frantic effort to give a lasting materiality to gesture also underpins Austin's rudimentary technology of alphabetic gesture notation. But rather than highlighting the richness of gesture in an age of oratory and pre-cinematic melodrama, Austin's system highlights the deficiencies of the alphabetic symbol when it comes to recording human gesture in full.

Alphabetic movement

The earliest traditions of European dance notation are strictly alphabetic, in the sense that these systems used letters of the Roman alphabet to encipher the units of a dance language. An example of this is the abovementioned Cervera system, used in the fifteenth century to record social dance. In fact, letter code systems were widely used for the recording of various European dance forms for over two hundred years, up until the development of symbolic movement notation. Two important works on dance notation put forward in the late nineteenth century provide historical antecedents for the systematization of a modern movement alphabet. One of them is Friedrich Albert Zorn's *Grammar of the Art of Dancing* (1905, first published in German in 1887), which made use of stick figure pictograms placed under accompanying music notation. The system was based on a finite set of human movements, once again based on the alphabetic model. The other one is Vladimir Ivanovich Stepanov's *Alphabet des mouvements du corps humain* (1892), which attempted a similar feat. Stepanov broke down movement into basic contrastive units, which could be represented in the form of music notation and a few supplementary symbols. He believed that the collection of symbols available in this system represented an alphabet, with the help of which one would be able to record with precision any position and any movement of the body.

It is important to add that both these systems were used to record ballet. The Zorn and Stepanov systems reaffirmed the idea that ballet could be dealt with as a language of movement, whose theoretical purview included an understanding of the grammar, syntax, and even the alphabetic ordering of balletic knowledge. These systems assumed that an alphabetic ordering of the knowledge of movement could provide a complete account of any human movement, or at least any movement used within the language of ballet.

Ann Hutchinson Guest has pointed out that the reader or interpreter of alphabetic notation is faced with an age-old problem: it is difficult to provide sufficient detail of a movement to make possible the future reconstruction of steps and style, even for those familiar with the recorded movements. Although she has argued that the same does not apply to symbolic systems of movement notation, especially Labanotation, both the alphabetic and symbolic approaches to the codification of movement are problematic. The problem with alphabeticism is not that it uses letters of the Roman or some other alphabet to encipher human movement, but that this system breaks down a language of movement into an arbitrary number of indivisible primitives. Even though Stepanov does not use letters, his system is still alphabetic. It makes no difference whether the symbols used to represent movement are letters or Labanotation symbols. The problem [Hutchinson] Guest highlights in relation to letter-coded dance notation systems is applicable to any dance notation system based on the representation of movement through a finite list of symbolic units.

The principles of an alphabetic approach are spelled out in [Hutchinson] Guest's Language of Dance system (LOD). Entirely grounded on a linguistic modality of communication, LOD argues for the understanding of dance as an alphabetic system based on the conformation of movement letters, which combine to make up movement words. According to her (Hutchinson 1977), dance is a language of functional and expressive gestures and body configurations through which nonverbal communication can be achieved. But insofar as the system is ultimately subservient to verbal language, LOD is assumed to have basic "parts of speech" (movement verbs, movement nouns, and movement adverbs), which are joined up in the construction of movement grammars. These movement grammars, she holds, define a relationship between different movement words and the functions that bind them to a movement sentence.

There is an obvious problem with the approach championed by [Hutchinson] Guest. She may not consider LOD alphabetic in the strictest sense of the word, given the fact that her system does not make use of Roman letters. Nonetheless, the premise of LOD is grounded on the assumption that corporeal movement can be divided into units (analogous to the unit of a letter), and that these units can be linked together to make words and phrases, which in turn generate a modality of discourse analogous to speech. The trouble is that alphabeticism is not only a way of ordering units according to a particular standard: it is also a way of thinking language in relation to linearization, to speech, to spoken discourse. Alphabeticism is also a cultural ideology. But before I move on to problematize an alphabetic approach to movement notation and representation, I would like to present a more contemporary example of how linguistics subordinates the understanding of human movement to the categories of speech.

From kineme to dyneme

The linguistic approach to the study of human movement is evidenced in a number of theories that have tried to apply general linguistics to kinetic activity. Ray Birdwhistell's theory of kinesics is one example. Kinesics is a system developed in the 1950s that is used for the interpretation of nonverbal behavior. Birdwhistell (1970) estimated that no more than 30 to 35 percent of the social meaning of a conversation or an interaction is carried by the words. He was concerned with the instrumental use of the body to produce a paralanguage, an auxiliary language or body language—a language that could essentially communicate the remaining content of social meaning. As such, Birdwhistell subjected full bodily movement to the regime of the phonetic. Although he is not concerned with a theory of human movement as such but with a theory of linguistic communication that is expressed via the body, his theory of kinesics poses a fundamental problem, both in terms of the limitations of speech and the limitations that a system of writing such as kinesic notation imposes on the representation of full bodily movement.

Like other alphabetic approaches, Birdwhistell's kinesics begins with the assumption that nonverbal forms of language can be broken down to indivisible units, known as kinemes. Whereas a phoneme is a basic unit of a language's phonology, which is combined with other phonemes to form meaningful units such as spoken words, Birdwhistell's kineme can be described as the smallest con-trastive kinesic unit that may bring about a change of meaning within body language. Linguistics inevitably focuses on the interplay between sound and meaning, and so does kinesics. Bodily movement is intended to *mean* something, complementary or supplementary to spoken communication. However, this would mean that movement is not a language but an auxiliary language at best.

No one would dispute that there is an approximate number of phonemes necessary for the production of any phonetic sound construction in a given language. In the case of the English language, there are approximately forty phonemes. The English alphabet, which is based on the Latin-script alphabet, has a finite number of letters (twenty-six). With twenty-six letters one can write any word in the English language, and with forty basic sounds one can make any phonetic construction of the English spoken language. But how many units are needed to make up any gesture of movement of the human body? The finitary logic of alphabetics works well in the former case. But this logic becomes rather problematic when considering movement languages. After all, how many positions can the body take? How many movements can the body make between positions? A ballet expert may be able to put a figure on this, but only within the ambit of ballet.

Birdwhistell (1970) proposed that there is a limited number of kinemes available to the nonverbal behavior of an average American. Body language is therefore treated not as a personal repertoire but a cultural repertoire. Strange as it may sound, in this theory all Americans speak the same body language. Birdwhistell set up a list of fifty or sixty kinemes as the basic units of average American nonverbal communication. So although he did not consider kinesics to be universal, he did generalize his system within a local universe (i.e., American nonverbal communication). Birdwhistell's theory of kinesics has found plenty of opposition, and I do not wish to add any further criticism. While it may seem ludicrous that one could define a general system of bodily language for a country as diverse as the United States, the idea is perfectly sensible in a computational approach to motion analysis.

Thus, computer scientist Richard Green has argued more recently for an *alphabet of dynemes*, which according to him are the smallest contrastive units of computer-readable human movement. The dyneme model, by Green's own admission, is based on speech recognition models using, once again, the phoneme model taken from general linguistics. Like Birdwhistell's kineme model, Green has proposed to pin down the number of units of movement that a specific computer vision system can detect from 2D or 3D recognition. The result is a formal system that orders movement into a finitary order, so that complex sequences can be simplified in terms of a combination of elementary components.

Green's continuous movement recognition (CMR) framework forms the basis of a computer vision segmentation of human motion. According to Green, this alphabet is made up of 35 dynemes, which computers can use to recognize the skills featured in a given video or animation sequence.

Dynemes make up movement words through the creation of probable movement sequences using vectorlike connections or motion vectors, which are computationally derived. So even though the framework here is germane to a computational-linguistic approach, many of the basic conceptual parameters of CMR are in line with Birdwhistell's kinesics and [Hutchinson] Guest's LOD, at least as far as the alphabetization of human movement is concerned. According to Green, the dyneme paradigm "enables CMR systems to track and recognize hundreds of full-body movement skills thus laying the basis for effective human-computer interactions associated with full-body movement activity recognition" (2008, 214).

Bearing this in mind, we may conclude that the computational analysis and recognition of human movement is forking into two very different approaches. On the one hand, computational approaches to movement analysis and recognition are reinforcing alphabeticism, by determining a limited set of units of movement to track and recognize kinetic patterns in 2D and 3D contexts. Computational media, especially within network forms of communication, are simultaneously problematizing this alphabetic regime, in order to facilitate nonlinear and nonfinite forms of kinesis in virtual environments. Before I turn my attention to a postalphabetic system of movement representation and ordering as an alternative way of thinking movement in a digital-era context, I will assess how this ambivalence is deep-seated within the creative practice of movement.

Forsythe's alphabetic modulations

William Forsythe's choreographic work is based on the idea that movement can be read and interpreted as a production of bodily structures folding and unfolding in a geometric space composed of points that are extensively interconnected. From this basic principle, Forsythe can build a catalog of procedures, many of which are already conventionalized in the language of ballet. Thus, he draws on an alphabetic tradition in ballet, in the sense that ballet is a language founded on a finite set of core positions, which can be used as elementary motor units. Not all the basic units in Forsythe's alphabet are balletic, though. Thus, he has also described these key units of composition as keyframes, pointing to a direct crossover between his contemporary dance approach and animation. It is this need to systematize the component parts of movement, and to order them into a catalog- or dictionary-like system capable of serving as an aid to choreographic memory, that precipitates a new sense of choreographic alphabeticism, or what Forsythe and Kaiser (1999) call "motion alphabets."

André Leroi-Gourhan (1993) has spoken of alphabetic systems as an "external memory," particularly in reference to the automation of alphabeticism represented by technologies like the dictionary and the encyclopedia. According to him, the dictionary is a highly evolved tool of external memory, in which thought is broken down into a vast number of fragments. Leroi-Gourhan goes so far as to suggest that the level of documentation that these technologies facilitate is comparable to that of mechanical animation. He concludes that the automation of alphabetic thinking reached its peak "when actuated by separate cams that endowed each of its organs with a fraction of memory; the encyclopedia is a fractional alphabetically arranged memory each of whose isolated mechanisms contains an animated part of the whole of memory" (262). In other words, the system is like an animation of alphabetic thinking, as the breakdown of parts is intended to provoke a recomposition of these parts, a stringing together or splicing that the reader achieves when reading (animating) the static pages of an alphabetically indexed book. Forsythe's idea of a movement alphabet represents a significant departure from this encyclopedic notion of alphabetic organization for two reasons: the alphabet is written by the body, and held in a physical memory; and the alphabet is not a collection of static units that can be recomposed through interpretation and repetition. The units that make up Forsythe's alphabet can evolve. This means that his alphabet can be modulated and deformed in a way that the more rigid technology of speech-based alphabeticism cannot. Forsythe writes:

> I created a non-balletic vocabulary of 135 movements, which I then taught to my dancers until they knew it backward and forward. No matter where or when the dancers move through the zone of one of those movements, they immediately know its place in the sequence. It's like rapidly scrolling through a list of names in a computer program. We use our alphabet in connection with the kinesphere—the total volume of a body's potential movement. Dancers are always conscious of their kinespheres, which exist in the air around them. For us, it becomes a huge field for jogging memory. Let me give you an example of how exactly how this works. When I cup the back of my neck with my hand, it's as if I was swatting a mosquito—and so, using this arbitrary association, we say that I'm spelling the letter "I" for "insect." Now suppose that while I'm dancing, I suddenly find my hand cupped around my knee, which reminds me of the insect element. Bearing in mind that my focus is always on the beginning of a movement rather than on its end, I will have to fold my neck down to that point in space rather than performing it standing up, as in the original alphabet. Now, keeping to the sequence of the movement alphabet, I can perform the movement either directly before or after I—that is, the movements associated with either H or J. In this kind of dancing, I can lose my equilibrium within a dance phrase, then remember everything from the point of that dislocation, so to speak. My body exists in the sphere of its own memory. (Forsythe and Kaiser 1999, 67–68)

Forsythe has explored the creative use of movement alphabets in a number of works, not least *Alien Action* (1992), where dancers performed operations based on the elemental motions represented by each letter in Forsythe's alphabet. But insofar as each letter can be modulated by a given dance operation, the modifications produced more letters, which in turn recalled more operations. Forsythe speaks of a total immersion system (Forsythe and Kaiser 1999). Modulation provokes a level of complexity that spills beyond alphabetic order onto a postalphabetic system. A key to this modulating evolution is the ability of the dancer to transform spatial information according to various prescribed operations (e.g., mental rotation, reflection, imagined self-translation), but not in the prescribed stylistic manner of ballet. These transformational operations found in Forsythe's technique offer a more self-generative model for the bodily organization of information, leading to higher-order groupings, which increase the representational capacity of so-called dance geometries. One example of his alphabetic modulation is the technique of "rotation inscription," which according to Forsythe is the ability to write with virtually any part of the body (Forsythe and Kaiser 1999). This technology is central to Forsythe's thinking, insofar as it lends a complex three-dimensional character to the activity of drawing and writing modulated balletic forms.

Modulation also enables a less rigid use of the traditional language of ballet, based on a synthesis of alphabetic ways of thinking/remembering movement and a use of digital technology that is distinctly postalphabetic. Thus, Forsythe's choreographic works are often caught between a language of words and letters embedded within balletic tradition and a postalphabetic recursive and exponential logic of algorithms. Unlike the finitary order of balletic alphabeticism, Forsythe's algorithmic approach creates a fundamental tension between two very different types of language machine, which are expressive in turn of two ways of thinking and dancing. He suggests that, for his piece *Eidos: Telos* (1998), he further expanded on this idea to problematize not only a balletic knowledge of movement but also a singular end-directed logic. Thus he gave himself and the dancers the following general instruction: "Take an equation, solve it; take the result and fold it back into the equation and then solve it again. Keep doing this a million times" (Forsythe and Kaiser 1999, 64). Forsythe seems to be suggesting that the combination of alphabetic and postalphabetic thinking is in fact a reprogrammed version of an age-old method: counterpoint.

Forsythe is right in claiming that there is nothing new in this recursive way of moving. In fact, the intervention of infinitely recursive logic within the finite logic of alphabetic memory had already been addressed in computational approaches to the dance as early as the 1960s. Forsythe's method resembles not only Laban's but also those of pioneer artists in the field of computer-generated dance and animation, notably A. Michael Noll and Manfred Mohr. Like Forsythe, both Mohr and Noll addressed explicitly the creative composition of multidimensional space in computer art, particularly in terms of a counterpoint between computer alphabets and nonalphabetic data processing systems. For instance, Mohr fractured the symmetry of a cube (as well as *n*-dimensional hypercubes), using the structure as a "system" or "alphabet." He wrote:

> I saw a fantastic alphabet, three dimensions projected into two dimensions. The system of the dimensional idea is to have more and more complex elements to play with; it's like playing a very long piano. The cubes lose their sides, start flashing and dancing wildly, according to some kind of calculated randomness. So after I studied this cube I started making drawings. Let's say a cube turns slowly from left to right. The centre is complete but towards the outside it loses its sides. I did a whole bunch of drawings from this. But then I looked at the cube and split it in two and rotated each side. So now each side is rotating separately, randomly. Then I went one dimension higher. (Hattrick 2012)

For Mohr, the disturbance or disintegration of symmetry becomes the emergent behavior through which computers can create new shapes and pathways between shapes. Because of the exponential levels of transformation available to computer-generated animation, calculated randomness can create much larger sets of units—much more than the modulated alphabet of Forsythe technique. As the system reaches high-order groupings, and as this "alphabet" becomes more and more complex, it loses its determination as a finite system, or indeed as a system of a magnitude that is sizeable from the perspective of a human brain. Human memory—alphabetic and finite as it is—cannot possibly grasp the complexity of the processing that a computer carries out. Thus, the computer appears to create a system that is entirely random or calculatedly random. This disintegration or randomness challenges the alphabetic order and forces us to recognize that the computer can think and calculate beyond human capabilities, and that it can store information beyond the capacity of a human memory.

156

Postalphabeticism

The upshot of computer-aided data processing is that information can become postalphabetic in a number of ways. Three fundamental changes to the alphabetic regime are worthy of attention. First, writing has been reconfigured in a postalphabetic context through the decline of the *signifier* and the rise of the *signal*. Machines do not recognize language in the linguistic signifier/signified binary made famous by Ferdinand de Saussure in the late nineteenth century. Machines do not read alphabetic signifiers that "mean" something in an arbitrary regime of symbolization. Digital machines read information in terms of on/off electrical states or +/- magnetic states, which can be universally scripted as ones and zeros. Second, computerization of knowledge has also deposed the alphabetic regime through the use of various scripted programming languages that are coded using letters and numbers. The regime of the alphabetic has given way to the regime of the alphanumeric. Indeed, the two are often incompatible, which is why it is often necessary to develop an interlingua: a connecting protocol that allows the computer to process alphabetic text. For instance, because machines process information alphanumerically, alphabetic text has to be processed via hypertext markup language (HTML), commonly used for the processing of text online. Third and last, computerization of knowledge challenges alphabeticism insofar as the ordering of knowledge is no longer linear and catalogical. Knowledge of movement is no longer stored in movement dictionaries and glossaries, like Austin's treatise on gesture or Stepanov's alphabet of human movements. Rather, it is stored in data motion capture libraries and complex networks that can be accessed via search engines that trawl and crawl vast domains of information. No longer is this a Gutenberg galaxy but a Google galaxy, where everything can be accessible in one place: information searches, emailing, instant messaging, data analytics, mapping, translating, scholarship, books.

One must couple all this with the fact that technological apparatuses have become increasingly mobile. Touch screen interfaces, voice and gesture recognition, haptic feedback technology, teleoperators, and holographic interaction are some examples of how man-machine communication can be performed kinetically and wordlessly. As Arthur and Marilouise Kroker point out, there is a postalphabetic future going on now in the world of the digital, possibly because the letters of the alphabet are too slow to keep up with the speed of electronic communication: "A paradigm-shift in the form of ideas in which writing itself bubbles to the electronic surface, searches anxiously for its lost chain of (alphabetic) signifiers, dances hesitatingly across the old literary divide between metaphor and metonymy, finally realizes that words are on their own in a liquid digital world" (2005, 326–327).

The postalphabetic regime not only signals the decline of static writing. It also signals a possibility for writing itself to acquire flexible and mobile modes of transmission. Alphabetic culture exerts pressure on a standardization of writing, particularly in terms of an inhibited orthography. Within a technologized environment, however, the rules of spelling and calligraphic convention are superseded by the divergent possibilities of electronic communication, which encourage speed and economy of expression. Emergent modalities of text production found in electronic media, for instance in the domain of instant messaging, presuppose a more flexible use of words and letters, as well as a more uninhibited orthography. Because of the kinetic character of web and mobile technological communication, language is driven to evolve by a principle of economization, according to which technologized text has become shorter, faster, more reductive, and altogether unorthodox. Examples of this might include l33t speak and the rebus, which combine letters and numbers to produce alphanumeric forms of text messaging (or if you prefer: "t3xt m3z4g1ng').[2]

Likewise, stick figures have colonized electronic forms of text production, once again undermining the regime of the alphabet. Stick figures are a timeless representation of human bodily poses.[3] Instant messaging not only demands a more economic mode of text representation, or indeed a style that reflects the alphanumeric nature of electronic communication. It also demands, going back to the analogy made by Arthur and Marilouise Kroker, a dance of letters and symbols. A good example is the stick figure emoticon, typically used in texting and other types of electronic communication to denote an affective undertone. The emoticon is represented usually as a facial expression, which can be represented using a standard keyboard. Circumventing the absence of a stick figure glyph, electronic texting and messaging has found novel ways of drawing facial and bodily figures using basic keyboard characters, almost as if there was a need within electronic forms of communication to bring the body back into electronic communication. Thus, electronic emotica allow text messengers to draw, for instance, smiles:) frowns:(gaping mouths:0 winks ;) and so on. Beyond this, electronic text and instant text messaging are also populated by kinetic and animational content. An example of this is the Emoji character, which typically provides visual reference within text communication.

Some Emoji characters are typically animated in order to provide a more dynamic style of textual communication: one such depicts a face blowing a kiss while winking, which can also be represented as the emoticon ;-X. The incorporation of a language of stick figural animation within electronic messaging is taken a step further toward cartoon animation in the case of Stick Texting, an animated texting app for iPhone or iPad that provides detailed action scenes and animated situations that challenge the conventional text-based and static nature of send-and-receive electronic messaging. Likewise, with the case of Arthur Elsenaar's piece *rEmote a.k.a Compose Your Own Emoticon* (1995), the writing of text through facial expression is explored within a performance art context where the wired-up face of the artist is directly connected to the Internet, allowing remote users to control Elsenaar's facial expressions and produce an array of highly unconventional emotica (more on this to come).

158

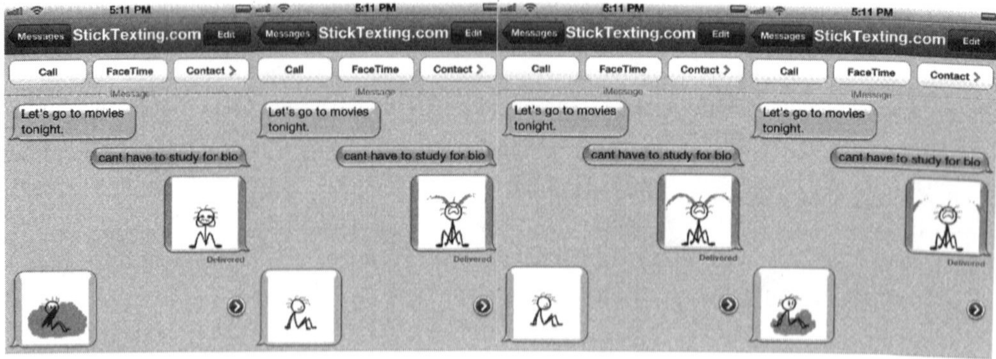

8.1
Stills from Stick Texting, app for iPad and iPhone
featuring animated text messages developed by
Mitchell Robiner. © Stick Texting, 2012 (courtesy
of Mitchell Robiner).

This encroachment of animational and distributed modes of communication within electronic text messaging is not an isolated phenomenon. In fact, the tendency to animate electronic text opens up a much broader question concerning the transformation of alphabetic forms of communication in a digital-era context. Can it be that alphabetic communication is being challenged to the point of being ostracized in some technological contexts, especially instant messaging? The visualization and animation of phone texting and online messaging can be addressed within a more general discussion concerning the broader shift toward the movement of information and the need to make the representation of language move at the screen or interface. My discussion is veering toward an analysis of the effects of technological mediation in the transformation of the language and mediation of movement. What I am about to argue is that we can no longer speak in terms of a knowledge *of* motion, but a knowledge *in* motion. Thus, human motion also refers to communication systems that have evolved to show us a universe of representation that is increasingly mobile, animated, and kinetic. Whereas in an alphabetic regime all things appeared still, and knowledge was never conflated with motion—hence the classical Greek dialectics of kinesis and stasis—in a postalphabetic regime movement and knowledge become synonymous. Digital intelligence is defined by motion.

9

Mathematical mechanics

Henceforth the term "interlingua" will not be used to refer to the link between notation and animation, nor to the international auxiliary language that goes by this name. Interlingua, as I intend to use the term, refers to a bridge designed to facilitate communication between human and machine. As such, this chapter explores a cross-traffic between the formal languages of mathematics and mechanics. The marriage of these two paradigms results in one of the most widely used languages of movement in the contemporary computer era: kinematics. It also results in a transdisciplinary field of studies that provides one of the most holistic frameworks for the scientific and artistic study of movement: biomechanics. This chapter is intended to provide a very basic historical contextualization, before I launch into a discussion of how movement is affected by digital technology in the final part of this book. My contention is that mechanization drives the transformation of a certain family of mathematical languages, and that this transformation of mathematics in turn guides the advancement of new machinic technology. As this feedback unfolds, knowledge of a synthetic kind of human-machine movement builds up, provoking a coevolution of the mathematical and the machinic, the biological and the technological.

Credit for the first mechanistic study of human and animal movement must go to Italian physiologist and mathematician Giovanni Alfonso Borelli. Borelli not only shared many of Aristotle's ideas regarding the mechanics of animal movement; he even borrowed the title of one of Aristotle's works. Borelli's *On the Movement of Animals* (1680) would be hugely influential on the mechanistic sciences of the eighteenth and nineteenth centuries, landing him in recent years the grand title of "father of biomechanics." Insofar as Borelli saw animal and human bodies as though they were machines, he described the body's musculoskeletal system as a series of simple levers, pulleys, and wheel axles that could flex, extend, rotate, and bend. His theory of the "animal-machine" marks a turning point in the sense that this thinker could understand movement in relation to a universal language, a mathematical language, that can be embodied by humans, animals, and artificial bodies (machines). The paradigm that emerges from Borelli's vision opens a passage, like the concept of the abstract-concrete machine I mentioned in the introduction, from mental to motor, from mind to body, and ultimately from human to machine. In breaking the ontology of movement into its trajective condition, into its double pincer, Borelli's work marks the beginning of a modern conception of movement as a cultural phenomenon that is open-ended and unstable. Biomechanics introduces an epistemology of movement that is thus liable to cultural and material transformation through the folding of abstraction and concretion via technological integration.

Borelli argued that in order to read the human moving body, it was not enough to use an abstract representation of solid geometry. What he needed was a concrete version of that language—a geometric mechanics, if you like. Drawing on Aristotle's idea that when we move we naturally draw geometric shapes, Borelli recognized that the geometric descriptions of animal movement could be used as instructions to create a kind of Meccano set of an animal's bodily architecture. Borelli wrote: "To understand the [moving organs of animals] we need geometry which is the unique and appropriate science to enable one to read and understand the *divine book written on animals*" (1989, 2, my emphasis). In other words, he could look at an animal as though it were a living language (a divine book), communicating the rational and formal ways in which nature builds and designs moving bodies. If the language could be written into a "book," could this book be translated? That is, can biological designs be applied to artificial machines? Borelli's insights point to a radical paradigm shift in the cultural conception of the body in motion, which is of paramount importance in the development of a contemporary culture of kinesis. In what follows, I will explore how biomechanics provides a discipline for the writing and rewriting of this "book" and how kinematics provides the language to write it, and not only within biological but also within artificial systems.

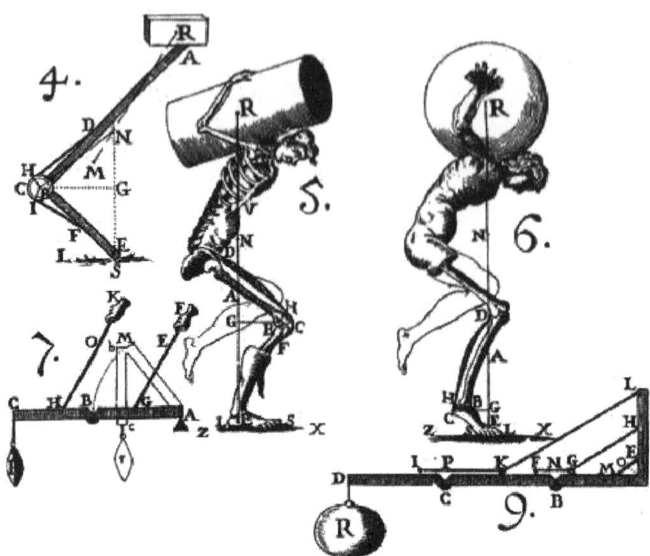

9.1
Detail of Giovanni Alfonso Borelli's illustration of the biomechanics of human movement, table 7 in his *De motu animalium* (1680).

In order to come to grips with the discipline of biomechanics, one must first understand not only classical geometry but also a modern language of mathematical mechanics, most often associated with the work of Isaac Newton. This is because Newton offered a radical reconception of mathematics as the principal language of natural science and natural philosophy. Before I consider how this novel understanding of mathematics might have triggered a modernization of the biomechanical knowledge of total movement, it is worth looking briefly at some of the underlying philosophical principles. Newton's mathematical philosophy ties in with an eidetic frame that is not modern at all but goes back at least to Aristotle. Newton was concerned with an understanding of universal movement that implied an agency so similar to God as to make no difference, and also quite similar to Aristotle's notion of the unmoved mover.[1] Newton saw this God as having properties of a physical agent. As such, even though Newton admitted that God existed outside human understanding, he also argued that God could be said to have auditory and optical faculties—what Newton famously called the *sensorium Dei*. God is neither duration nor space, in Newton's eyes, yet he endures forever and is everywhere present. God is taken as absolute and singular for the same reason human beings remain one and the same throughout their lives, which according to Newton is due to their organs of sense. Sense, therefore, is the constant that connects the finite and the infinite, the human and the divine. The difference is quantitative, not qualitative. Newton's God is an infinite version of a human sensorium, an all-powerful set of eyes, ears, and brain capable of perceiving and understanding everything. God is a system of organs without a body. And because this God senses everything, it also moves everything.

Newton's philosophy demands a language to qualify its philosophical claims. It demands a formal way of describing this universal entity that senses everything and gives dynamic life to everything, and which finds itself represented, if only in a minuscule version of itself, in the movements of humans and animals. More specifically, this natural philosophy demands a bridge between the language of abstract and universal forms (geometry) and the language of physically constructed bodies (mechanics). Newton conceived this new mathematics in the form of his so-called equations of motion, which enabled him to create a synthesis of geometry and mechanics. The bridge between these two disciplines was possible thanks to a new language, an interlingua—what is now known as kinematics, or the geometry of motion. In addition, Newton invented the differential and integral calculus, also to describe phenomena involving general movement and change.

Partly because the calculus was in fact a shared invention (Leibniz came up with the same idea at around the same time), there is no single uniform notation for differentiation. Instead, several notational forms for the derivative of a function have been proposed by subsequent mathematicians, which makes the notation of mathematical differentiation prone to cultural variation. Indeed, the notation of equations of motion is not universal either, which is why there are different ways of writing Newton's laws of motion. And insofar as the usefulness of each modality depends on the context of mathematical inquiry, and because in some cases it is advantageous to use more than one notation in a given context, the writing of these mathematical languages points, yet again, to the difficulties posed by representation of motion, even at the mathematical level. Thus, the ambiguities I have identified in systems of movement notation like Labanotation/Kinetography Laban are also present in Newton's notation of the calculus and in the writing of his equations.

The language Newton wedged between pure mathematics and practical mechanics provided a missing link in an eidetic and philosophical view of the universe. At the same time, it also provided a solution to the scientific observation of physical phenomena, which geometry alone could not explain. Newton wrote that if geometry is commonly used as the study of magnitudes and mechanics is the study of motion, the language in between—he referred to it as "rational mechanics"—would be a "science of motions resulting from any force whatsoever, and of the forces required to produce any motions, accurately proposed and demonstrated" (2003, 232). As Newton himself acknowledged, his equations of motion were general enough to be applied to any moving body whatsoever—animate or inanimate, human or machinic. What follows from this determination is that Newton's nomenclature can be widely circulated among practitioners in the fields of mechanics, biomechanics, robotics, and computer science. The question I wish to pose next is whether a body of equations that was conceived in such a general way could be applied to describe human movement in particular. There is a short answer to this question: of course it can; equations of motion are commonly applied in human movement science. What concerns me is not how, mathematically or scientifically speaking, these equations are formulated, but how the language is open-ended and sufficiently modulated to allow for the writing of many different "books" on the human body, going back to Borelli's metaphor. How can these equations be treated as cultural artifacts, used to write the program according to which human bodies and machine bodies are instructed and trained to move?

Braune and Fischer's equations of movement

The first major application of mathematical mechanics to the study of anatomical human movement was carried out by Wilhelm Braune and Otto Fischer in late nineteenth-century Germany. Unlike Marey's approach, Braune and Fischer's experimental science was not restricted to a kinematic *picture* of motion. Instead, their method focused on a kinematic *computation* of motion. This is a major achievement in the history of movement science, although, as we will see, in seeking to find a computational description of articulated human movement, this work also revealed major deficiencies. Their method can be framed in terms of three distinct steps toward a mathematical abstraction of live human movement: (1) the capture of real-time data and observational study of a natural language of physical movement (gait), (2) a determination of the kinematics of the sampled movement, (3) algebraic calculation of this data using a tridimensional coordinate model.

Braune and Fischer captured not just any segment of the human body. Instead, they broke down the body system into 12 rigid segments, each of which could be interpreted in purely quantitative terms. By an application of Newton's equations of motion, and by using fairly conventional nomenclature to notate their finds, these scientists were also able to transcribe tridimensional recordings of real-time movement into so-called "movement equations" (Braune and Fischer 1987). In fact, they designed chains of equations, in order to describe the kinematic links involved in an articulated human movement. Thus, they created arithmetic formulations such as: forearm + hand, lower leg + foot, trunk + head + arms, and so on. This natural bodily arithmetic determined by the biomechanical structure of the human body prompted Braune and Fischer to create movement equations that were necessarily constructed as different expressions appearing in the different parts of the body involved in movement.

The complexity of the task is evident from the great number of movement equations the body generates during movement. Likewise, the tabulated data featured in Braune and Fischer's book *The Human Gait* is of considerable complexity, resting on a tridimensional coordinate system worked out by themselves. They thus acknowledged that the language of movement equations was fraught with a number of technical difficulties, not least because of the extremely complicated mechanical circumstances presented by the human body. And so while they identified the method to achieve their task, and set out a computational approach that is used to this day, their method also highlights its own limitations. Their copious tables and calculations, many of which were incorrect, drove the need for technological advancement in the capture and data processing of human movement. After all, their experiments were carried out in pursuit of exact findings, so that scientific knowledge of human motion could be applied in key disciplines including military performance, sports biomechanics, gymnastics, and the movement arts.

It is important to add that Braune and Fischer's work is characterized not only by the use of a modern method that combined mathematical modeling, kinematics, and computation, but also by the pioneering use of one of the first modern motion capture systems. They compared their multicamera system to a microscope, insofar as the technology allowed them to identify the fine-grained details of human movement. They wrote, "as every improvement in the microscope must entail progress in the knowledge of the structure of different organisms, any improvement in our method of recording movement inevitably widens our knowledge of the laws of movement" (1987, 116). This can be interpreted as an example of how the technologization of the vision of motion becomes entangled with a scientific epistemology and discourse. At the same time, Braune and Fischer's admission that the technology posed a number of problems, and that major refinements in its application were needed to improve setup, calibration, unobtrusiveness, and accuracy, all point toward an ongoing need for motion capture technology to advance, and for discourse to advance with it. This is precisely the direction in which the coevolution of motion capture technology and photogrammetric mathematics has pushed the knowledge of movement, and the equational scripting of movement. Thus, Braune and Fischer's idea of using movement equations combined with a technological medium of data capture was taken up, for instance, by Otto von Gruber's projective equations for stereoimaging (1924), Earl Church's so-called equations for resection (1945), and Helmut Schmid's principles of multistation analytical photogrammetry using matrix notation (1953).

Kinematics

Whereas biomechanics is a science (and art) of mechanistic movement, kinematics is the language. Closely associated with the language of differential calculus and Newton's equations of motion, kinematics refers to a synthetic geometry of movement categorically different from the mathematical language of dynamics. So if the construction of an epistemology of human movement has so far hinged on an understanding of solid geometry as a "fiction of motion," to borrow the definition put forward by Aristotle once again, and if geometrical topology is a language of mapping operations, then kinematics pries open a new epistemology grounded on the understanding of geometry *as* motion.

But there are at least two fundamentally different ways of representing this basic language: as kinematic equations and as kinematic notation. They may sound similar, but they are not. The difference between them is similar to the one described earlier in relation to computer animation and notation. The argument I have been building over the course of this chapter is now becoming more explicit: different ways of representing mechanistic movement also create different histories of material representation, and different histories of machinic knowledge. Synthesis and cooperation between these two paradigms is not easy. Kinematic equations are direct representations of physical phenomena, which in the era of computation can be used for the purpose of motion control and automation. For instance, kinematics is usually applied to design and automate the articulated movement sequences of artificial bodies (e.g., robots or animation characters). Kinematic notation, on the other hand, was a system of symbolic representation used to describe the movement of machines, which has become all but obsolete. To unpack these ideas further, I would like to consider in more detail the politics of representation arising from these two paradigms.

The term "kinematics" first appeared in a dictionary of science entitled *Essai sur la philosophie des sciences* (1838) by André-Marie Ampère, who coined the term to refer to a geometry of movement distinct from dynamics. The equations used in this geometry of motion, also known as kinematic equations, rationalize and abstract the behavior of a physical system in terms of its motion as a function of time. Compared to its sister field of dynamics, kinematics deals with a more restricted number of variables. In fact, kinematics deals with only five time-related variables: displacement, initial velocity, final velocity, acceleration, and time, denoted by the letters S, U, V, A, and T—hence SUVAT equations.

Readers who are unfamiliar with SUVAT equations may wonder how these contribute to an account of a cultural theory of the language and mediation of human movement. I cannot think of a single major work in cultural theory devoted to the understanding of equations as cultural artifacts. And this is a problem, given the ubiquity of equations in the programming of technologized movement in a digital era. So even if there is no cultural theory of the equation to frame my discussion, even if equations hold an aura of inscrutability for a general audience, there is no escaping the fact that the construction of mathematized and technologized movement resides in the equational description of kinetic activity. When looking at animated characters in video games, or admiring the most recent developments in human robotics, the nonexpert may be forgiven for focusing on material features. However, these digital beings are animated by the internal language of kinematics, which implies that the scripting of their movement is achieved extensively via code or via equations of motion. The "book" of artificial human movement is indeed written in the language of kinematics.

There is another side to the story of kinematic representation, however, one that brings us back to the basic problem posed in these chapters: why does arbitrary notation so often fail when it comes to the technologization of human movement? The language of kinematics was greatly improved by German machine theorist Franz Reuleaux, who also invented the first system of symbolic notation for machinic kinematics. While Borelli is called the "father of biomechanics," Reuleaux might be the no less important "father of kinematics." In fact, Reuleaux created a kind of universal language and alphabet, which he compiled in a dictionary of machine movement first published in its English translation in 1876 under the title *Kinematics of Machinery: Outlines of a Theory of Machines*. Reuleaux drew largely on Charles Babbage to systematize a symbolic system for the representation of machine movement, which he called "kinematic notation." Unlike kinematic equations, Reuleaux notation did not make use of letters assigned to abstract quantities (SUVAT). Nor did the system rely on assignment of letters to parts of the human body, as many movement notations systems do. Reuleaux notation is a system for machine movement description that essentially maps kinematic constraints onto symbols that represent three aspects of machine movement: a machine part symbol, a form symbol, and a relation symbol. The striving for a universal language of movement, as we have seen, is met by a similar striving for generality in the understanding of machine movement, which Reuleaux took up in an effort to record in universal written form the movement of any machine whatsoever. If Laban attempted to internationalize and standardize the symbolic writing of human movement, Reuleaux notation could be said to have attempted the same in the ambit of machine movement. Except that Reuleaux notation did not manage to achieve the comprehensive application that Laban's system did. It is also worth pointing out that, although the attempt to develop a more analytical and logical representation of machine movement was intended to avoid cumbersome drawings and diagrams, Reuleaux's notation was unsuccessful not least because it was too difficult to adopt. The demise of kinematic notation once again provokes the question: How can movement be captured via the indirect medium of arbitrary symbols without undermining the direct and immediate nature of total movement?

Although Reuleaux notation did not succeed in becoming the standard means of writing machine movement, his work established the language of kinematics within the fields of engineering and mechanics, where it is firmly rooted to this day. Rather than focusing on the movement of mechanical apparatuses, the contemporary language of kinematics has evolved to cover a number of novel applications, particularly in the fields of robotics, computer-aided manufacture (CAM), computer-aided design (CAD), and computer-generated imaging (CGI). Within this digital-era context, motion control encompasses two sublanguages: forward and inverse kinematics (or FK and IK for short). These sublanguages refer primarily to the use of kinematic equations in robots, moving machinery, or animation characters. IK is perhaps the more common of the two, at least within artificial human movement design and engineering, as it provides an answer to the key computational problem of calculating joint parameters in order to obtain a desired end position. Although there are many different applications of IK across a plethora of different technologies, what is common to the IK model is a breakdown of the motion plan of a robot, machine, or digital character into given trajectories. Thus a robot or animated figure can move in a designated fashion, by a rationale of joint actuators or motor parts that are stitched together into a chain of movement. The breakdown of movement over the course of this kinematic chain is perhaps one of the principal objectives of digital kinematics.

IK offers a language that is intuitive insofar as it is goal-directed. It also reflects a natural way of performing movement. As Aristotle pointed out, the logic of movement is not reflexive but impulsive—movement is driven by necessity and desire, and by inner moves that are physicalized directly. We do not move because we tell ourselves to: we simply do it. Inverse kinematics allows digital characters and robots to achieve goal-directed movement, so that whoever is using a kinematic tool does not have to stop and reflect on how the movement is achieved. Movement is performed; it remains a doing and a making—a practice—rather than a hypothesis. Unlike notation, which, as I mentioned earlier, cannot easily be automated, the basic computational mathematics underlying IK robotics and animation allows for an intelligent knowledge of movement, which can be performed automatically or without deliberation. This point illustrates the underlying premise of this part of the book: whereas the notated mediation of movement slows down our connection with performed movement by representing it in an arbitrary and purely symbolic fashion, forcing us to stop and interpret the symbols, the mathematical and computational paradigms of kinematics are more effective in commanding a technological system to *perform* movement directly. A computer performs a kinematic instruction automatically, so when a computer-generated dancer moves on a screen, we do not see the language of kinematics but only its performance. When we move, we do not tell our brain to send out an instruction, nor does the brain provide a written instruction that our intellectual faculties must interpret externally. This direct language from brain to body, or from computer to digital body, questions the role notation and other forms of linguistic symbolization can play in the ongoing technologization of motion.

The negation of a movement notation paradigm implied in the title of chapter 7 ("No Notation") is justified because automated communication technology cannot afford delays. To return to the point made by Arthur and Marilouise Kroker, electronic communication is too fast for alphabetic writing, and in order to keep up one must accept that the slow regime of the alphabetic (or in this case of the symbolic notation of machine movement) has been taken over by the fast regime of movement performativity: i.e., by movement languages that *do* something, that provoke a machine to move, as opposed to giving symbolic accounts of it. Languages that fail to *do* movement demand disembodied meaning. Even though symbolic notation will never die out, and the same could be said about alphabeticism, what is proclaimed in a world of postalphabeticism and post-stave notation is not the end of old regimes, but their ostracism within a kinematic technologization of movement, and within a new media world where languages *do* movement (hence movement performativity). To sum up, whereas the symbols in Reuleaux's kinematic notation *mean* movement, inverse kinematics *does* movement: it is the soft architecture that allows the digital character on screen to move; it tells the robot to perform movement to a desired position, even if this end-oriented program is effaced from the experience of seeing the digital or robotic body move. If kinematic notation is written onto the page so we can see the language symbolized and represented before us, kinematic equations are written onto bodies, as Borelli would say. Kinematics is invisible to an external gaze in the same way that the language of motor control commanded by the brain is executed directly onto physical movement without the subject's conscious awareness of the existence of that motor language at the neurophysical level.

Control

Nikolai Bernstein has to be credited with introducing this basic idea: motor control is characterized by the brain's capacity to write a nonsymbolic (or if you like, a natural) language, a motor program that commands the body to move. By the same token, that which programs the biomechanical body is not so much a discipline or a technology of the body, in the Foucauldian sense, but a system of control. So my final question is not who writes the book of the biomechanized body nor who reads it, but who (if anyone) is in control of it. Is it the machine or the human? Or is control also shared? Is it found in a trajective space in between? Motion control is of paramount importance in my overall argument, even though so far I have not paid sufficient attention to this issue.

The idea will have become familiar to many of us, given the popularization of motion controllers within the orbit of console game technology. Examples include Nintendo's Wii Remote, the ASUS Eee Stick, Sony's PlayStation Move, and HP's Swing. While such consumer products have made motion-controlling technology readily available and highly popular, the underlying kinematics of digital characters and robots remains effaced from the view of a game user. The user of a video game plays—but he or she does not access the knowledge of a language underlying the motion on screen.

The example of motion controllers can be expanded to the idea of "social controllers," or socially normative mechanisms that govern the way we move, that determine the places where we move to and from, that program the motives (the desires, appetites, intentions) that provoke our movements (physical and mental). This is the lesson of the Soviet experiment carried out at the Central Institute of Labor, which I mentioned earlier, which tried to understand the language of industrial movement in order to control the production of automated factory work and lead a utopian program of social engineering. But it would be too simplistic to argue that such mechanisms of social control apply technology to the orchestration of people's everyday movement. What contemporary technology can do is identify our position, keep track of our behaviors and our kinetic activities, and thus give visibility to our every movement (online or in physical space). As we start to move in relation to that system of ubiquitous visibility, as we start to adjust the way we move to a GPS map or to any other tracking device, we begin to move in relation to technological motion visualization, and thus technologies begin to gain a certain sway over our everyday kinetic experience.

In his "Postscript to Societies of Control" Deleuze defined control as a "mechanism giving the position of any element within an open environment at any given instant (whether animal in a reserve or human in a corporation)" (1992, 7). The definition can be tinkered with in order to satisfy the conceptual framework underpinning the current debate: control relies on instruments that determine where things will move and where they will end—like inverse kinematics. Control is also defined by systems of motion visualization and motion codification that can track movement or can draw the trajectories of objects and people, giving computational representations of this movement, and thus giving us the capacity to reprogram these trajectories as manipulable instructions. If we live in a society of control—not a society of disciplination—as Deleuze argued, it is because a cultural shift has occurred from disciplinary behavior to programmed behavior. More importantly, we have shifted to a cultural condition of possibilities in which machines are not only biomechanically designed like Borelli's Meccano sets but are also intelligent, so that smart technologies can identify and process rational languages autonomously and automatically.

Deleuze made another interesting point regarding the historicity of machinic agency, which is also worth fleshing out: "types of machines are easily matched with each type of society—not that machines are determining, but because they express those social forms capable of generating them and using them" (1992, 6). In Deleuze's theorization, beyond the mechanical machine and the energy machine lies the "third machine," the computer, whose power to control is greatly enhanced by the fact that computers are artificially intelligent. In the era of the computer, according to Deleuze, "what counts is not the barrier but the computer that tracks each person's position—licit or illicit—and effects a universal modulation" (7). Thus, the significance of the third machine in characterizing and defining the era we live in—the digital era—can be explained given the power of computers to read, to program, and to track the movement of other machines, and even of human beings. They have the power to understand languages that make things move. The question is whether this is really a society of control. After all, control presupposes that a central system, a central brain, can coordinate the movement of a body, or at least keep track of it. That is the premise of Bernstein's investigation, and the field of motor control that stemmed from such investigations. But what happens when—as is the case with electronic forms of motion computation—many brains form a distributed intelligence, producing such complexity of information that movement can no longer be centralized and coordinated from a single center? Indeed, rather than Deleuze's society of control, we live in a society *out of control*.

And so we come to my conclusion. As I understand the term, interlingua bridges a division between being human and being other (a technological being in the broadest sense), producing a very different ex-stasis to the one described in earlier chapters. We learn to become something other than ourselves not only by seeing movement represented in the extension, but also by coming into contact with technological otherness, with this being outside our physical selves that technologized corporeality and technologized movement affords. But in what way do we return changed? Why should we even want to return to our anatomical selves after having experienced the ecstasy of technologized movement?

The agency that controls us from the other side is not necessarily a nation-state, a church, a political party, an organization or corporation, but a system of distributed relations constituted in and through technologized communication. The anonymity of this agency means that the content of a new technology cannot be controlled, because digital technology in general has gained the capacity to evolve without anyone's centralized and commanding influence or censorship. Having gained this degree of autonomy from the human hand that feeds them, technological systems (e.g., the Internet) can begin to affect the way we behave as though they had an agency of their own. Our human movements have become defined by our technologized mobility, and this mobility is in turn determined by a technological capability that is increasingly uncontrollable given the vast proliferation of smart technologies of communication and motorization, and given the fragmentation of technological brains into different operational systems, different languages, or different "determinations" of movement perception, to borrow the term from Bergson (1983). Decentralized and distributed, we now move in a condition of technological indetermination, increasingly reliant upon independent or interdependent devices to guide us through our kinetic life experience. We now experience movement through motion-assisting technologies like the global positioning system, radio frequency identification, real-time locating systems, and a plethora of other tracking systems that tell us where things are in physical or virtual space. In a world that has lost its capacity to see itself from a centralized and panoptic perspective, the tracking of individual trajectories and objects becomes the only means of finding oneself in the midst of such complexity.

MOTION TECHNOLOGY

PART **IV** MOTION TECHNOLOGY

10

Dyadic progression

The language of the universal binary originated not with a contemporary understanding of digital computing, but with an ancient philosophical system. Binary languages stem naturally, according to Aristotle, from the physical issuance of locomotor progression. Aristotle's thesis is useful in developing an understanding of what a digital language of movement entails. His entire theory of animal and human progression rests on this assumption: the same principles that govern general motion must be found in the activity of walking. So the act of walking is an expression of the Pythagorean concept of a universal, primal division of the Monad into the Dyad, the one into the two, which is expressed as the duality of kinesis and stasis.

Aristotle assumed that joints and limbs must be anatomically necessary if one part of an animal moves and the other rests. To clarify, the human gait ought to be studied in terms of a position at rest (a stretched limb) and a position in motion (the flexed limb). In the case of human walking, when one leg is at rest, this limb is one straight line. When the leg is in motion, it is flexed, and so the angle of flection produces two lines. The same applies to any joint and limb articulation. The language of progression is always the same: one limb made up of two joint parts, and one action made up of two states (motion and rest). Aristotle's teleological conclusion is that, just like universal movement, human and animal motion occur in terms of a logical association between rest and movement. Kinesis and stasis are thus associated not by chance but by universal necessity. One may conclude that from this physical condition, which according to Aristotle is universal, stems a universal language.

Aristotle thus stumbled upon the idea of a universal system of representation based on two values. But its universality is true only in principle, since the actual performance of walking is in fact individualized and subjective: each body or walking machine walks in a different way. Each system of representation of walking—from footprint notation, to the natural odography of foot printing, to Marey's machinic odography—is culturally different. Aristotle even suggested that this universal sense of progression was applicable not only to humans but to automatons: "the movement of animals resembles that of marionettes which move as the result of a small movement, when the strings are released and strike one another." He added, to reinforce this coincidence: "Animals have similar parts in their organs; namely, the growth of their sinews and bones, the latter corresponding to the pegs in the marionettes and the iron, while the sinews correspond to the strings" (1961, 465). This idea could be taken one step further: the will or the intelligence to move does not have to be performed by a human agent. Just as the physical act of walking can be automated by the puppet, the mental act or the thinking and programming of the movement can be automated by an artificially intelligent being.

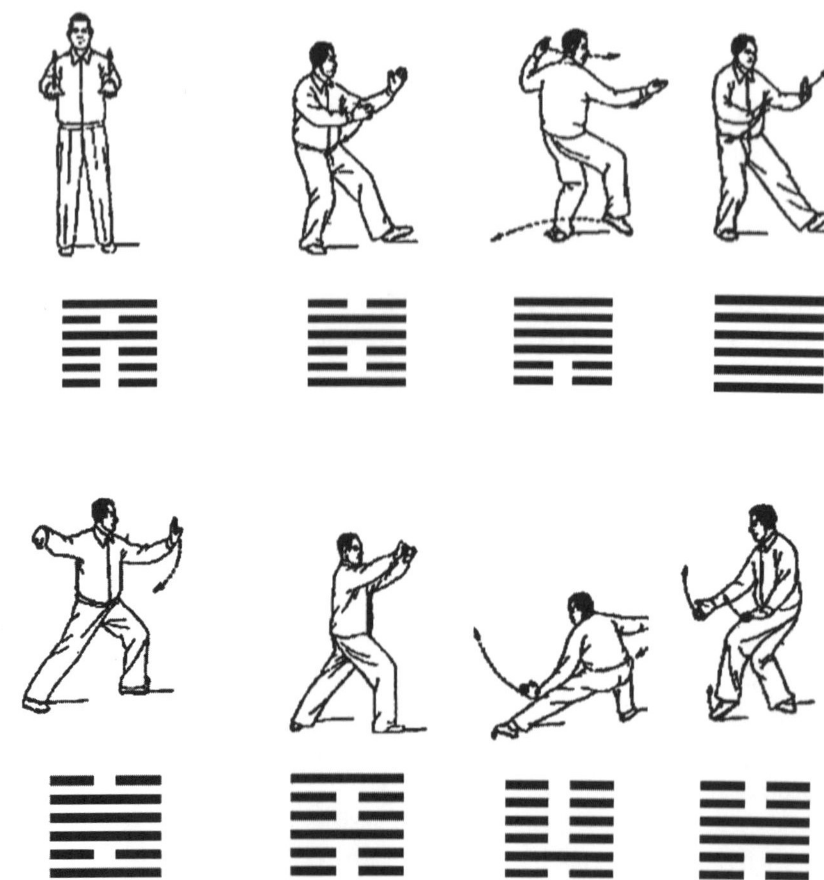

10.1
I Ching hexagrams with the equivalent
body positions used in the language
of tai chi ch'uan.

Indeed, computer technology can supplement biomechanical knowledge of the digital puppet's movements with a mental intention, affording much more than a biomechanical motor—for the electronic computer offers a degree of artificially intelligent movement. The electronic computer offers the language to program the intelligent execution of electronic movement, at the basis of which is the universal language of binary digits (bits). In the final part of this book, I will address the effects of current computer technology in the transformation of human movement languages, the computerization of kinetic formalisms, and the expanded kinetopoietic possibilities that digitally generated motion can afford.

Tai chi ch'uan, or the invention of digital movement

One way of seeing this history of digital movement unfold toward full automation is via the classical Chinese divination text, the *I Ching* or *Classic of Changes*, one of five canonical Confucian texts. The *I Ching* contains a chart system made up of hexagrams, or geometric six-point star figures—64 of them in total (see figure 7.2). Each of the six points in the hexagram is made up of three rows of lines. In addition, there are two types of line: broken and unbroken. The broken line is yin and the unbroken line is yang. Many types of natural polarities can be expressed in terms of yin-yang binary, including light and dark, high and low, life and death, male and female, and, perhaps most importantly, motion and rest. Thus, when a hexagram is cast, each yin and yang line will be indicated as either moving (changing) or fixed (unchanging). By combinatorial means, lines can change to their opposite. The system is self-generative, based on the coming together of polar opposites—male and female, motion and rest—over a period of time.

That the system could be developed into a form of physical movement training is evident from the application of the *I Ching* to tai chi ch'uan, or tai chi for short. In its original inception, tai chi was developed not as a form of martial arts, a leisurely physical exercise, but as the physical expression of Taoist philosophy. The effort of achieving an ideal state of spiritual well-being, as proposed by Taoist philosophy, is directed toward tai chi as a physical expression of a supreme potential principle. *Tai chi ch'uan* translates to English as "great goal" or "supreme ultimate," indicating that the technique is believed to physicalize a philosophical and spiritual objective. The language of tai chi thus has a twofold effect: it engages the practitioner in both a physical exercise intended to promote attentiveness and a mental exercise intended to extend self-knowledge. In its more traditional conception, this movement language is intended to create a state of in-betweenness (that is, between the boundless unpolarized circle and the polar yin and yang). In this way, tai chi establishes a midpoint or harmony, utilizing combinations of different bodily postures to produce significant therapeutic effects with minimal effort.

Because each of the 108 postures of the tai chi alphabet expresses a different philosophical concept, and the bodily posture can be considered a motor representation of a coded philosophical idea, tai chi provides a complex set of combinatorial possibilities that help articulate different binary progressions through physical movement. From this purely formal perspective, tai chi proposes the codification of natural movements in a language of bodily positions that expresses the same combinatorial framework provided by the *I Ching*. Thus, each position in tai chi is derived from a specific hexagram.[1] Like the universal binary, tai chi is a language of progression, in the sense that it can help articulate strings of individual units of bodily positions into a sequence. Thus, tai chi expresses in very simple terms a basic idea underlying this book: the language of the discrete can be embodied through the paradigm of bodily positions, which are the smallest contrastive units of a formal movement language, and bodily transpositions, which are the logical links between one unit and the next. Tai chi can be defined as a motor representation of binary language, in the sense that yin-yang dualism can be interpreted as the lifted or unloaded foot versus the foot at rest, or as the orientation of a movement going forward versus backward. According to Antonio Camurri et al. (1986), the postures of tai chi can indeed be represented in binary notation. Formal combinations of tai chi postures thus become interesting not only from a somatic perspective but also from a purely formal perspective, i.e., in terms of numerical patterns, as in the case of the tai chi sequence:

000001 000011 000111 001111 011111 111111

111110 111100 111000 110000 100000 000000

According to these authors, tai chi is quite remarkable for "its modernity in formalizing aspects of human behavior (natural movements, in particular), which is the focus of contemporary artificial intelligence" (Camurri et al. 1986, 95). Indeed, humanoid robots like the Nao robot developed by the French company Aldebaran are programmed to be able to do tai chi in addition to a number of other kinetic activities, because the robot has also been programmed to obey formalized aspects of human behavior and natural movement. Nao has a wide array of locomotor activities which, in effect, enable the machine to think movement at a basic degree of artificial physical intelligence. Unlike many of the automatons mentioned earlier (Aristotle's puppets, da Vinci's Mechanical Man, Borelli's animal machine, or Schlemmer's *Kunstfigur*), all of which are purely mechanical, Nao is not only computationally intelligent but also possessed with capacitive sensors that allow it to "feel" movement. As such, Nao can respond to being touched, and can recognize when one of its peers is in the same room.

If tai chi is a form of binary digital movement and positions can be readily scripted in terms of binary digit notation, the assimilation of this language by a robotic engine is not at all surprising. What is interesting, however, is whether a comparison of Nao's tai chi and a human's performance of tai chi can help identify aspects of movement a robot performer might not be able to perform. What aspects of an embodied knowledge of movement found within tai chi does Nao fail to understand?

What dimensions of embodied movement transcend a purely formal interpretation of this movement language, as performed robotically? Clearly, robotic performance of a movement language is limited compared to a human's performance. On the other hand, is it possible for Nao to perform movements that a human being cannot execute, thus also expanding the possibilities of motor performance beyond anatomical conditioning?

Leibniz: On digital movement

In the mid-seventeenth century, the German mathematician and philosopher Gottfried Wilhelm Leibniz proposed to substitute the base ten numerical progression with a simpler progression that proceeds by twos (see Leibniz 1863). Leibniz wanted to find true characteristics in numbers and the numerology behind things, and thus he can be credited as the progenitor of the modern conception of the digital. However, like Aristotle, what Leibniz was after was a universal language of thought that could have been expressed by cultures far from the Western canon. Leibniz's inspiration therefore came not only from Aristotle but also from the *I Ching*. In the same way that Taoist philosophy could be incorporated into every aspect of life including a language of movement, Leibniz was able to install the binary in many different areas of everyday life.

As Wilson (1989) has argued, Leibniz proposed formal descriptions of living creatures in terms of two values (1 and 0). Wilson gives the example of the determination of a subject's moral composition, saying that Leibniz associated the entrance of evil into the world with nothingness, which is the antithesis of the good or One. In other words, nothingness enters into the composition of moral character in the same way that 0 enters the binary system. Crucially, Leibniz's thesis extended to a theory of binary digital movement. In 1698, he wrote: "creatures are varied according to the different combinations of one with zero or with the positive and privative" (quoted in Wilson 1989, 273). The image evoked in this passage is reminiscent of the basic concept of the tai chi, which is to find a balance between the nonpolar and boundless whole (the circle) and the polarity or tension of the yin and yang. Indeed, Leibniz's thesis is closer still to Laban's binary of effort and recovery, or Lewin's theory of force field restrictions, in the sense that physical movement is formalized in terms of an undecided condition between forces that encourage us to move and those that stop us from moving.

Living creatures are thus caught up in an interplay between force and inertial resistance, between motivation and lack of motivation, between movement and zero movement. Leibniz described these binary values as "protopathia," the primitive force of resistance, and "protopoeia," or the primitive active force (cited in Wilson 1989). We can evolve a theory of digital movement from Leibniz's thinking, according to which movement can be formally represented as a ceaseless counterpoint between these categories. But because it has to construct different ways of articulating the relationship between resistance and force, the binary language of movement is also a creative activity. To combine the different possibilities of a binary progression requires not a mechanical procedure but a creative understanding of how a language is performed, and how it is actuated in a cultural context. Thus, implied within Leibniz's theory is a dual understanding of movement as a creative force (*poiesis*) and as an uncreative or canceling force (*pathos*). Whereas the realization of protopathia accounts for the material and biological properties of movement, particularly through the resistance and inertia caused by the materiality against which kinetic force interacts, or the physical and health limitations of a corporeal body, the realization of protopoeia accounts for the presence of a spiritedness within material objects and for the mind inside matter, what Leibniz called the ensouled machine. Thus, for Leibniz the Monad or One is simply a combination of the active and passive powers of mobile creatures.

Indeed, his thesis can be reprogrammed in terms of a kinetic poiesis or kinetopoiesis—a creation through movement, which is liable to the endless ebb of expended force and resistance, of effort and recovery, of action and inertia, and of positive and privative energy. Over the course of this book, we have seen that movement is not merely represented as a record, or a formal inscription of numbers or lines. Beyond this mechanical representation, there is an inventive utilization of the language of movement as creative practice. As we have seen, to represent movement it is not enough to produce an inscription. Just as a creative writer must know more than just how to inscribe letters onto a page, to produce a kinetopoietic act one must know how to use a formal language of movement creatively. In this case, one must be able to perform a creative interpretation of the tai chi, or indeed a creative physicalization of Leibniz's binary model of living creatures (i.e., living creators of movement).

Although there is some indication that Leibniz might have been concerned with the binary representation of human bodily movement, he was more interested in finding a language of thought. What he was after was a universal language that could express pure ideas before these become symbolized and thus liable to culturally specific forms of representation and interpretation. He was after a kind of ideography. It is conceivable, however, that within this ideal language a representation of thought might have been possible in terms of the written expression of innermotion. We will never know, since an exact account of the language Leibniz had in mind has never been given. In order to integrate his thinking within this debate, it is important to recognize that his efforts were directed toward a language that is a combination of philosophical, scientific, mathematical, and metaphysical thought. Thus, it was not a language to be expressed in a corporeal way but in a metacorporeal way, thus serving as the medium of expression of the human spirit—the anima inside the body or machine (the ensouled machine). But who is to say that the language of inner thoughts imagined by Leibniz cannot indeed be folded outwardly so as to be expressed in the extension? Why can't a language of pure innermotion be danced in the way the tai chi dances Taoist philosophical principles or Sufi dervishes whirl into a sense of ecstasy that fulfills Islamic mysticism? In other words, why can't the body also be a conduit to the expression of a universal language of spiritual thinking?

In fact, Leibniz drew on the scholastic use of the term *mathesis*, meaning "knowledge," while expanding on Descartes's unfulfilled project of a *mathesis universalis*. Leibniz did not consider his binary the only language that could fulfill Descartes's ambition; he also applied himself to a number of new mathematical inventions, including the infinitesimal calculus, in order to accomplish this universal knowledge system. He wrote: "the human race appears to me comparable to a group of people who wander in confusion in the shadows without a guide or an order, without words or other signs for directing their movement" (quoted in Wilson 1989, 7). Although Leibniz probably refers here to the movement of thought, for me the more inviting question is whether formal languages of movement can guide the connection between inner and outer, thus integrating the creative and pattern-constructing habits of human beings in terms of the guided creation of shapes that are both physical and mental, like the shapes of a binary digital progression in Camurri et al.'s digital tai chi.

Thus far I have provided a basic idea of how Leibniz might have conceptualized the beginnings of a modern digital way of thinking, which could be installed in all places including the formal representation of corporeal movement. However, and as I mentioned earlier, it is still not clear what kind of language he had in mind, nor how this language could be written down. Rather than simply assuming that a synthetic language could provide the means of substituting calculation for reasoning, and rather than saying universal thought was fundamentally calculative—a thinking via numbers—Leibniz suggested *mathesis universalis* should not be confined to a single domain of language, not even the mathematical domain. Crucially, his project highlighted the limitations of any given language system, whether mathematical or linguistic. The project also highlighted the need to create a combinatorial art that could lead to the modulation and evolution of languages. The difficulty with this project, as with any attempt to formalize a language of inner moves, is the question of representation. What kind of characters would this knowledge adopt?

Over the course of his investigations, Leibniz grappled with the problem of how a universal language should represent its denotation, so that universal mathesis would not impose a burden on memory. His foundation for the invention of a *characteristica universalis* or a universal notation stemmed from his belief that while artificial things can normally be defined functionally in terms of regular relationships and rules, which are mirrored in notation, notation can also lend itself to expressing natural things: for instance, natural opposition.

Because Leibniz never described his characteristica in operational detail, many commentators have been left wondering what exactly this notation system would have looked like, and whether it would have differed from the hexagrams used in the *I Ching*. Leibniz's combination of algebraic calculations with musical notes and astronomical signs, and his desire to create an alphabet of human thought that drew on non-Western glyphic traditions including Egyptian and Chinese hieroglyphics and chemical signs, suggest that the kind of notation system he had in mind was a synthesis of a great number of scriptive traditions. There are similarities between Leibniz's characteristica and

Laban's notion of primary action signs, mentioned earlier. Yet no such universal language is possible, except in the computational sense of a universal computing language, which I discuss later.

Leibniz machine

Judging by his interest in the automation of reasoning, one of the major problems Leibniz set out to address was how to apply universal language to mechanized procedures that do not necessarily require human reasoning, such as inputting-outputting, question-answering, or command-effect. He wrote that his universal knowledge would deliver a new vision to the intellect—it would be a new kind of instrument that would increase the power of the mind much more than optical lenses strengthen the eyes, and would be as far superior to microscopes and telescopes as reason is superior to sight (cited in Wilson 1989, 34). It is obvious that Leibniz's binary language finds its technological medium in the domain of universal computing.

Leibniz got the idea for his calculating machine from a pedometer, or step-counting machine.[2] He explained: "When I saw, many years ago, an instrument with whose help one could count one's own steps without thinking, the idea came to me that all arithmetic could be achieved through a similar type of device" (quoted in Wilson, 1989, 26). That Leibniz's calculating machine was derived from a pedometer is not entirely without consequence, as the connection between calculation and walking, or counting steps, highlights a basic conjunction between stepped movement and computational logic. Indeed, Leibniz's association between a walking machine and a calculating machine supports an argument that I wish to address seriously, especially as my debate is shifting in the direction of a more contemporary technologizing of movement. If thought is the internalization of movement according to the mentality-motility connection I have been making over the course of this book, should there not be a similar connection in the case of artificial forms of thinking? In other words, is mechanized thinking also the internalization of mechanized movement? Leibniz certainly seemed to think so.

In 1694 Leibniz completed the first physical model of his machine, which is in fact the first digital mechanical calculator—a direct precursor of the modern digital computer. The machine is known as the Step Reckoner, a name that refers to the basic mechanics of the apparatus. To make the machine "walk through" a calculation, Leibniz used a special cylinder, known as the Leibniz wheel, featuring teeth of incremental lengths which, when coupled to a counting wheel, provided the basic engine of this mechanical calculator. The Step Reckoner was designed with an input section featuring eight dials with knobs to set the operand number, and a rear accumulator section or output section, which produced the result of the given operation. Leibniz's invention also featured a multiplier dial, which operated like a telephone dial. Essentially, one could dial the number of times a simple arithmetic operation was to be performed, between 0 and 9 times. Although the size of the machine built by Leibniz only allowed multiplication of a given operand number up to 9, the principle could be extended to any multiplication table: if one could build a machine with a dial of infinite numbers, then the machine would be able to calculate mathematical infinity.

This historical connection between physical walking and calculating step by step, or between physical walk and calculative walk, is central to the development of a digital way of thinking and a digital way of moving that has existed since antiquity. In a manner of speaking, the computer era started in ancient times.[3] The moment we begin to think and move in relation to discrete steps—countable steps—a digital sense of progression (physical and mental) naturally emerges. This evolving history of represented binary digits, from manual to machinic and from machinic to electronic, ratifies the connection between the mental act of progressing via the calculation of numbers and the physical act of progression by physical steps. In fact, the idea that machines "walk" and that their processing of discrete information is conducted step by step is not entirely lost in contemporary understandings of digital computation.

The principle of step-by-step calculation is also found in more direct ancestors of the modern computer, such as the Turing machine. Although Turing machines are intended as hypothetical devices rather than constructed apparatuses, they fulfill the same step-reckoning logic as the Leibniz machine, at least conceptually. Scanned symbols are printed backward and forward onto the device's tape (or memory), producing a progression, which is also referred to as "walking." And in the same way that the path along which a person walks is the recorded memory of that person's presence in space, so the trajectory left behind by the walking Turing machine is a computational memory. Thus, a computer produces inner moves or thoughts via algorithmic steps, with an algorithm defined as an internalized or logical way of walking, step by step, from input to output following basic rules of computational logic.

If calculating and computing machines could be said to walk, it is not because they mimic the activity of human walking. Nevertheless, physical walks and computational walks have in common this two-state sense of progression (at once mental and physical). Physical and mental movement then become part of this integrated process this book refers to as total movement, in the sense that the physicalization of a walk is the motor representation of an inner logic, and vice versa. This folding of inner and outer, of physical and calculative notions of stepping and step-reckoning, reformulates the book's title thesis in the contemporary digital-era context. In this context, intelligent computerized systems, and the capacity for contemporary systems to think more complex sets of operations and algorithmic moves, also touch on the capacity for contemporary technologies to be more mobile. In other words, because contemporary technologies are more intelligent, and because they can carry out increasingly complex calculative or step-reckoning operations, their mental dexterity is reflected in their capacity to control automated movement, and to self-generate movement. Contemporary computing affords increasingly abstract and powerful ways of walking. Rather than the straightforward and linear walks of Aristotelian logic, contemporary computation can thus manage nonlinear walks (random walks or quantum walks). Electronic computation can handle step-by-step linear progressions of formal logic that can be recursive, looped, or calculatedly random.

Going for an algorithmic walk

In his "Formulary for a New Urbanism" (written 1953), French political activist and poet Ivan Chtcheglov wrote that walking constitutes the latest stage in a long historical morphology. Chtcheglov's idea of a revolutionary urbanism, which was unstable, diffuse, and nonlinear, was best exemplified in his idea of the *dérive*, or drifting, a concept that was also taken up by French intellectual and political activist Guy Debord and the Situationist International. In seeking to generate discourse out of landscape through aimless walking, the dérive experiment proposed to bring back an environmental way of inscribing one's own bodily time and space onto urban surroundings. This idea resonates with the thesis of this chapter: there is a connection between walking, or between stepping and counting steps, and the creation of abstract systems of calculation and reasoning. For Chtcheglov, walking around the city is not only a morphology; it is a way of thinking and articulating streams of counter-cultural thinking that string together spatial and temporal situations into a poetic or kinetopoietic discourse. To amble around the city is to represent the counterlogic of drifting, which opposes the linear and goal-oriented regime of a technocratic, bureaucratic, and capitalist urban mobility.

Walking is also an encounter with memory and history. After all, one can walk over someone else's footsteps, and thus one can transform the activity of walking into a kinesymbolic activity, a means of reading narratives written by past bodies into the landscape. In walking through a historical space like the city of Paris, Chtcheglov was also proposing what he called a "symbolic urbanism" (1981, 168) which could give new meaning to that historical space. Crucially, Chtcheglov located the historical relevance of drifting as a means of knowing within a contemporary cultural context, which he described as being symptomatized by a "thousand ways of modifying life, with a view to an ultimate mythic synthesis" (169). And insofar as drifting is a new way of walking, a new morphology, so the dérive can be considered an activity that involves not only experience but also representation (and the materialization of memory). It is a way of representing an alternative and countercultural way in which people assume their condition as members of what Chtcheglov called a "mobile civilization" (169).

Psychogeography, as this practice is now commonly known, presupposes that drifting is a means of connecting a city in space and time, not through a random walk—in the broad sense of this term—or through a game of chance. For Chtcheglov, a psychogeographic representation is a good replacement for Sunday Mass: it is more effective in making people enter into communication with the ensemble of energies of the collective. Drifting is therefore not random; its intention is to create a new collective that is guided by a plan other than the everyday plan to go to work, or to go shopping, which might fulfill the capitalist logic of the mobile city. Dérives carried out by members of the

Situationist International used another compass to experience urban surroundings; for instance, by chasing smells or navigating Paris using a map of London. Debord (1981) expanded on Chtcheglov's formulary, and contended that the dérive is a technique of rapid passage through varied ambiences involving playful-constructive behavior and an awareness of psychogeographic effects that are quite distinct from the classic notion of the stroll (1981, 50). For a start, the dérive is not a linear step-by-step representation of a cityscape—it is not a walking syllogism. Conceptually, the dérive invites a modern logic into its physicalized representation. It elicits a logic that has no predetermined endpoint, and which does not move straight. In Debord's words: "In a dérive one or more persons during a certain period drop their relations, their work and leisure activities, and all their other usual motives for movement and action" (1981, 51). This immersion in a mobile civilization is a significant artistic and cultural representation of a way of thinking or acting that enables an alternative cultural expression of mobility. Rather than besuited businesspeople walking busily to and fro, or the delivery man, or the everyday pedestrian on her way to work, the drifter abandons this official position, this social role, and becomes whatever the journey allows. Having said this, Debord warned that the dérive included both this letting go and its necessary contradiction. Psychogeography is informed by a science of environmental spaces and by an act of traversing urban and rational spaces in a way that is conducive to a kind of data analysis. The dérive turns the practice of walking into a calculative negotiation of the city's inherent geometries. Debord concluded: "The objective passional terrain of the dérive must be defined in accordance both with its own logic and with its relations with social morphology" (1981, 52).

Since the exploration of this new urbanism entails establishing trajectories and memories of walking that involve calculating directions of penetration, the dérive draws not only on ecology, cartography, and topography but also, in more recent conceptions of psychogeographic drawing, on the formalism of computer algorithms. Thus, in contemporary psychographic practice, algorithmic walking refers to a physical urban stroll that is programmed in the manner of a computer algorithm. For instance, algorithmic walking might involve following a predefined series of psychogeographic commands: take the first right, the second left, then the first left, and then repeat. Halfway between a random and a structured way of traveling, algorithmic walking or generative psychogeography was pioneered by Dutch psychogeographer and performance artist Wilfried Hou Je Bek. In his 2004 piece *.walk* (dotwalk), Hou Je Bek devised what he called "generative psychogeography," intended to explore city spaces by translating psychogeographic walks into a kind of pedestrian computer. Hou Je Bek imagined a Universal Psychogeographical Computer (UPC), a peripatetic and foot-powered machine. The performance of this ideal machine sets out to produce a "fundamental concept that might be used to program non-electric computers" (in O'Rourke 2013, 90). In addition, the UPC comprises examples of what Hou Je Bek calls a "pseudocode," which can be exchanged when two psychogeographers meet to produce an "export code" (90). Likewise, if the body is "wetware," then the walk can be referred to as "walkware."

Generative psychogeography will undoubtedly contain a computation in the strict sense of the word, and the procedure will involve the performance of an algorithm in the strictest sense. The use of computer-specific terminology is not intended to be scientific but playful and self-reflective, so that the performance may precipitate a different understanding of the computerized city. According to Hou Je Bek, generative psychogeography is: "1) The ability of the directions to enslave the participant; to create the desire to find out where this all 'will lead to', 2) the real unexpected 'new-ness' of the stroll and 3) the actual enhancement of the agent's cognitive map with new images and experiences of the city" (Hou Je Bek n.d.). At the same time, the pedestrian software is a commentary on the computerization of urban space, so that in treating the city as hardware, which is literally walked along by the *.walk* software (i.e., the stroller), the difference between the physical and the computational understanding of walking and calculating can be overcome.

The adoption of an algorithmic way of moving is also a trademark of William Forsythe's choreographic work. In Forsythe's words, "algorithms are little machines made of language. ... They naturally take things apart and put them back in very unexpected ways" (quoted in Manning 2009, 22). The algorithmic program he commands himself or his dancers to perform requires a language, a vocabulary of movements that is not known in advance but is discovered in the process of moving. As in Hou Je Bek's algorithmic walks, the shape of an algorithmic dance step in Forsythe's work is obtained by trial and error—that is, by simply testing the algorithm and seeing if it produces a shape, a structure, or a pattern that communicates a choreographic idea of sorts. Forsythe has also extended this process beyond choreographic practice in the narrow sense, to participatory installations where the dance or walking algorithm can be intended to create combinatorial structures by which audience members arrange themselves in space to generate patterns. In either case, Forsythe's algorithms enable the choreographing of bodies and spaces in such a way that one cannot predict what will happen to the dancer/mover in any given sequence. The only way to know is to execute the program. Like John Cage's chance music and Merce Cunningham's chance dance—which, incidentally, are also inspired by the *I Ching*—the kernel of the performance is that the dancer or musician creates a situation where the white canvas catches whatever falls on it. "And where does the beauty begin and where does it end?" asked Cage. "Where it ends is where the artist begins. In this way we get our navigation done for us" (Cage 2010, 108). One might add that, in an algorithmic sense, we get our movement done for us.

Digital brains

The language of binary digits suits physical systems in two states—e.g., plus and minus, positive and negative. Indeed, electronic signals suit binary code to a tee because of the ease with which on and off states can be scripted as zeros and ones. This combination of the language of the binary and electrical circuitry results in what is nowadays a basic, even universal mode of communication: electronic computing. So Leibniz's binary has become a universal language after all, if only within the context of the electronic computer. We can measure the way electronic communication has changed a number of everyday activities by listing Internet terms that carry the prefix e- (for "electronic"): e.g., e-book, e-commerce, e-mail, e-banking, e-democracy, e-trade, e-cash, and e-theater. In the strictest sense, "e-communication" stands for communication that is carried out online. The electronic processing of information and the binary system used to support it can be conceptualized as a theory of electronic movement that is expressed as both innermotion and outermotion. Three key points support this thesis: first, electronic forms of communication rely on the coding of physical signals into two states, thus enabling the sort of abstract-concrete machine I spoke of earlier. Second, the human brain could be said to utilize the same framework to provoke thought, in that the enervation of nerve cells that provoke neurophysical movement are also determined by two-state physical signals. Third, the human brain and computer brain are analogous from the point of view of the digital programming that supports the performance of movement—hence the title "digital brains."

Communication theorist Colin Cherry argued in the 1950s that the transmission of signals is by definition a physical activity (audible, visual, tactile). Signals, according to Cherry, are physical embodiments of a message (1957, 61). Signal-based communication is constituted via the physical transmission of a signal, which is taken up by a recipient through some physical and sensory interface. This, in turn, elicits response behavior. Once again, no arbitrary notation is needed, only a direct physical impulse encoded as a signal. Hence, the communication via stimulus-response protocols is direct, speedy, and economic. There is no need to waste time in symbolizing the signal, because the signal produces a response automatically. Within formal representations of signal processing, a recipient needs to be able to interpret the physical stimulus as a signal, which is where code comes in.

For Cherry, the fundamental principle of the signal is the idea of discrimination, which he defines as the mathematical understanding of signal processing that first arose in the era of telegraphy and telephony. Yet signals convey communicative content in a way that is abstracted from all questions of meaning. The importance of a signal transmitted along wires or air does not concern value or truth imperatives as in the case of words; the effective communication of signals follows from a different determination, which is selection or discrimination. Once a recipient has been selected and the medium is optimal for a signal transmission, the signal will simply be transmitted to that recipient. Assuming a conventional way of codifying signals has been agreed upon, the signal can therefore be received and the content of the signal can be communicated. According to this basic logic, the electronic signal of a telegraphic relay is ultimately readable thanks to a specific code used to conventionalize the interpretability of the physical signal, which in the case of telegraphy is the Morse code. Earlier when I discussed the writing of movement via pneumatic signals, I touched on Étienne-Jules Marey's chronographic code. What concerns me now is the integration of electrical signals, physical movement, and binary-digital or algorithmic forms of codification within the same technological medium. I will focus on the way electrical signals trigger physical movement, and how the movement of physical bodies can be programmed automatically, so that their movement can be controlled by machines.

The first major historical step toward an understanding of bioelectricity was taken by Luigi Galvani in the 1780s, when he discovered that muscle contractions could be generated by an electrical fluid or substance in the nerves of animals—for instance, in a frog's legs. Galvani described the phenomenon as "animal electricity," but the generation of physical movement through electrical charge soon became known as galvanism and was adopted by a great number of contemporary scientists, aficionados, and artists. Galvanism was later revived as part of a therapeutic electrophysiological science and muscle stimulation technology pioneered by French neurologist Guillaume Benjamin-Amand Duchenne de Boulogne. Duchenne advanced a technique known as electropuncture, according to which individual muscles could be stimulated by applying voltages across electrodes on the skin. Besides investigating the precise location where muscles can be made to move by electrical stimulation, Duchenne applied his method to a detailed survey of human facial muscles and the excitation of those muscles to produce gestures of distinct emotional character.

A second major development in the understanding of an electronic motion paradigm is due to advances in neuroscience, particularly brain anatomy. Spanish pathologist, neuroscientist, and medical artist Santiago Ramón y Cajal, sometimes referred to as "the father of modern neuroscience," produced a vast catalog of drawings illustrating the delicate arborizations of brain cells, thus paving the way to an understanding of neural structures as highly complex architectural networks. Crucially, Ramón y Cajal identified that brain cells are discrete entities, not continuous, and that they communicate with one another via a process of signal transmission and reception—what is now known as synapse. This so-called neuron doctrine was further confirmed by the discovery that neurons are specialized cells capable of passing signals to individual target cells via a complex process that regulates neurotransmission in two fundamental ways: via chemical synapse and via electrical synapse. Thus, synaptic communication relies, much like signal processing in an electronic circuit, on the passing of electric current that causes voltage changes in the brain cell.

Drawing on synaptic transmission, Soviet scientist Nikolai Bernstein claimed that motor control also happens as a result of binary operations comprising a number of relatively autonomic subsystems, or synergies, each performing their own task while integrated by the central nervous system. The realization that neurons are densely arranged, and that they facilitate information exchange through electric currents and electrotonic influences, agreed with Bernstein's understanding of the structural physiology of human movement. In fact, Bernstein advanced his famous theory of localization in motor control by arguing that the brain organizes a map of interrelated stimuli into a localization scheme, similar to that of electronic circuits, in which the same structure can be preserved over various topographies (1984a, 92). "Localization" in this case refers to a structural and nontopographic arrangement reliant on necessary commands that are transferred from these associations onto the muscular system. Bernstein hypothesized exact "formulae of movement" (97–98), which involved the arousal of nerve tissue via the activation of a dormant or latent code. He then assumed that the motor system must unfold at this neural level as a temporal structure involving stamped-in connections between what he called engrams, creating an engrammatic form, which is the structural physiology of movement. Bernstein called this the motor program.

In his essay "Trends in Physiology and Their Relation to Cybernetics," Bernstein (1984b) further elaborated on the connection between the regulation of biological and machinic complex systems and information and communication involved in motor functions. Motor performance, he wrote, is guided by a coded program similar to that of an artificially automated system. He concluded that an organism could construct and combine material codes that reflect countless forms of activity from tropism to the most complex forms of directed action. Bernstein also argued that it was necessary to take up this cybernetic approach in order to indicate and study the differences (and similarities) between living and artificial systems. This is the very same question that American mathematician John von Neumann—the so-called father of the modern computer—took up in his unfinished book *The Computer and the Brain* (1958). Von Neumann described the similarities and dissimilarities between computers and brains—or the two automatons—as involving principles of overall organization and control similar to those used by Bernstein.

Von Neumann (1958) began by recognizing that the nervous system is digital. The basic aim of this system is to generate and propagate nerve impulses in a variety of aspects—electrical, chemical, mechanical. He was concerned with the logic of its propagation, which is essentially reproducible in terms of unitary electrical disturbances generated by the nerve cell. Since the nervous pulses can be viewed as two-state markers (i.e., absence of a pulse or presence of a pulse), these states can be represented in binary language as digits 0 and 1. For this reason, von Neumann contended that the nervous system has "a *prima facie* digital character" (1958, 91). The neurons appear "as the basic *logical* organs, and hence also the basic *digital* organs" (100, my emphasis). This is the same two-state relationship that Bernstein (1984a) assumed to be responsible for the planning and sequencing of neurophysical movement. Instead of a neural propagation of impulses, however, von Neumann described the propagation of electrical pulses in transistor computers in terms of a liaison between emitter and control electrodes.

According to von Neumann, the central nervous system transmits numerical data by periodic or nearly periodic trains of electrical pulses. A sort of frequency-modulated system of signaling is at work here, in the sense that pulse intensities are translated into numerical frequencies. This idea leads him to the most distinguishing difference between the nervous system and computing machines: the nervous system is a computing machine that can manage its exceedingly complicated workload at a low level of precision and a high level of reliability, according to which no known human computing machine can operate. The computer, according to von Neumann, should thus be described as a substantially simplified version of the brain. As such, the two are underpinned by very different languages—the language of the brain and the language of mathematics. Whereas human languages are largely historical accidents, von Neumann argues, showing no absolute or necessary form, the so-called language of the brain is a necessary short code that is essentially different from those natural languages, which our common experience refers to. Von Neumann's book finishes with the following insight: "when we talk mathematics, we may be discussing a secondary language, built on the primary language used by the central nervous system" (1958, 82). In other words, mathematics is a symbolic layer of representation that builds on the natural language of the brain. Language is an accident resulting from our encoded brain.

e-Motional performance

This brief historical analysis leads into the contemporary digital era, in which the exploitation of electrical voltages, physical movement, and code have been extensively integrated within various practices involving electronic motion control. The integration of electrical signaling, physical movement, and computer code can be treated as a major cultural factor in the transformation of the representation of electrically and electronically processed physical movement. Because electronics utilizes the variations of electrical amplitudes to capture and transmit signals, signal processing can be exploited by a number of other apparatuses beside the computer. Indeed, this exploitation of electrical signal processing and computer coding is a point of departure for a profound cultural reconception of human motion as e-motion. Within this paradigm, materiality and message cannot be disentangled. Corporeal movement cannot be understood as a purely physical or material phenomenon; it is not a phenomenon in which the physical body exists as an independent and standalone entity. Body and code are fused, matter and language cross over, and what stems from their copula is an unstable substance, a trajective agency that defines the digital not in terms of a concrete materiality, but a materiality that is abstract-concrete.

This reprogramming of movement reignites Bernstein's proposal of a cybernetic approach by way of a cyborg paradigm of movement, which deserves a passing gloss. Whereas the biomechanical paradigm I discussed earlier is grounded on the associations of human and machine at a strictly mechanical level, from an information-theoretical and cybernetic standpoint the human body can be viewed as a synthetic system whose motions can be manipulated by means of code and electrical control signals. In other words, the cybernetic paradigm goes beyond the mechanical integration of human and machine to include the integration of any natural and artificial system, especially in terms of a feedback between natural and artificial intelligences.

As Arthur Elsenaar and Remko Scha explain: "a point of view that was already implicit in Galvani's eighteenth-century experiments with frogs' legs is particularly relevant today because it opens up the possibility of employing the human body as a display device for algorithms that run on digital computers" (2002, 17). The medical technology utilized by Duchenne in the nineteenth century acquires a paramedical function in the field of performance art, especially cyborg performance. Australian artist Stelarc is often credited with a leading role in the genealogy of cyborg art, and although I do not find much scope left here to pronounce myself on this artist's work, it is certainly worth pointing out that Stelarc pioneered a kinetopoietic interpretation of the language I have been discussing in the previous pages, in the sense that he gave an artistic and embodied expression to the connection between a computational language of motor programming and a technologized body connected to the machine. The work is significant here not only in terms of the hardware used, and the construction of a cyborg model within an artistic practice. What is significant is that the invention of a cyborg here also relates to the synthesis of a computational and corporeal language of motor programming and motor control. Having invited Stelarc into this discussion, I must also revisit a question I raised earlier in relation to the biomechanical paradigm of human movement: Who controls this book written on the body? Both biomechanics and cybernetics provoke the key issue of control, i.e., the power to determine where things will move and where they will end. Stelarc's work speaks quite directly to the Deleuzian idea of a society of control, in a way that is both graphic and bodily explicit. Stelarc uses his own body so that it can be moved by audience members or by an automated motion controller. For instance, in *Split Body* (1994), the automated part of Stelarc's body was programmed by the audience through a touchscreen interface in the gallery space. More recently, Stelarc has moved to muscle control regimes that are not mandated by the audience, but by random and largely unpredictable instructions. As such, *Split Body* also conveys a sense of what I referred to as a society out of control; that is, a society that is coordinated by a decentered intelligence and in a state pure kinetic ecstasy (i.e., living outside its own physical and anatomical determination). The anatomical body can be said to be obsolete, drawing on Stelarc's famous pronouncement, insofar as it can be controlled electrically and artificially. Moreover, it can move in ways other than in physical space, for example in electronic space. Thus, not only is the *body* obsolete; so is bodily movement. e-motion highlights this double opening of the bodily and bodily movement paradigms, both in the direction of electrical charge controls and electronic (online) forms of movement. In his *Ping Body* performance (1996), Stelarc electrically captured, and then electronically coded, his involuntary gestures, thus transforming them into a representation of Internet movement patterns. A special program was used in this piece to send Stelarc's gesture signals to more than 30 Internet domains worldwide, measuring the relay time taken, and then using this metric as further input to control his electrified limbs.

Arthur Elsenaar (2013) has also taken up the possibilities of e-motion by exploring algorithmically controlled human faces, or what he calls "the language of facial e-motion," through the
application of muscle interface devices. Elsenaar has argued that most of the muscle contraction
configurations that the human face is capable of performing are never used spontaneously by people,
and that many of these configurations cannot even be produced without external electrical stimulation. Thus, e-motion paves the way for the exploration of complex emotional states, according to
this artist.[4] In Elsenaar's use of the term, "e-motion" refers not only to the radical reprogramming
of movement via electrical stimulation or the programming of movement via computer languages,
but also to the provocation of new configurations of the inner content of movement at an emotional
(or e-motional) level. As such, the creation of what this artist calls "artifacial expression" presents
the peculiar difficulty of creating a cybernetic inter-face, in the most literal sense of the word.
Elsenaar's work shows the expressive possibilities of the human face to connect, or interface, with
an all-controlling computer.

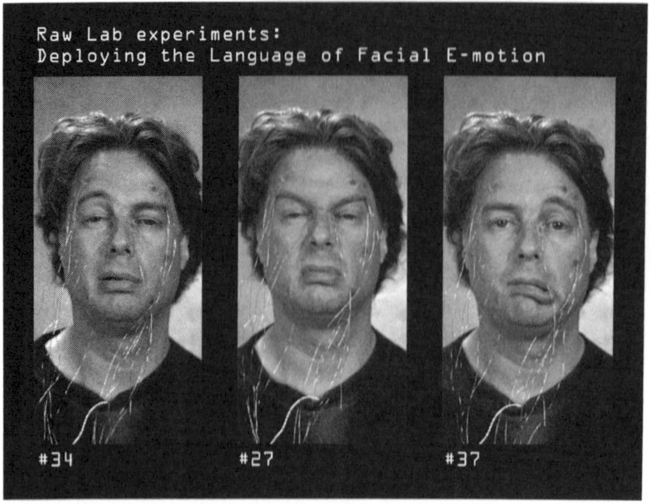

10.2
Composite image of Arthur Elsenaar's "Facial
Choreologic probing" experiments, featured
in Raw Lab. Video: Josephine Japerse and
Jeroen Meijer (courtesy of Arthur Elsenaar).

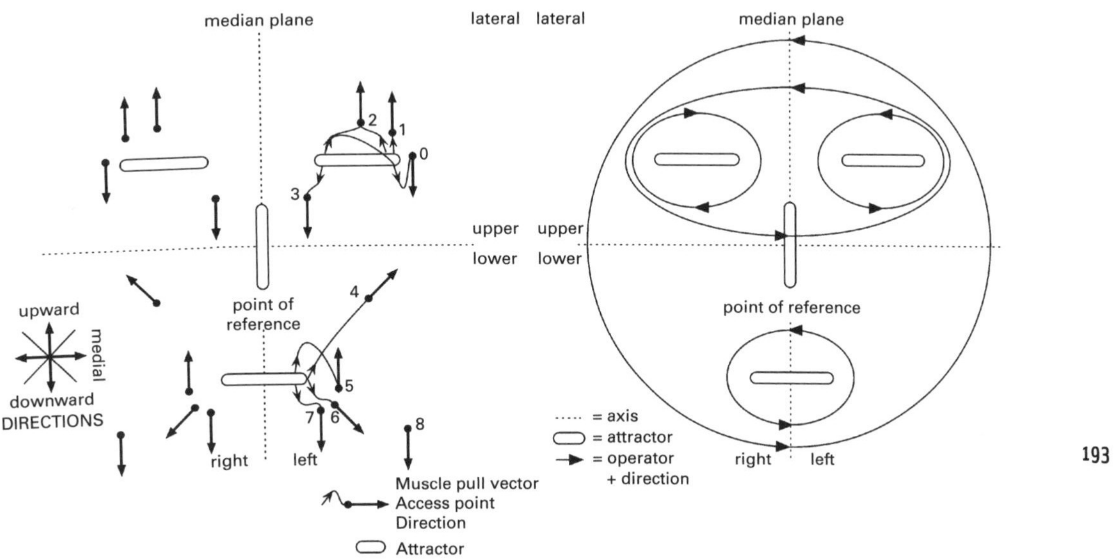

10.3
The language of facial e-motion: a schematic
picture showing logical structures of the face as a
choreologic surface by Arthur Elsenaar (courtesy
of the artist).

10 DIGITAL MOVEMENT

The work of artists like Stelarc and Elsenaar raises the issue of motion control. Going back to Nikolai Bernstein's experimental studies, the seat of control has traditionally been associated with the central nervous system. However, the question of a brainless control—that is, a system of control that is governed by a technology without a central brain, but a network of separate brainlike engines collaborating to produce a thinking system (like the Internet)—provokes a drastic new way of understanding the controlling agency behind human movement. These performances also highlight an inversion of the joystick paradigm of motion control, according to which technologies are used and manipulated by users, rather than the other way round. So the question now is: Who controls movement? The kernel here is not how to represent and symbolize, how to notate, for reasons that I have already made clear. In a post-stave notation context, where signifiers have become signals, what matters is who controls the transmission of signals and what this code is intended to provoke at the receiving end. If within this society out of control that has opened up around us information processing determines where things will move in the midst of data complexity, and where they will end up, then controlling the signal or the code is a sign of empowerment. It is not a bodily power and a discipline, in the Foucauldian sense, but a power to utilize language and inscription to command and control. If there is a motion controller that manipulates avatars on screens, or that manipulates Stelarc's obsolete body and Elsenaar's artifacial choreographies, what kind of agent is it? Clearly, what controls the book written on human bodies is not necessarily a "technology of the self," which Foucault (1988) defined as self-control through obedience and through mastery of one's own body and mind. Here is a technology of the selfless, or the self that is distributed and thus no longer self-controlled, but controlled instead by a cybernetic system, or by a power that resides in between. Halfway between human and nonhuman, halfway between physical and virtual, between live and prerecorded, the language of technologized motion opens up a massively complex articulation of control relations. This contemporary world of electronically controlled movement reveals an agent that is no longer centralized by a Godlike brain that controls and causes all things to move. And while this agency might seem a world away from ancient speculations regarding a digital language of movement, which is where I began this chapter, at a formal level they are not. The ancient connection between the binary language of human and automated movement reveals that as soon as movement is represented in formal ways, as soon as movement enters the orbit of language, and as soon as it exits the domain of the purely physical and thus becomes liable to abstraction (and abstract forms of representation), movement performance and control also leave the domain of the purely human in order to advance toward a more unstable ontology, a more trajective agency that is neither human nor machine, but which is shared and distributed.

11

The legend of Butades

Pliny the Elder used the legend of Butades—a Greek tile maker from the sixth century BCE—to explain the origins of drawing. According to Pliny's version of the story, Butades' daughter had fallen in love with a youth who was soon to leave for another town. Love-smitten, the maiden drew the outline of her lover's shadow on a wall. Based on this outline, Butades went on to model the face of the young man, and then baked it in clay. Legend has it Butades pioneered the use of shadow drawing to make lifelike models of the human body. The technique, known as sciagraphy, is mentioned by a number of ancient writers, including Plato, who referenced it in his *Republic*. The myth of Butades touches on a key characteristic of any medium designed to capture live bodies or bodily movement—for instance, in terms of the extraction of an outline (in this case a shadow) from a living source. The process is very similar to the rendering of virtual characters from motion capture data in contemporary computer graphics. Pliny's story explaining the origin of drawing is better fitted to an explanation of the origins of motion capture.

To return to the myth, it is interesting that the need to create this human model based on a shadow should stem from the imminent departure of the young lover, and that sciagraphy in this case should preserve the person's physical presence. But Butades' technique does not only create a bridge between the living body and a life-sized inanimate model; it also represents an attempt to resist an absence, or to project the absence of a physical body onto a plane of artistic representation. As Derrida wrote in his *Memoirs of the Blind*:

> The narrative relates the origin of graphic representation to the absence or invisibility of the model. Butades' daughter does not see her lover, either because she turns her back to him ... or because he turns his back to her, or again, simply because their gazes cannot meet: it is as if seeing was forbidden in order to draw, as if one drew only on condition of not seeing, as if the drawing were a declaration of love destined for or suited to the invisibility of the other. (1998, 175)

For Derrida the body disappears not when the lover goes away, but as soon as the maiden decides to draw the young man's shadow. Because Butades' gaze is fixed not on the youth but on his shadow outline, the tile maker is no longer seeing the youth; he is seeing his projection. This description suggests that representation is a means of invisibility, a disappearance of the body from the process of capture. Indeed, in recent theorizations of motion capture graphics, the description of bodiless movement seems to corroborate this idea. For Derrida, the act of representing and drawing live models inaugurates an art of blindness. By the same token, insofar as the technology of motion capture is typically used to extract data out of a captured subject, and to use this outline to create digital characters that are supposedly more lifelike or hyperrealistic, one could argue, following Derrida's trail, that motion capture graphics inaugurates an art of disembodiment. Although

Derrida's argument is persuasive, I wish to argue the contrary. My intention in what follows is to challenge Derrida's theorization, and the theorization of motion capture as a technology that provokes movement without bodies (without physical and anatomical bodies, that is). As English philosopher Ralph Cudworth (1996) said, paraphrasing Aristotle, the idea of having the power to move "without a body" seems absurd; all sensed souls are corporeal because there is "No walking without feet."[1] Yet why would Butades need to create the lover's sculpted face out of a bodily shadow? Why not model it from memory? To draw the lover's face from memory would defeat the purpose of Butades' work, surely, for his goal is to preserve the physical lover in the form of a sculpture.

Derrida claimed that the art of drawing is in fact drawing the viewer away from the object of representation. But this assumption is dubious. The purpose of creative drawing is not to record, to preserve, to reiterate, to carbon-copy an original, but to create something new out of the old. Thus, and returning to the Butades legend, it is not the process of turning the young man's face into an artifice, or "artiface" as Elsenaar would have it, that causes the disappearance of the youth. Yes, the lover is now gone, and all that is left is Butades' sculpture—and indeed Butades' daughter has no other contact with her lover except her father's clay sculpture. But this clay face is not intended to be the original lover; instead, the clay face is a new lover—a virtual lover. A completely different face has been generated out of this sciagraphic drawing. And so the process involved in sciagraphy, as in motion capture, is not disembodied. Motion capture is, by definition, grounded on the capture of bodily movement; it is not a separation of corporeal movement from the corporeal body, for no corporeal movement can ever be issued without a corporeal body. The point I wish to stress is this: the nature, or if you like, the ontology, of this body is more unstable within a motion capture animation process. The movement that motion capture seeks to record is always physical—it is never anything other than physical and real-time movement. But motion capture technology can extract this physical movement from its occurrence as a single performance in the physical world, and then use the recording as data (as shadow) to animate another kind of body—a nonhuman and nonliving body in a virtual or robotic environment.

The difficulty with defining motion capture is not made easier by the fact that this medium takes various names: digital puppetry, virtual theater, digital rotoscope, performance capture. Furthermore, the term motion capture (or "mocap") refers not only to a technology or a technological setup (an instrument); it is also used for a technologized language of movement, involving the formalized description of movement coordinates and movement data for its subsequent computational analysis and computer-generated and high-speed computer processing. Alberto Menache's book (2000) on the emergence of this technology and its application to animation production is useful as a starting point, particularly insofar as this author provides a working definition: "Motion capture is the process of recording a live motion event and translating it into usable mathematical terms by tracking a number of key points in space over time and combining them to obtain a single three-dimensional (3D) representation of the performance." Menache adds: "In brief, it is the technology that enables the process of translating a live performance into a digital performance" (2000, 1). In more practical terms, motion capture technology refers to a variety of systems that have evolved since the 1970s and 1980s, supporting different setups and protocols for the capture of movement. Motion capture also involves the photogrammetric analysis of a performer's movement (more on this to come), which is typically obtained after the subject is recorded wearing special equipment featuring a number of markers near each joint to identify motion by positions or angles.

To attempt a theoretical and analytical debate on motion capture in general, and at such a late stage of this book, would be far too ambitious. My concern must be narrowed down to a simple question, which further reinforces the goal of this final part of the book; to wit, how might a current technology transform the language of human movement? How does motion capture provide an example of how the language of human movement evolves along with its technologies of representation? Does mocap provide changing conditions of material and cultural inscription, performance and interpretation, thus providing novel means of kinetopoietic creation? If Menache's definition of this technology is to be accepted, then motion capture is by definition a process of translation. However, translation presupposes that what is happening in this case is a conversion of one language to another. What mocap does is not a translation but a mapping, a passing from one domain of movement (live) to another (digital) via a process of codification.

Eidetic capture

In his *On the Gait of Animals* Aristotle proposed an experiment to observe the natural geometry produced by the body in motion, writing that if a man were to walk parallel to a wall in sunshine, "the line described [by the shadow of his head] would be not straight but zigzag, becoming lower as he bends, and higher when he stands and lifts himself up" (Aristotle 1912). Because the passage in square brackets is corrupted in the original and the precise meaning of the sentence cannot be made out, other interpretations have been put forward suggesting that Aristotle was in fact referring to an actual contraption that would use a reed to draw the geometric shape of human movement onto a wall.[2] Whatever the case may be, there is no doubt that Aristotle had in mind a primitive motion-recording device. In fact, I would argue that his analytical view of movement can be described as "mocap vision" long before the invention of motion capture technology in the contemporary sense.

Just as Aristotle could imagine conducting this experiment in ancient times, so technologies can be envisioned long before they are actually invented, built, or first tested. We have already seen how digital computation was conceived, in effect, in antiquity. Thus the history of motion capture is not limited to the invention of its current technology, but includes the first conception of a process to record live human movement and turn it into abstract mathematical determinations. If mocap thinking is a way of seeing and understanding movement based on the extraction of move-

199

ment information from live bodies, then the conception of motion capture is due not so much to a technological feat, but to the desire to analyze movement and to break down its component parts into granular segments.

Mocap thinking: What happens to the body

In what follows, I will touch on two key theoretical debates that have captured the attention of academic scholarship. The first has to do with what mocap does to the live body when it maps sampled movement onto digital formats. The second sticking point for cultural, performance, and media theorists is the question of mediation itself, and how mocap can be compared to other familiar forms of mediated motion, especially cinema and photography.

The question of what happens to the body in mocap media is the subject of a predominantly polarized debate: either mocap does away with the body, or else it allows an affective traffic of corporeality. Thus, mocap is theorized either as a bodily or a metabodily form of live-digital mediation. From the metabodily side, the paradigm of a "no-body movement" or a "dance without bodies" introduced by Martine Époque and Denis Poulin in the early noughties offers an interesting starting point. Époque and Poulin's film *CODA: The Finale of No-Body Dance* (2006–2014) is a mocap version of the finale of Stravinsky's *Rite of Spring*. What concerns me is not that motion capture provides these artists an original technological tool to compose choreographic movement; after all, the use of motion capture in dance and performance goes back at least a decade, to the collaborations between OpenEnded Group and Merce Cunningham. Unlike in the *Ghostcatching* paradigm (1999), also proposed by OpenEnded Group (in this case with Bill T. Jones), the dematerialization of the body via mocap is realized by Époque and Poulin in terms of a body that is made up of tiny particles. Particle animation software lends itself to the formulation of a paradigm of movement based on a dematerialization of bodies into particles, or into bits of information (what these artists call info-choreography). On the other hand, even though the filmic representation of movement through particle dynamics is by no means novel,[3] the combination of mocap and particle dynamics offers a less commonly trodden path for theoretical investigation. What emerges from this paradigm is the idea that a dance of particles can make up the body, at the same time that the body can make up a dance.

Popular science author Gary Zukav has taken up this same analogy between particle physics and dance to speak of the movement of subatomic particles as an indeterminate state. Of some of the most notable physicists who have led the way in the evolution of quantum physics, he writes: "Now they become the dance: and the dance becomes them" (1979, 17). The same applies to subatomic particles: they move and interact in order to make matter, and matter then moves these particles in turn. In the case of what Époque and Poulin call "infochoreography," the dancing of data and the "databasing" of dance become an interestingly liminal and unstable territory to explore new trajectories for digital movement creativity. Époque and Poulin argue that dance movements can be created without the need for a body. But even if mocap releases the dance from the dancer's body, it does not entirely do away with the bodiliness of the captured movement. Even if we do not see the original and corporeal body in the final mocap animation, we nonetheless see *bodily* movement. Even if the youth is not present for Butades' daughter to see, his embodied trace is. And because this new form (this sciagraphic or digital model) is ultimately traced back to a living body, and because the final rendition is fashioned out of traces of embodiment, it makes no sense to speak of a movement or dance *without* bodies. Movement *outside* bodies, perhaps. Movement *beside* the body, certainly. What is going on here is not the emergence of a language that forgets the body, a language of blindness (going back to Derrida). It is a language that involves a mapping, so that what starts live ends up digital.

CODA's celebration of the motion of particles—a dance of neutrinos—does not entirely do away with matter and materiality; on the contrary, it reveals matter at its most fundamental level, at the level of elementary particles that explain why bodies have mass, and why bodies can move. To my view, this metabodily argument does not fully obliterate the elementary constitution of matter, which makes up animate and inanimate bodies. I insist: there is no motion without a body: human, celestial, atomic, subatomic. The great paradox of movement is that at the heart of all things, in that subatomic chiasmus where fundamental particles move, matter and movement become unstable ontologies. Trajectivity reigns. Thus, in the same way that there is no motion without a body (in a Newtonian physical world), there is no body without a quantum motion.

This conception of the disembodiment of movement via mocap is taken up by number of authors who have emerged from within digital performance practice and theory. Erin Manning (2009), for instance, has argued that from a Bergsonian and immanent philosophical perspective, mocap is *not* capable of going beyond the predefined perimeter of already actualized human gestures. She explains that mocap does not contain qualitative and dynamic contents, and is no more than a quantifiable execution, a physical displacement from A to B. Stamatia Portanova (2013) takes up Manning's analysis to highlight the problematic use of numerical technologies to register the embodied experience of the dancer. For Portanova, motion capture announces a virtual domain where virtual characters move without bodies. But let us not limit this analysis to a criticism of what motion capture does *not* do, or what it is *not*.

Portanova has argued that mocap cuts the organic flow of movement, and in the resulting storage it reopens motion to recombinatory potential. Also adopting a Bergsonian theoretical perspective, Portanova speaks of the medium as a kind of memory that transforms the cut into an abstract object. She introduces the coinage "mov-objects" to help conceptualize this idea, writing that mov-objects account for the "remembered ideas of movement," adding that "the codified nature of motion-captured movement data libraries" means they are "ideas continuously returning in many dances, together with their infinitely downloadable, reusable potential" (Portanova 2013, 63). In sum, the mov-object builds the connecting bridge between the concrete, or concretely physical, and the virtual determination of movement. In Bergsonian terms, this technology opens the passage from matter to memory, or what I call the abstract-concrete machine.

There are two problems, as I see it, in Portanova's metabodily argument. First, the preposition "without" in her book title is slightly problematic. I prefer to think of mocap as a medium that produces movement *out of* bodies. Secondly, and I will address this problem separately, there is a flaw with the Bergsonian and Deleuzian framework, since these thinkers provide a basis for the theorization of cinema and the movement image, not of motion capture (which is *not* an image-based form of mediation, as we will see). Likewise, and from a phenomenological perspective this time, Susan Kozel (2007) has spoken of mocap as enabling an intersubjectivity. She images motion capture performance as a form of intercorporeality, a performance of alterity, a duet between the body and its other. However, I would argue that the language of mocap is not intersubjective at all. The trouble with intersubjectivity (I am returning to Lacan) is that it concerns a subject that understands another subject. Lacan's passage from thought to language is not intersubjective. Like Lacan's topology, the topological medium of mocap is trajective (I am also returning to Virilio now), not least because the mapping function in mocap technology does not refer to a passage from subject to subject, but from subject to object and back. It is this trajective passage across totally different ways of bodily being (from live to digital) that concerns me. What we are all dealing with, to be sure, is a passage across different movement ontologies.

Thus, mocap technology can be used to reinforce a basic theoretical premise of this book. It is not that mocap produces an alter to the original ego, a bodily "other" that mirrors the living body, which seems to be Kozel's argument. It is not that the technology forgets the body, as metabodily theorists suggest. It is not that mocap creates a line of stepping-stones from live to digital, from A to B, going back to Manning's critique. The language of motion capture is not only numerical and discretizing; it is also topological and continuous. Thus, the medium is not exactly a means of abandoning the physical, or a provocation to stay at the level of quantitative abstraction. Because it has to map the numerical data onto a digital plane of representation, a continuity function is necessary, and the topological dimensions of mocap language must be preserved. To sum up, mocap is not a medium that *walks* from A to B, as Manning claims, but one that *maps* A onto B. In other words, A does not stay behind. A is of course a reference to the live body. A is not forgotten: elements of it are mapped out and injected onto another ontology of the body (B).

Like the example of the mug and the doughnut in chapter 4, the mathematical language of topology does not involve discrete and broken transformations—the transformations available within the domain of solid geometry. Because selected elements of a live body are transferred directly and continuously onto a digital avatar (even if the stylistic representation of this avatar involves reimagining the virtual body as a ghost or as a particle body, suggesting the dematerialization and desubjectification of the original body), there is no forgetting of the original, there is no cutoff point after which we no longer connect back to bodiliness. There is no point in the mapping from mug to doughnut at which one might claim a separation between the two. The preposition "without" (i.e., movement "without" body) suggests an opposition or cut. To return to the Butades legend, it is important to point out that the sciagraphic sculpture is different from any other sculpture of the long-gone lover. Because the sculpture was made from a bodily outline, it retains an affective and qualitative sense that other models might not. It contains a trace, like a smell caught in a piece of clothing. Mocap retains that smell of the body. That is why Butades' daughter can fall in love with this virtual person that her father has created for her. The Butades sciagraphic model is not a model of the original lover. It is not an intersubjective self. It is not an alter ego. It is a lover that the daughter has found in a new dimension of her love: in the domain of the fetish. She now owns an object that does not have a life of its own but which she has animated by means of her own fantasy.

Mocap: Beyond the movement image

Motion capture has not received the kind of attention Deleuze gave to cinema, or Barthes gave to photography, or Derrida gave to drawing. This lack of scholarly attention is evidently due to the fact that motion capture is a fairly recent technology, having emerged in its modern guise in the 1970s, and within the relatively confined circles of university research. Since it penetrated mainstream entertainment production only in the mid 1980s and early 1990s, it is not surprising that there is no motion capture equivalent to Deleuze's books on cinema. But this does not explain why no major work in the past ten years has embarked on a critical study of this medium technology—beyond the practical guides, demo files, tutorials, manuals, and primers.

It is important to highlight that motion capture does not provoke a vision of motion in the same way that cinema does. The second major problem with contemporary critique is a failure to recognize that motion capture is a medium in its own right. Abandoning the concept of the "movement-image" and abandoning the cinematically biased and image-oriented theorizations of Bergson and Deleuze is the first step toward theorizing mocap independently of the cinema. In his critique of what he called "knowledge of a cinematographical kind" (1983, 323), Bergson condemned cinema for seeking the ultimate divisibility and motionlessness of things. He was especially critical of knowledge that is generated when the subject attaches himself not to the inner becoming of things, but instead is placed outside them in order to recompose their becoming artificially, by taking snapshots of the passing reality. Bergson added: "we hardly do anything else than set going a kind of cinematograph inside us" (323). Of particular concern to him was dialectical intellectualism, which he considered to be a strategy by which thought agrees with itself. He also criticized the need to see and think through solid objects, and via logistic means that culminate in geometry, adding: "the intellect feels at home among inanimate objects, more especially among solids" (1983, ix). It is this triumph of geometric thinking that enabled the rational intellect to claim full understanding of movement from a static perspective, and through an illusionary and projective medium (cinema).

We can now speak of knowledge of a motion capture kind, in which the subject does not perceive and seek representation from the outside, by taking snapshots, but from within a corporeal base, by extracting gestural information directly from the body, so as to reach a level of mathematical abstraction and of linguistic formalization. As soon as we abandon a way of knowing through projected images and discard this "cinematograph inside us," the Bergsonian critique seems inadequate to a discussion of a medium that does not resemble cinematographic and photographic capture at all. In fact, Maureen Furniss (1999) has argued that it is more appropriate for mocap to be compared to music recording and to compositional methods similar to electronic music, especially "sampling," a term that typically refers to bits of prerecorded music, dialogue, or other sounds that are recorded and mixed into a new composition. Brad deGraf and Emre Yilmaz (1999) have proposed an analogy between mocap instrumentation and the saxophone, commenting that mocap is "a new kind of jazz." Through real-time control of three-dimensional computer renderings, mocap synthesizes the qualities of puppetry, live action, stop-motion animation, game intelligence, and other forms into an entirely new fusion that can play freely with quantifiable movement—not just the image of movement. This sampling of movement does not play well in any format, style, or genre, which is the point of deGraf and Yilmaz's saxophone analogy. Mocap plays great jazz—a jazz of movement, that is.

This conception provides a much-needed reconception of the medium that abandons any assumed dependence on cinematic and image-based analogies. It helps us to better understand that because the camera systems behind motion capture are intended to record photogrammetric data rather than images, the sampling of movement afforded by mocap is infused with computational recombinations; hence the comparison with the language of music, and jazz in particular.

Even in the case of optical sensor systems (say, as opposed to nonoptical techniques), what matters is the information that self-reflective markers might relay in a formally represented way; that is, as computable data. As I pointed out earlier, one basic language that underpins the optical modality of motion capture technology is photogrammetry, which is a mathematical description extracted from photographic space. As such, optical motion capture is more about photogrammetric data analysis than visual interpretation, since the actual visual "look" of a captured body might be intended to change once the data is mapped onto the "look" of a digital avatar (assuming the application of motion capture is digital animation).

Photogrammetry is an inherently "opseographic" language, going back to Peter Weibel's concept (1996) and to a debate I started earlier surrounding Marey's chronophotographic experiments. Insofar as chronophotographic geometry (see chapter 3) allowed Marey to read geometric figures that emerged from a visual output (a photographic print), he was able to invent an analytical process involving a *reading over the seeing*. The same applies to more evolved forms of photogrammetry, and to applications of photogrammetry to optical motion capture, as these began to evolve in biomechanical research during the 1970s and 1980s.

Photogrammetry is especially useful in motion capture for recovering the exact positions of surface points (typically indicated by self-reflective markers), and for recording the motion pathways of designated reference points located on a moving object. The key term here is "recovery." The technology is known as motion capture for a reason: because these motion pathways cannot be seen or followed with the naked eye in real time, let alone recorded. Photogrammetric analysis feeds the measurements from remote sensing and the results of imagery analysis into computational models. This results in a computational understanding of movement that can successively estimate, and with increasing accuracy, the actual stereoscopic relative motions within various fields of movement research.

Because the language of motion capture once again reinforces the ongoing mathematization and logical formalization of human movement, albeit in the domain of mathematical computing, this technology does not radically transform the relationship between movement and representation that we have touched on throughout this book. As I mentioned at the beginning of this chapter, contemporary motion capture is, at an eidetic level, a fulfillment of Aristotle's vision of a shadow-capturing device that could reveal, beyond the image, a series of geometries of motion. What does change, however, and what is radically transformed by this contemporary technology, is the materiality of representation. Far from the basic shadow projected onto a wall, the mocap digitalization of movement expands the possibilities of motion analysis and motion recomposition, and vastly enhances the concrete objects that this language is employed to give movement to: from shadows on a wall, to motion capture robots, to mocap dance, to mocap digital animation, to digital puppets, to motion- and gesture-controlled machines and gadgets.

A theoretical understanding of the language of motion capture must therefore abandon the image and take up mocap as a communicational, instrumental, and affective traffic of the body and bodily movement into the orbit of writing. According to Rotman (2008), there is no limit, at least in principle, to what is written about or of the body using mocap technology. Rotman sees gestural language (for instance as codified and mapped within mocap media) as having a vast, unrealized, and as yet untheorized or critically narrativized potential. He has proposed that what is mediated in capture media operates under the regime of the enacted or reproduced, rather than the symbolized. Motion capture is *not* a symbolic form of movement representation and motion-processing technology, in the same way as notation is (see chapter 7). Rotman goes on to qualify his argument: "the phonogram and tape recorder do not notate sound in the form of symbols but write it—record or capture it—as a direct signal to an apparatus able to reproduce (a perceptually indistinguishable version of) the captured sounds" (2008, 42). He also argues, and this echoes a point I raised earlier, that while notation effects a discrete algebraic framework based primarily on sound symbolization and relational structures of prior difference, motion capture presents a continuous, topological model. I insist that this medium does not *walk* the path from live to digital, step by step and discretely; it *maps* it continuously.

Kinect effect

On June 1, 2009, under the code name "Project Natal," computer giant Microsoft announced a new line of motion-sensing input devices for their video game console Xbox 360, a competitor of Sony's PlayStation and Nintendo's Wii. Project Natal was named after the city in northeastern Brazil as a tribute to the Brazilian-born Microsoft director of the project, Alex Kipman. Now regarded as a "father of Kinect," Kipman described Kinect upon its launch as a never-before-seen experience: "This is much broader than just entertainment. Moving from an old world, where you have to understand technology, to a new world, where technology understands us, is a computer-industry-wide move" (Kipman 2010, unpaginated). In effect, the project name was also chosen because "natal" means "birth-related," reflecting Microsoft's vision of this technology as the birth of a new generation of home entertainment.

Kinect's most immediate goal was to provide a new gaming interface using acoustic and visual sensors to detect a player's movements in 3D space, and to finally do away with the traditional joy-stick paradigm of game control. Kinect would allow game users to interact with their console/computer using gestures and spoken commands, making hands-free control a more engaging way of playing electronic games. In effect, as Kipman suggests above, the intention was for the technology to provide a sensorium, a set of eyes and ears that could be turned into commodities, or shelf components. The device could be placed in a living room space and become an integral part of everyday home life. It would thus bring the universe of motion sensing to the home, and at an affordable price. As a consumer product, Kinect opened up an entirely new market engaged in the consumption of motion.

Perhaps the most revolutionary aspect of the device is not its status as commoditized motion capture, but its innovation as a noncommercial software platform. Microsoft released a Kinect Software Development Kit (SDK) in 2011, which allowed developers to write Kinecting apps in programming languages like C++/CLI, C#, or Visual Basic, leaving the technology open and free to hacking—not in the pejorative sense of the word, of course. By tapping into the Kinect sensor's data stream, hackers were invited to create their own version of a Kinect motion capture set and reimagine the technology in any way they might wish, and not only within the confines of a computer game. The openness of the software platform, coupled with its status as an affordable household commodity, led to its staggering commercial success. As of the time of writing, Kinect has sold more than 24 million units worldwide.[4] Kinect won the 2011 MacRobert Award for engineering innovation, followed by T3's Gadget of the Year award (2011) and Gaming Gadget of the Year prize (2011). During the world premiere of Kinect for Xbox, held at the Electronic Entertainment Expo (E3) in Los Angeles that year, the device was unveiled in an arena stage show produced by Cirque du Soleil. The performance included an iconic scene during which a child actor climbed over a giant model of the Xbox logo, a sphere adorned with a glowing green X, while a live-controlled avatar of the boy was seen projected onto a massive backscreen.

The image of a new generation of game players emerging from the Xbox sphere brings us full circle, to a conception of the kinetic sphere (now a "kinectic" sphere) with which I began this investigation (see chapter 1). During the launch event at E3, Microsoft also unveiled the name of its new product: a portmanteau of the words "kinetic" and "connect" that points to the core of Microsoft's ambitions. But this portmanteau also redirects my attention to an ancient notion of the sphere as a conceptual model that explains the natural forces of connection (*phylia*) and repulsion (*neikos*). Indeed, in addition to providing the intended affiliation and sense of connection between player and avatar, Kinect has generated a feeling of repulsion, leading to the emergence of a strong voice of criticism, even within the gaming community. In some cases, the immersive and kinesthetic experience enabled by the device can lead to a disconcerting and disconnected gaming experience, leading the Canadian television show *Extra Credits* to call Microsoft Kinect the "uncanny valley of input devices."[5] Kinect disconnects, according to detractors, not least because it provides a physical immersion within an interactive system that does not, in fact, respond to live movements in an intuitively physical way. So, in the same way that a rubbery and humanlike robot may seem less human than a highly stylized robot, for the simple reason that its likeness is coupled with its totally unfamiliar and unhuman conduct, Kinect's connection between player and avatar via hands-free control can also be unsatisfying. Indeed, the "uncanny valley" that robotics scholar Masahiro Mori famously proposed to describe our reaction to the appearance of humanlike robots applies as well to reactions to the way we interact kinetically with machines.[6]

On the other hand, the technology can immerse the user within a sphere of movement that is highly commercialized. My critique here is not so much about the representation of formal movement within a specific Kinect-compatible game product, as it is about the overarching commercialization of movement through hands-free-console-controlling environments. Figures show that in 2012 the average American Xbox Live Gold user spent 87 hours a month in front of their Xbox—an increase of 8.7 hours from the previous year—and that users consumed 18 billion hours of entertainment through Xbox Live in 2012.[7] Kinect's commoditization of human movement is a double-edged sword. On the one hand, the effect of having "kinectified" the home allows motion-sensing technology to further divert human-to-human interaction to human-to-gadget interaction, and to the production of gaming products that turn movement into a form of commercial consumption. Kinect can (and indeed should) be critiqued as an instrument of commodity fetishism, in that its popularization can be blamed for transforming the perception of kinetic relationships from being a relationship among moving bodies or game players to being a relationship between consumers and screened motion.

I return to the maiden in the Butades legend. Her love for a young man is transformed into love for a clay object. Affection turns to fetishization. The same may apply to the technologization of movement via Microsoft Kinect; and this brings us to a much broader question, one that I can only present here as a topic for further inquiry. (I would like first to point out that, as with any popular media technology, no moralizing judgment can be made on Kinect's cultural transformation of the kinetic experience.) As with any technology, there are two sides to the Kinect revolution. Given its wide availability, low cost, and open-source software platform, Kinect's impact has extended far beyond the gaming industry. SDK and other independent platforms for Kinect have transformed human-computer interaction in multiple industries, including education, healthcare, retail, transportation, and the movement arts. For instance, with increasing economic globalization and workforce mobilization, immersive experiences enable people across geographically distributed sites to interact collaboratively, using Kinect for videoconferencing, telepresencing, real-time capture for transport and telecommunication, kinetic online interfaces, and so on. Microsoft speaks of a "Kinect Effect" to describe the way this device, originally intended to revolutionize the way people play games and experience entertainment, has also revolutionized a number of other industries, research activities, communities, and services. A dedicated webpage in the Microsoft Xbox website called "The Kinect Effect: How the World Is Using Kinect" highlights some of the more recent applications of the technology. Examples include applications that help children with autism, aid in stroke patient rehabilitation, offer surgery assistance in operating rooms, and create "kinectic" art. Within this context, KinectHacks.com is perhaps the most extensive independent community dedicated to the promotion, further development, and sharing of Microsoft Kinect user-made programs. According to the community's mission statement, "the vast potential possessed by the Kinect, accompanied by the creativity and ingenuity of various Kinect users and code developers ... will pave the way for future technologies that will help both the private and public sectors of society."[8] This website also features a top ten list of Kinect Hacks. As of April 2014, this list included Kinect or "fitnect" interactive dressing room, Kinect-augmented urban models, Kinect multitorch surface for architects, and Kinect 3D scanner.

This fast-changing technology is about to change yet again, and not only because of the unveiling of version 2.0 of Microsoft Kinect. In November 2013, computer manufacturing giant Apple confirmed the purchase of Israel-based PrimeSense for an estimated US$360 million.[9] PrimeSense was responsible for the depth sensor technology behind Microsoft's Kinect—that is, before Microsoft built its own sensor. Apple's purchase of PrimeSense presages a new history of consumer motion capture that is yet to be unleashed by that multinational corporation. Because Apple has been secretive about its plans at the time of this writing, the future of homemade motion capture is as yet unclear. One may suppose that Apple is interested in embedding motion sensors in iOS devices, Macs, or Apple TVs, thus using 3D sensor technology to create ways of controlling devices without physical contact—that is, through gesture and motion recognition. This would explain not only the purchase of motion-sensing technology experts PrimeSense, but also Apple's filing for a patent entitled "Real Time Video Process Control Using Gestures." This technology would allow users to "throw" content, thus giving users the ability to transfer data from one of the firm's products to another using contact-free hand movements. With motion sensing now rolled into Apple's signature devices, the future of motion capture lies not only in the living room but also in portable device technology. In this frantic pursuit for innovation within our technologized economy of movement, the synergy between motion capture and mobile technology is the latest in a recent historical transformation of the human kinetic experience. From total movement we come to a point of total techno-kinesis: our commodity devices are fast turning into mobile, portable, wearable, and movement-recognizing smart technologies.

12

Local-global

In this final chapter I will discuss a contemporary technology that supports a very different paradigm of movement, freed from its determination in proxemic space and from a physical sense of temporality. I will turn my attention, that is, to the way movement is conceived on the Internet: to an understanding of movement in terms of electronic location within global networks, and the way these parameters can interact to provoke an enveloping of local and remote. Movement online, I argue in this chapter, is inherently paradoxical or double-stated. Unlike with physical locomotion, where movement can be defined in purely locational terms and a moving subject can never access a global sense of movement all at once, the paradigm of e-motion discussed here affords movement that is at once locational and translocational, at once local and global—hence glocomotion.

To illustrate this concept, I will briefly introduce two spaces associated with the Science Museum in London: the Antenna Gallery, a space for the dissemination of technology and environment news in an innovative and electronically savvy way, and *Listening Post*, a multimedia installation created by Mark Hansen and Ben Rubin, which was purchased by the Science Museum in 2007 (the piece was exhibited in the Science Museum for a period of two years). The Antenna Gallery is a fully integrated interactive multimedia gallery space, conceived both as a physical and electronic site devoted to the dissemination of the latest news in science, technology, and innovation. The gallery functions as a community space, where visitors can share comments, polls, and immediate responses to the latest developments in science and technology. Comments made on the web are displayed in the gallery and vice versa, producing a two-way traffic between the electronic web space and the physical gallery space.

On entering the physical gallery, which is located in a large open space in the ground floor of the museum, the eye is arrested by a rear panel displaying a large LED message board. Although LED dot displays are a common sight in shops, railway stations, and other public spaces because they provide effective and flexible means of showing real-time information, this display is quite unique. The Antenna Gallery board is arranged in the shape of a network grid, where real-time messages typed in interactive kiosks within the gallery, as well as messages coming from the web, can be seen scrolling in all directions. Having the LED message board in a network shape provides further illustration of the concept behind the Antenna Gallery: the messages displayed in the gallery are the result of a collaborative network. Within this space that is also an antenna, an informational network, everything is moving. Information is continuously being updated; messages reflect the changing perceptions of visitors, as well as the ever-changing content of science and technology news. What we have here is an unstable space that is neither physical nor electronic, and in whose double-stated condition presence is realized momentarily in an ever-changing and mobile environment.

One other feature of the Antenna Gallery's display board involves the integration of local and global domains, at least from the point of view of motion perception. As with a conventional LED message board, the LED units in the Antenna Gallery message board are programmed to switch on and off rapidly. Although the dot matrix that makes up the display board is static, a perception of scrolling motion is achieved by switching lights on and off along this matrix. Thus, strips of dots making lines and word messages appear to move around the back wall, colliding and bouncing off each other, like trains moving along a railway network. However, although the museum visitor may perceive the lines and messages on this massive network board as scrolling back and forth, clearly they are not. In the field of motion vision, this effect is known as beta movement, an apparent motion often used in billboard displays.

With beta movement, it is not that the image is moving. Rather, the position of alternate elements in a sequence is changing, an effect that can be produced cinematically through frame-by-frame sequencing, and which can also be produced in key frame animation. If the position of the cross in figure 12.1 were to alternate from one square to the next in a rhythmic and linear succession from left to right and then from right to left, the cross would appear to move back and forth. This is known as motion integration, a process by means of which the brain extracts individual local motion signals at various parts of the visual field to integrate them into a global representation.

212

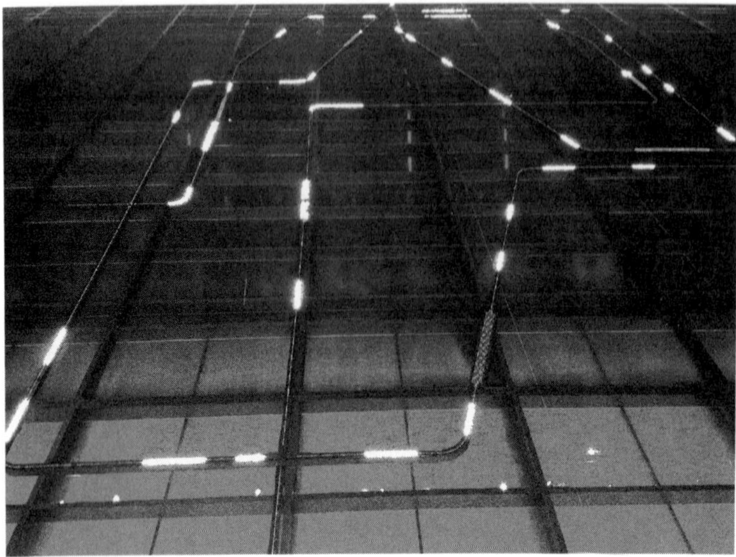

12.1
Display panel at Antenna Gallery, Science Museum London (photo by the author).

The relationship between local and global can be expanded beyond this visual regime. Indeed, like the shape of the museum display board, perception in this case also triggers the paradoxical confluence of a local and global sense of movement space. To understand how spaces like the Antenna Gallery are paradoxically poised between a local and a global determination, I would like to call on a theory of local/global relations pertaining to the language of mathematics, which, as we have seen throughout this book, is closely associated with formalized human movement. According to French philosopher and mathematician Albert Lautman, the integration of local and global is a guiding concern within modern mathematical research. His conceptual understanding of local–global relations can be defined as the study of any primitive element in a system, most often infinitesimal (local), which is followed through step by step until a whole, or global, emerges by juxtaposition (2011, 95). As the sense of local and global becomes more abstracted in Lautman's definition, integration does not necessarily occur in a single concrete mathematical example: the concept is general enough to be considered a major theme within a number of branches of mathematics. The same could be said of local/global integration in the context of electronic forms of movement. Indeed, this basic juxtaposition constitutes a major paradigm within current systems conceived around the idea of networked movement. Clearly, the sense of movement one encounters at the Antenna Gallery is not confined to bodily movement. In the case of the Antenna Gallery, the passage from local to global does not occur within the same system of representation, say between elements in the same mathematical language, but rather from a local sense of movement space (a user, or a body even) to a global sense that is perceived to have no physical existence in extension, or in physical stereospace.

The movement of information, and the emergence of a culture of online kinesis, is characterized not only by a conflation of local and global motion (glocomotion) but by a loss of physical connection with a networked sense of global space, and with a condition of perpetual movement and ceaseless activity—networks like the Antenna Gallery are defined by a kinesis without stasis. It is possible to say that with the rise of electronic network culture and Internet technology especially, it is not only the representation of movement that has radically changed. Everything about movement is different online: the spaces of electronic motion are no longer comparable to the stereotypical spaces discussed in chapter 1, nor is the sense of temporality (chapter 2), nor is the sense of the movement form. And yet, as we will see presently, online activity can be looked at as a technocultural form of movement nonetheless. Although these parameters have radically changed, they are still essential to online kinesis. Online kinesis still requires an online space, an online temporality, and an online movement form associated with what I call hypermovement, as it is realized at the interface.

The paradox of local and global integration can also be unpacked in a discussion of Mark Hansen and Ben Rubin's award-winning multimedia installation *Listening Post* (2001), acquired by the Science Museum in 2007. Often considered a landmark in the medium of net art, *Listening Post* is a portrait of the movement and sound of text transactions in online communication. Like the makers of the Antenna Gallery grid display, Hansen and Rubin relied on a novel visualization of online messages to create their "listening post." To create a visual and auditory sense of how text communication occurs online, they sampled live text from thousands of unrestricted chat rooms, message boards, and other public forums. They then showed these texts on over 200 LED message display boards placed on a large, curved panel. Computer-synthesized voices read or sang the messages as they scrolled and disappeared over this lattice grid. The piece is delivered in seven cycles or movements, each one of which is programmed separately to generate different visual, aural, and musical arrangements.

The correlation between message and network can be seen as an underlying subject of *Listening Post*. Although the piece is presented in an installation space, it also points back at the virtual spaces from which these electronic texts have been culled. The problem is that the viewer has no contextual information, so we do not know where these messages actually came from. Just as in the Antenna Gallery, there is no sense of by whom, where, or why these messages were originally sent. All we have is the message—the information—floating and dancing across screens. Thus, the post referenced in the title of this piece is neither local nor global but glocal at best—what Rubin calls a "big de-contextualization machine" (in Simanowski 2011, 198). This context-free space is nonetheless both a site for reflection and a site of sensation, inasmuch as the audience is engulfed by moving text and rhythmic sound. In the sense that the piece finds a way of raising kinesthetic awareness of Internet communication, Hansen and Rubin also find an entry point through which the abstract movement of electronic messaging can be reassembled into a visual, motor, and sonic field. So in the same way that perception of motion can be split between recognition of a local and a global domain of motion, so this piece can be seen as a tiny sensorium of the infinitely big entity that is the World Wide Web. Going back to Lautman's theorization, the local is tied to the global step by step. Like a fractal progression, we can move from one scale of the local-global to another to another, until the magnitude of this relationship is no longer perceivable by an optical field of vision, at which point we lose the system's sense of corporeality and its kinesthetic sensation. At the massively blown-up scale that is global online communication, movement is nearer abstraction, and it is almost impossible to grasp given its vastness. In the case studies discussed here, this lack of perceptual grasp is resolved because the audience can see and listen to the movements of online communication at a sizeable scale.

Perhaps glocomotion makes better sense now that we have examined the strange condition of movement within electronic media technology, where local and global, here and there, are juxtaposed, creating a state of decontextualization. It is important to note that this estranging sense of glocomotion can be provoked not only by the experience of web use but by a plethora of other technologies, including GPS, RFID, wireless mobile telecommunication, mobile computing, and environmental sensing technology. New generations of integrated spatial systems have become available as a result of recent technological advances in mobile computing and wireless communication, not least given the development of miniaturized computing devices. Across a wide range of applications, embedded systems provide data capture and processing services that create local/global integration. Thus, a provocation of a glocal decontextualization is occurring across various different technological systems and media. Anyone carrying a device with such capabilities, whether it be a wireless smart phone or a GPS-embedded iPad, can thus be inserted within an orbit of technologized movement that is neither local nor global, but glocomotional. This implanting of spatial computing in physical geographical environments has provoked a fundamental transformation of the way we navigate real space through GPS and network-assisted geography. We move within spaces that are not only conceived locally, or from an immediately physical perspective.

As this mapping of local/global emerges within increasingly dense and complex systems, so the processing of spatial information in omniscient systems requires the decentralization of information processing and the construction of distributed movement geographies. The map of the local-global is no longer realized by a single external vision, but by a collection of internal computing units cooperatively addressing tasks. In this network setup, no single node has access to the entire system state. In such conditions of global uncontrollability, spatial computing can happen anywhere, anytime. Spatial intelligence achieves a perfect ambience, what is known in the vernacular as ambient spatial intelligence (AmSI). In other words, the contemporary electronic paradigm of mobility is not a map that is physicalized in the way a paper map is. The mapping of local into global is produced by process of spatial abstraction and an invisible architecture constituted in and through computer networking. And this affects not only our sense of place or space, but indeed the way we represent our presence in that space, the way we conceive our own subjectivity through written or coded moves. As Rotman states (2008), the passage from writing to networks indexes a contemporary and ongoing upheaval of undetermined scope whose effects surround us. We have become distributed by the fact that we no longer represent experience in relation to our bodily locale, or within an immediately physical ambient space. With the body turning into a GPS point within a technologized ambient spatial intelligence, the fate of the subject, writes Rotman, is "to be subsumed—assimilated into, repositioned and overlaid—by digital forms of self-reference, by modes of self-enunciation intrinsic to, and only possible within, the instantaneities of a digitally recalibrated space-time and reconfigured agency/presence facilitated by interactive and distributed electronic networks" (2008, 110). Such a mouthful demands a bit of unpacking.

The language of e-motion

Before I bring this investigation to its conclusion, I will visit three remaining sites of analysis. First, I will argue that communicational transactions occurring in the Internet are formal, under the conditions laid down by its basic protocol (IP). Following a brief examination of the example of Hypertext

Transfer Protocol (HTTP), I will conclude that even the movement of communication and information within web space requires a language of movement, such as HyperText Markup Language (HTML), for the purpose of processing text in distributed information exchange. Second, I will consider the possibility of tracing the movement of individual web navigators, in order to suggest that in the same way as outermotion can be traced to yield traceforms, or indeed in the same way as innermotion can be traced to yield liaison forms, movement at the interface can be tracked to yield what is known in the vernacular as traceroute. Third, I will argue that once a user recognizes that there is a language inside web navigation, and that one's online moves leave traces behind, the notion that online communication is spaceless or motionless becomes untenable. An awareness of the "instantaneities of digitally recalibrated space-time," drawing once again on Rotman's theorization, can be visualized and spatialized, an idea that is exemplified by Bell Labs' Internet Mapping Project.

This leads me to the question of protocol. Internet communication is bound up with the question of transference. To communicate online, one has to transfer a unit of communication (say, a message) to someone or something else, via some medium or connection pathway. The Internet is a place of pure in-betweenness and relationality defined by its client-server architecture. Within this trajective architecture, communication occurs as a distributed web of relations between individual computers (clients) and the providers of a web resource (server), via a network (the World Wide Web). The visualization of this distribution is effaced, however. While online, users do not typically see this triangulation, nor do they see the virtual space—the architecture—inside which their web navigation activities are taking place. Nor do they necessarily know the language that is used to formalize this communication. A web user might not know where, in physical space, a particular server is located. The user might never know his or her IP address or hostname. All the user knows, while navigating, is what the user sees on the screen: webpages, pop-ups, animations, text—i.e., glossy electronic imagery and text, a merely visual and textual layer that effaces the underlying protocols and languages of the Internet. What we see, according to media theorist Lisa Parks, is "the economic mobility of digital corporations ... which reinforce the corporation's status as data portal, carrier or delivery system" (2004, 39). According to this analysis, although web users are encouraged to imagine themselves as navigating, most users have little or no understanding of the material conditions and infrastructure of this navigation space. Web users can also be technologically illiterate, transported by the technology without any awareness of how they are moving, or indeed *who* is moving them.

Until the user's requests are met by an HTTP message ("404: Page not Found," or some other net jargon), and until the pretense of information cool is exposed, a deeper layer of language beneath the glossy images will remain elusive. We become aware of the language underlying our e-moves when something fails to happen, when a move is met with a dead end, a glitch occurs, or something is not found. Failure in this transfer can happen for ordinary reasons, as for instance in the case of power failure. Transfer can be affected by connectivity problems as well; otherwise, we can expect data to "move" from a given location to a remote network, opening up the cool universe of the web onto our computer screens. Those moments when code creeps into the experience of web navigation are what concern me, however, not only in relation to error messages but to the general layer of formalization underlying online communication.

Internet Protocol (IP) is the basic formal platform in the World Wide Web: without it nothing would move, electronically speaking. Internet Protocol relays datagrams across network boundaries through the process known as routing, which involves selection of paths in a network. This function is what effectively enables internetworking, and thus makes the Internet come to life. Although a user might take connectivity as an invisible feat of technology, connection (and by extension movement) is a physical operation involving signal processing as well as the transfers of datagrams (i.e., linguistic operations).

Although a user may perceive the Internet as having being written in a given natural language, in English or French or Mandarin, it is written in a number of Internet protocol languages. Thus, rather than speaking of an international language when referring to the World Wide Web we are better off speaking of an "internetional" language. To ensure the transfer or "movement" of text, for instance, it is necessary to speak and understand the protocol of HTTP, or to speak the language of HTML. Whether the language that appears on any given webpage is English or Mandarin does not change the internetional character of online language. Within the conditions of Internet text transfer, the languages we encounter as we navigate are the same as the images: they are surface layers of a deeper Internet universe. Deep beneath are internetional languages relayed via alphanumeric code.

HTTP is the foundation of text-based communication in the World Wide Web. It might be helpful to recall that the Internet functions as a request-response protocol in communicational exchanges or sessions between clients (e.g., web browsers) and servers (e.g., applications running on a computer hosting a web site). A client submits an HTTP request message to the server, to which the server returns a response message. To further channel information in the Internet, HTTP requires protocols of informational transfer or transport protocols. The movement of information in cyberspace has to be formally coded, that is, so that once sent, a message can be read. Thus, a formal HTTP message is both machine-readable (the response contains a status code) and human-readable (the response displays a reason phrase), as in the case of the unsuccessful response message "HTTP/1.1 404 Not Found." Although there are a great number of standard and nonstandard HTTP responses, status codes fall into five distinct categories: informational or temporary (100s), successful (200s), redirected messages (300s), client error (400s), and server error (500s).

Ian Chambers (2002) has argued that the gap that emerges between language and mobile citizens can no longer be assumed to be the direct expression of a precise national, cultural, and geopolitical identity. Instead, the uncoupling of identities from fixed homelands, and the sense of identification through language in more nomadic contexts, finds itself caught up in a continual process of translating and being translated. This state of transit, which Chambers has addressed in literary expressions or television realism, is most evident in the context of what I dub internetional language. This new condition of textualization within Internet language, and the layers of translation and transit required in online communication, reroute my discussion back to an earlier debate on the transformation of natural languages and the mutation of alphabetic writing into moving, animated, and ultimately postalphabetic forms of textual communication. Text moves not only because it can be animated, however, but because the language behind this written representation is also moving, shifting, alternating from one language domain to another. Because in traversing a space like the Internet we have to navigate a distributed space where no single language takes precedence, except the language of Internet Protocol, the sense of language inside the World Wide Web is always in transit: it is moving. Although my own exploration of the Net is localized within my own languages (English or Spanish), upon entering the World Wide Web my language becomes a medium to enter a translinguistic realm—the realm of an internetional translanguage that is articulated through formal means like HTTP or HTML.

Lisa Parks has argued that the idea of language as medium is particularly relevant in an era of global digitization, where the materiality of the world becomes code. She raises a number of relevant questions that point back at the rubric of local/glocal. For instance: "If language is one of the rubrics through which we know and understand technologized movement, then what are the implications of having the capacity to translate foreign languages at web interfaces into one's native tongue?" She adds: "Put another way, does the user really 'move' if machine translation in effect effaces the foreign language environment and the challenge of navigation through it?" (2004, 47). According to Parks, it is because of this transit of language, this linguistic liquidity, that our understanding of movement at the interface is fundamentally altered. If the technology has radically transformed our contemporary culture of movement, it is not only through a transformation of the human body that moves (robotic movement), nor indeed through a transformation of vision into vision-computation (motion capture), but also through the transformation of movement into an electronic form of translinguistic and translocal representation.

Technologized movement is even more susceptible to a radical paradigm shift in the case of Internet communication. Online movement involves a complete destabilization of the sense of local language, provoking a sense of glocal expression characterized by the transit between various language domains (human and machinic). And even though web users can easily manage to avoid colliding with languages other than their own, thus retaining a sense of native expression within their Internet activity (just like the glossy images and glossy texts appearing at the superficial level), the notion that the Internet is germane to one particular language is of course misconstrued. In order to move through the entire space available online, the web user must continuously overcome interlinguistic gaps, in the encounter with HTML code or HTTP messages or indeed in having to navigate through electronic textures that speak any language: an e-Tower of Babel.

Tracing movement at the interface

The next site of analysis I wish to explore concerns the representation of movement at the interface in relation to the formation of e-traces. There is a fundamental difference between movement forms at the interface—what I call e-trace—and the movement forms discussed in earlier chapters. In the process of routing, or of typing URL addresses onto a browser, online activity generates at least two distinct ways of expressing kinetic traces. Despite lacking any physical sense of spatial proximity or distance, online activity generates specific connection pathways that are drawn up automatically by the computer, as well as chains of visited webpages that are drawn up intentionally by the user. The possibility for hypermovement is fundamentally chronemic in both cases. Movement is observed at the interface through time: i.e., through speed, through connectivity, through transitions between different instantaneous stages of an online session. Hyperspace thus emerges from this fundamentally temporal determination.

219

In the same way that Marey saw human and animal movement in terms of paths occurring in physical space, so Internet activity can be recorded and represented because of its temporal determination as a path in virtual space. Unlike Marey's subjects, however, and unlike physical movement, the online agent is moving in a nondistant and aproximal space—a space that is in no way stereotypical or anthropomorphic. Put differently, everything is temporally abstract within hyperspace. Contrary to Marey's traces, which are movement times that emerge naturally from physical space, e-traces are spatialities that emerge from aphysical time. For this reason, the pathways created by users online are always time-consuming: while online, we inhabit sites that take time to access, and that can be redirected after a specific amount of time, or can expire. If movement at the interface can be understood as the specific path(s) through which data moves at a certain rate and at a certain time, then the first question to be reckoned with is how these different pathways can be created and how they can be represented. In what follows, I will consider two ways in which an e-trace can be drawn up: either via traceroute, a computer network diagnostic tool used to display and measure transit delays of paths across an IP network, or via clickstream, which is the record of places visited by a user while browsing the web.

Traceroute was born in 1987, after American computer scientist Van Jacobson amended a program used to find the path data packets will take between a local computer and a remote network host. Jacobson's program was invented to "see" the path taken by a computer when accessing a network, measuring transit delays in the process. What traceroute helps "visualize," as it were, is the temporal history of routes in terms of the time-stamped round trip established in client-host interaction. In order to establish a path between local machine and remote host, it is necessary to determine a so-called time-to-live value (TTL), also known as hop limit. The values are time-stamped, in the sense that traceroute identifies delay latency values in milliseconds, in order to measure and map out the best possible pathways to connection. The implementation of Jacobson's original program enables, for example, the specification of the number of queries to send per hop, or the time to wait for response. According to Parks, since most interfaces are designed for maximum efficiency or what she calls "informational cool," the surface representation of Internet communication effaces traceroute data, in the same way that it avoids HTTP messages (unless there is a problem). That traceroute data is readily available but is not well known implies, she writes, "that it would almost be too horrifying to see one's own online trajectories, because it might involve a recognition of the self as data moving at unrecognizably high speeds" (Parks 2004, 40).

Having said this, there is a less impersonal or more subjectified way of representing movement paths at the interface. It is important to recall that when "moving" online, users carry out three typical operations: hyperlinking, bookmarking, and browsing (internal searching). According to Theusinger and Huber, these three modes of activity enable "different types of moves" over the course of a typical Internet session, including "forward steps (e.g. from node A to B), backward steps (e.g. from node D to C) as well as forward jump steps indicated by the arrow from H to I" (2000, 1). These three types of moves, they tell us, can be described as the "footsteps" of a web navigator. Like the dendritic representations of innermotion discussed earlier, e-motion can be graphically represented in the form of a tree, more specifically a decision tree, which reveals how users decide the pathways they create in hyperspace. These decision trees not only indicate the path taken by a web walker; they can also be indicators of average length of clicks and other bits of transactional information.

The recording of this activity is involuntary, because every page viewed by a visitor is captured in a web log as a separate record. This makes up a path, otherwise known as clickstream, which is captured in the form of a log file. Clickstream is then a series of page requests, in which every page requested is temporarily log-filed: the result is a history or memory of web activity. The objective capture of hypermovement is of enormous significance, not least because in seeing the pathways taken by individual users at the interface one can understand relationships and gain data-analytical awareness of trends, habits, and patterns of web use. For instance, webmasters can take advantage of being able to track portal activity. Paths can be subsequently analyzed to determine the sequences in which users have navigated specific websites. Understanding of clickstream data provides stakeholders in the orbit of e-commerce with key knowledge of movement at the interface, which can be harnessed to customize or improve user experience, or to attract customers to particular advertisements or offerings, as well as help design real-time online engagement. One question raised by traceroute and clickstream paradigms of electronic movement is this: What kind of theoretical and conceptual frameworks can be used to give a narrative or discursive body to these forms of movement representation?

The theoretical analysis of e-motion is an area of as yet unrealized potential. And yet, while not much has been written on what hypermovement entails as an expression of electronic culture, nor how human movement has been radically transformed at the linguistic, representational, and experiential level while living online, there are frameworks relating to preelectronic forms of communication that can be used to help us create a theoretical picture for hypermovement. One framework that might be useful is time geography, a concept first proposed by Torsten Hägerstrand in the early 1960s. Hägerstrand attempted to map the trajectories and itineraries of everyday activities within socioeconomic space-time. The evolving transdisciplinary perspective offered by time geography offers a significant step toward a more integrative ontological framework and visual language of temporal movement. Hägerstrand's formulation of the individual as path maker within specific situational contexts is particularly relevant within the context of e-motion. According to Hägerstrand, an individual's daily activities from home to office to shops and back home can be plotted, modeled, and analyzed to reveal a great deal of information about the subject: "life paths become captured within a net of constraints, some of which are imposed by physiological and physical necessities and some imposed by private and common decisions" (Hägerstrand 1970, 11). As such, social worlds can be described as networks of movement paths in time and space—an idea that foregrounds the dynamics of hypermovement. Other life paths are constrained by possibilities imposed by purely technological conditions, which is the case with clickstream tracking.

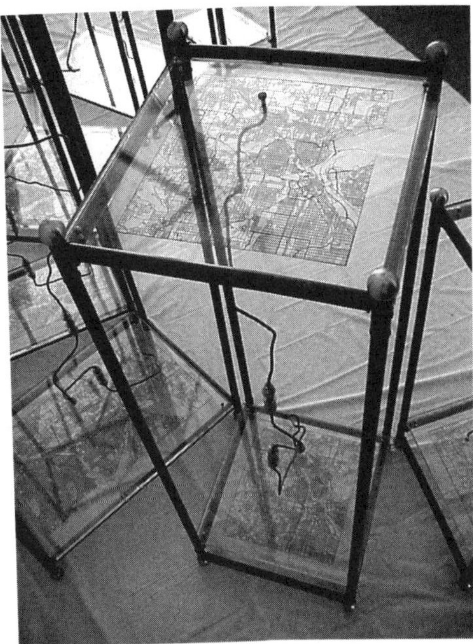

12.2
Time Pieces, by Marilynn J. Taylor, an
assemblage of seven three-dimensional
maps drawing on Torsten Hägerstrand's
models of time-space cube, representing
a weekly record of pathways along a
local map (courtesy of Marilynn J. Taylor).

Using models taken from solid geometry, Hägerstrand provided a number of examples of what this language of time geography could look like. Examples include the space-time aquarium (or space-time cube) and the space-time prism. In effect, he proposed a novel system of graphic notation. Inasmuch as his time geography notation remains somewhat abstracted from the embodied experience of mobility it seeks to represent, it may seem unfitting to a study of physical mobility, but it can be a useful tool to reveal the re-moved space-time of online path-taking. Indeed, whereas the knowledge of movement on the Internet has been mastered extensively by experts in the field of business intelligence, it is worth pointing out that if Hägerstrand's system, or some equivalent, can be applied to an investigation of online path-taking, then the intelligence provoked by online movement can be theorized and knowledge of hypermovement can be harnessed beyond the confines of e-commerce. Online movement patterns can provide an important area of study for cultural theorists, and even for practitioners wishing to represent the movement of information online as movement art. Time geography is one transdisciplinary framework—not the only one, of course—that can be employed to rescue the objectification of movement at the interface from an e-commercial intelligence.

Net cartographies

Parks also offers an interesting critical reflection on the representation of the kinetic screen. She problematizes the widespread acceptance of the idea that technologies of communication like the Internet afford a placeless globalism, what in media theory going back to the writings of Marshall McLuhan and Manuel Castells has often been referred to as the annihilation of time and space. Earlier I noted that the local-global integration afforded by projects like the Antenna Gallery and *Listening Post* can provoke an indeterminacy in a visitor's sense of online spatiality and motion, thus conveying the paradox of glocomotion. In what follows, I will argue for the need to understand the kinetic possibilities of cyberspace not as an annihilation of time/space, nor as an annihilation of the bodily medium, but as a more complementary position whereby moving at the interface involves neither placelessness nor place, neither bodiliness nor disembodiment, neither local nor global, but, I insist, a more liminal condition characteristic of electronic forms of communication.

While the Internet provokes a purely temporal or chronemic use of movement, as I mentioned earlier, time and space are folded onto each other. Thus, a peculiar type of space emerges from within the re-moved temporality of e-motion. Electronic communication creates an abstract space for itself, a space of pure representation. So it is not space that is annihilated but the proxemic observation of space. The Internet can thus be conceptualized as many temporalities without a definitive physical space, but temporalities that are projected onto a spatiality of their own, where they gain a nonphysical determination. What the Internet leaves us with is a space that has no distance—where opening a website in the UK or in China makes no significant difference from a proxemic point of view, but only from the point of view of the connectivity of a local client request in relation to a global network. In other words, an address such as www.google.com is neither closer nor further away from a user accessing it in the UK or in China. There is no sense of proximity to that address in a physical sense. There is only a temporal or connective sense to that address. The space of online activity emerges from this determination.

Earlier I also discussed the representation of innermotion (or the kinesis of thinking) in terms of liaisons that make up the architecture of logical movement. The movement of thought was represented as an arborescent structure made up of individual object and arrow interactions, which are basic units of representable logic. To better understand the relationship between this arborescent formation of thought and the externalized representation of thought in outer movement, I suggested using topological modeling. The Internet (to expand now on these earlier discussions) can be represented as a network topology; in giving the Internet a graphic representation or material expression, it is possible to recognize the sense of space, of movement, and even of bodiliness inside it. In the same way as it is possible to write down the movement of thought through parsing trees and dendritic graphs, so it is possible to represent the movement space of the Internet in terms of giant tree-like structures. Unlike the virtual structures of human thought, the Internet is a virtual dendrite that is generated by the activity of electronic communication, so it involves both a dimension of innermotion, or internalized thought, and of outermotion, or externalized movement perceived in the activity of web navigation. To navigate, then, involves both an inner motivation (a thought process) and an externalization of this process by a series of browsing activities and navigational maneuvers that involve seeing different things move *on* or *between* screens. Flicked-through webpages, pop-ups, online animations, embedded videos, underlined hyperlinks all help attract, reroute, and further encourage this traffic that makes up for the external expression of e-motion. Thus, in the same way that the body becomes a conduit to externalize the interiority of movement as thought, so the Internet can be conceptualized as a virtual body that externalizes the inner movement (the motivations, the thought processes, the search) that ultimately drives the navigation of a web user.

This leads me to Internet cartography, and the mapping and drawing of Internet topology. Although the Internet has been represented topologically in myriad ways, for the purposes of this analysis I will gloss one important historical case study: the Internet Mapping Project (IMP). IMP spawned at Bell Labs in 1997, spearheaded by Bill Cheswick and Steve Branigan in conjunction with Hal Burch of Carnegie Mellon University. The project involved collecting and recording routing paths from a test host to over 90,000 registered networks on the Internet over a period of several years. According to the authors, the visualization of the Internet results in interesting routing and reachability information. With around 88,000 nodes and 100,000 edges, the graph visualizations produced by the Bell Labs team are extremely cluttered. This poses a visual problem, in the sense that the complexity of the patterns generated makes the information hard to fathom from a purely visual

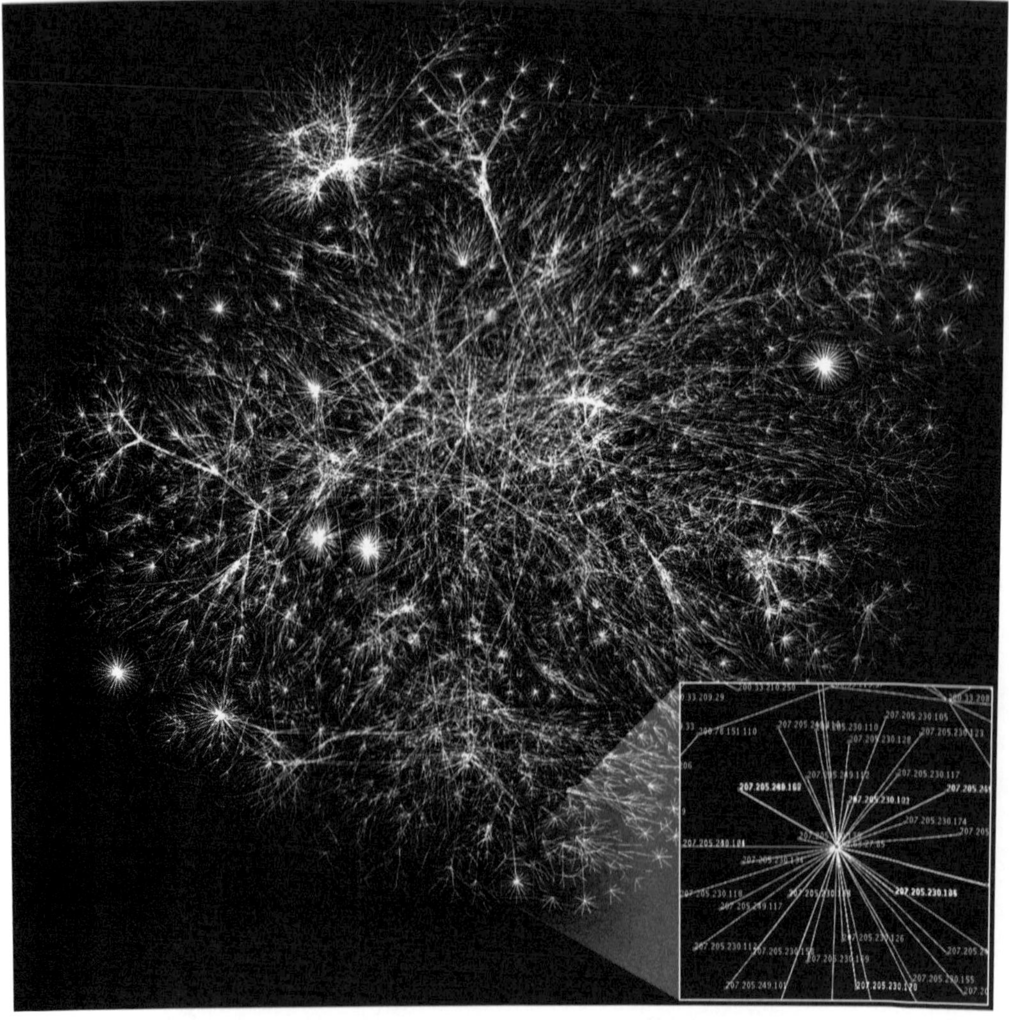

12.3
Opte map of the Internet (2004). © Opte project
(courtesy of Barnett Lyon).

point of view. This problem can be addressed by plotting a minimum distance-spanning tree that throws away the edges of the map. In addition, the map of the Internet can be color-coded, showing network-relevant data: IP address, domain information, location, and so on. The authors explain the map thus: "by obtaining a list of all announced networks on an internet, and discovering the [traceroute] path to each of these networks, we build a good picture of the 'center' of the Internet, and a kind of picture of what the Internet looks like as a whole" (Cheswick, Burch, and Branigan 2000).

Furthermore, according to Cheswick, the project's goal was to collect data over time and produce a kind of time-lapse film of the growth of the Internet. In providing a visual representation of location and network, the project resolves the paradox of local/global movement, but only through the further layer of abstraction and representation that is the IMP Internet tree. In fact, like *Listening Post*, which provides a representation of the sound of the Internet, IMP has no capabilities to draw the entire Internet or to visualize its entire expanse in real time. The size of the problem is such that it escapes the limits of any algorithmic calculation. The Internet has grown beyond sizeable magnitude; its movements and its expanse are so vast that only tiny segments of it can be processed at a time so that they may be visualized in the IMP tree, or indeed so that they may be sonified in the Hansen-Rubin listening post. Like the *sensorium Dei* of Newton (see chapter 9), the Internet is an infinite space, which our own human representations only manage to comprehend partially. The point of giving the Internet a representation is not to reveal it in full but to show a portion that can be grasped by our feeble human memory, and through a topological representation that yields nonmetric and nondistant spatial relations, or spatialized relations of Internet times within relatively small regions of Internet activity.

Kevin Kelly, cofounder of *Wired* magazine, has found a way of bypassing the problem of representing the web objectively, by starting another version of the Internet Mapping Project. In Kelly's version, the map is not intended to represent what the Internet looks like, nor the location of the center of this universe. Rather, his project reveals the way people imagine the Internet: what Kelly has tried to do is produce a compilation of images of the way people subjectively represent the space or indeed the experience of being online. This project thus could be said to champion the idea that any representation is a valid representation of the Internet, since this universe is highly subjective anyway. The goal of this Internet Mapping Project, as Kelly himself states, is to create a "folk cartography" (quoted in Blum 2012, 6). Andrew Blum reports that the representation of the Internet collated in Kelly's project shows two kinds of mental maps: chaotic expressions of a spidery infinity, and the image of the Internet as village. In other words, the folk representation of the Internet seems to convey a sense of movement or one of spatial socialization. What these mentalscapes reveal, according to Blum, is not so much the sense of the physical as a misconstrued sense of placelessness and nonphysical existence. To counter this, he proposes to sense the Internet as a place with sounds and smells, with physical details, with infinite edges and remarkably few centers.

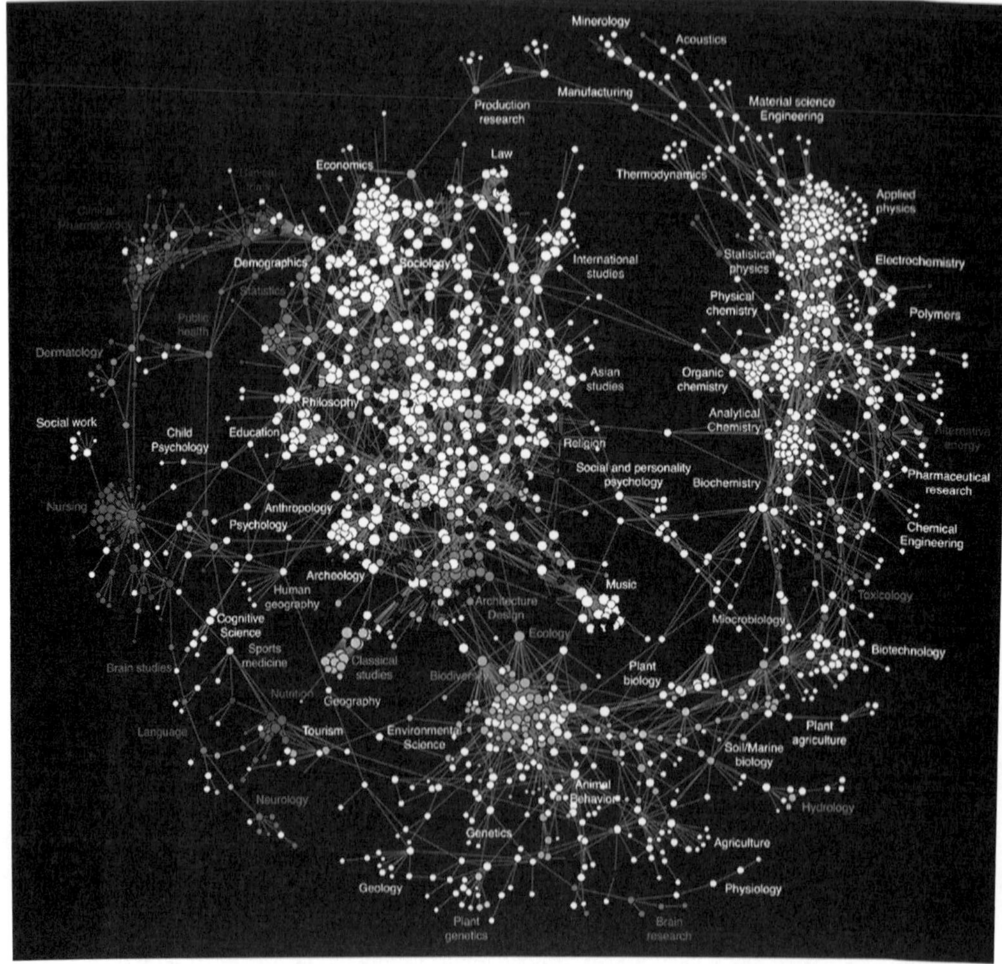

12.4
A map of science created by Bollen et al. (2009)
from clickstream data. Circles represent individual
journals. The lines that connect journals are the
edges of the clickstream model. Colors in the original
correspond to the AAT classification of the journal.

"The movement of data is difficult to nail down, but that doesn't make the particularities along its path any less real" (Blum 2012, 189).

In addition to traceroute maps, Internet maps can be drawn out using clickstream data to create cartographies that are derived from routine log interactions. One example of this is the "Maps of Science" produced by Johan Bollen et al. in 2009.[1] These maps were derived from an aggregated log dataset that contained approximately 1 billion user interactions, logged in the course of 2006 and 2007 by web portals operated by a number of key scientific publishers and aggregators, including JSTOR and Ingenta. This example is relevant not least because it provides an application of click-stream data visualization that avoids the more confined e-business model of clickstream analysis, thus helping us understand how other types of knowledge and intelligence stored online can be mapped. In this case, the map helps us visualize how academic knowledge spreads across the natural sciences, social sciences, and humanities. It is worth reiterating that the mapping of informational trajectories is of course not new, nor indeed an exclusive preserve of Internet data analysis, but that maps like these provide unique instruments for exploring the structure and evolution of search activities online. In the case of the "Maps of Science" project, following clickstream data analysis provides a much more organic and, if you like, kinetic sense of how academic knowledge changes and re-forms itself over periods of time. According to Bollen et al. (2009), clickstream data analysis has a set of attractive characteristics compared to citation datasets: for instance, "the number of logged interactions now greatly surpasses the volume of all existing citations." What these cartographies show are systems that change and grow like living creatures without central nervous systems.

Lessons from the tunicate

Rodolfo Llinás exemplified the idea that thought is the evolutionary internalization of physical movement by way of a curious case from the natural world. Creatures that are able to move must by necessity possess brain activity. Vegetal life does not think, because vegetal life does not move of its own accord. Thus, plants do not have brains. The example provided by Llinás is that of the sea squirt or tunicate, a type of marine creature that starts life as a tadpole-like larva equipped with eye and ganglion brain. The creature undergoes metamorphosis once it has developed sufficiently to find a suitable rock on which to live. It then becomes sessile and plantlike, at which point it digests its own brain. The point is illustrative in more ways than one. The brain and nervous system are an evolutionary step toward self-propelled movement. When the animal stops moving, it stops using its brain. It becomes "unintelligent": it eats its own brain. The Internet is an odd kind of tunicate. It is an infinite plant of projected human activity with no central nervous system and no central brain. It is highly kinetic (in an electronic sense) and yet it has no centralized brain. The Internet is a strange sort of tunicate indeed. If the lesson of the tunicate is that brain activity is determined by an organism's faculty of self-motorization or autokinesis, and if the brain is an evolutionary adaptation to allow organisms to move, then the Internet is an exception, for it has no central intelligence, or at least it does not have a brain that is centralized. If the Internet is a living thing, then it is living in a virtual universe where no center, no all-encompassing nerve system, is to be found, but where all things exist in the strange logic of glocomotion: a total relationality or complementarism (e.g., client-server, local-global). This is because the intelligence of this system is realized through the connections established by thousands of individual brainlike engines (servers) that make up the Internet's distributed intelligence. It is like a tunicate rooted to no concrete rock, to no solid ground, but only to its own self-propelled activity. The representation of the Internet as a tree or tunicate shows us that behind the minor physical activity necessary to conduct online communication is a predominantly intelligent activity: the visualizations of the worldwide web discussed in this chapter reveal a virtual organism that is a technologized form of innermotion (a technologization of human thought). But I repeat: the web is an intelligence without brain, or rather without centralized and fixed organs of intelligence. If the Internet is a representation of universal human pensement, it is a communal intelligence rather than an individual one. The intelligence is produced by interaction, by networking, by the temporal connections established between millions of clients and thousands of servers.

Monetizing movement

Movement at the interface reinforces an important argument I have made in this book: intelligence is the result of a thought process behind movement. Thus far I have argued that mobile thought generates mental intelligence, and that mobile physicality generates physical intelligence. This is, of course, a rather stiff conceptualization, since human movement, as I have repeatedly pointed out, is an integrated process involving both mind and body. However, division of knowledge in professional contexts tends to reinforce these rigid categorizations. Thus, physical intelligence can generate a number of strict skill sets or categories of professional skill, which can be embedded within highly specialized job specifications and professional types. Physical intelligence is one of many skills that might be conventionally demanded of choreographers, physiotherapists, kinesiologists, athletes. This division of knowledge is even more prominent in the case of a third intelligence, which is generated by knowing how things move online, or more generally how data moves. More generally, this third intelligence can be conceptualized, as opposed to physical and mental intelligence, as a kind *systems intelligence*—i.e., an intelligence that emerges from an understanding of how complex human systems and elements within the system (especially information) are mobilized. The question is: What kind of professional role, and what kind of industries, derive from knowing about hypermovement? Unsurprisingly, Internet intelligence is being harnessed primarily by data miners and information and intelligence analysts, a now well-established category of knowledge and expertise evolving within the orbit of business intelligence (BI). The fact that knowledge of data movement is commonly known as e-intelligence or business intelligence is not without conse-quence. e-Intelligence can be defined very broadly as the product of an understanding of how and why patterns of electronic movement (i.e., data) occur, and of capturing datasets in order to obtain a commoditized or objectified sense of Big Data. In effect, this is what makes an organization or corporation intelligent: its awareness of why, where, and whose information is moving. The specifici-ties of how individual businesses can turn mobile data into financial gain make a wide-open question, which I will not seek to address here. There is, however, a general use of data that concerns me: its objectification as commercial profit: i.e., the selling and buying of data, or to be more specific, the selling and buying of electronic mobility.

The sessionization and tokenization of user movements conducted by data analysts has evolved into a professional and expert field involving the fine- grained study of movement information for commercial purposes. Like the fine-grained detailed analysis of physical movement we touched on in earlier sections, the movement of users and information online is a massively complex field of study, and it can be followed through at minute levels of detail, even at a per customer or per inter-action basis. Traceroute and clickstream records are just two examples of how electronic movement is opening up completely different epistemologies of movement analysis, which are germane to a very specific kind of expertise, possessed of a unique set of technical and technological know-how. But if online movement has become an activity that is corporately monitored, surveyed, and indeed policed, given the danger of spyware, is movement at the interface as free as the inventors of Internet technology first envisaged it? Is the Internet, as seen through the eyes of a BI analyst, a free-moving dendrite, an expression of besouled and intelligent movement, a creative enterprise involving expressions of human experience? The short answer to this question is yes, except that the meaning of the terms used above has been radically reprogrammed compared to paradigms discussed in earlier chapters. Is it a world of unbounded creative expression and growth? Quite likely, but this is a creativity and an intelligence motorized to generate corporate growth and data money. Unbeknown to the user, we move not in an invisible great floating plant of free creativity, or in a world of bound-less electronic gloss, or in a communal consciousness, but in a mine of commercial and corporate activity. If we forget that the Internet is a temporality possessed with space, then we ignore that we are being seen, and that our every move can be captured and analyzed by business intelligence and business intelligentsia. There is a breed of everyday experts that can pinpoint where the rest of us move, how we move, why we move, and then predict where we will be moving next.

Lumeta is a corporate giant that describes itself, at least in its website mission statement, as the world's most widely deployed network situational awareness solution for large, geographi-cally distributed organizations. A spinoff of Bell Labs, and using an enhanced version of the same technology developed by Cheswick for the Internet Mapping Project discussed above, Lumeta is a fine example of how the Internet has become a projected environment for commercialization: a space where temporalities can be owned, rented, sold out. Lumeta patented Bell Labs technology in order to offer large corporations the service of mapping every IP asset, host, and node on a network, giving businesses a clear view of risks arising from network commerce. Insofar as today's distributed, ever-changing IT environments require complete network visibility in order to maintain security, compliance, and availability, the exponential growth of IP-enabled devices means that IT organizations require comprehensive investment of time and resources in network engineering and visualization of these architectures. What is true of large corporations is also true of government and local authorities.

Like motion capture technology, or indeed like the Kinect effect touched on earlier, the possibilities for using Internet technology for social, cultural, or medical purposes cannot be denounced as commercialistic and pernicious, quite simply because these moral pronouncements do not provide a complete typecast. What concerns me, however, is the way companies see in the Internet the potential to exploit the many data mines this landscape affords. As in the example of motion capture, the influence of major technology corporations over the production of knowledge surrounding Internet movement can lead to the inevitable control of movement by large corporations commercially powerful enough to roll over new technology into their portfolios and generate robust capabilities for business intelligence.

Time geographer Torsten Hägerstrand emphasized that while infrastructures are themselves constituted by and reproduced through movements, "people are not paths, but they cannot avoid drawing them in time space" (in Gregory 1985, 324). For Lisa Parks, what movement at the interface provokes is precisely the opposite: "a way of conceiving of people as paths drawn in the time space of the web" (2004, 41). This fetishist commoditization of movement and this commoditization of people's movement raise further concerns about how the transformation of technology affects not only the language of movement, or the representation of movement, but indeed the transaction of movement, the economy of movement, and ultimately our freedom to move. That the transformation of movement pathways into data that can be "mined" and commoditized and sold raises concerns about the technologization of movement from the point of view of the objectification of motion, and the purpose of this objectification. Ultimately, who gains from this knowledge? Whose intelligence is it, and how intelligent is it, if indeed it thinks that the exploitation of electronic movement is limitless?

Whereas in prior histories of movement glossed in this book technology served the purpose of objectifying movement, say for medical purposes, for scientific purposes, or indeed for artistic purposes, the current digital and data-consuming context hinges on the overtly commercialist purpose of this objectification. Like the technology of motion capture, which has transformed the mediation of live movement into a marketplace for the buying and selling of samples and libraries of movement, the monetization of e-traces and web paths can make navigating online a rather risky affair involving not only loss of privacy but also loss of freedom to move. If the innovative use of collaborative technologies has been tarnished by attempts to monetize streams of content, then clickstream money-making can take the meaning of exploitation to a new level. Monetizing and exploiting people's moves (physically or online) undercuts any consideration of the World Wide Web as a free space, or as a place unfettered by commercial boundaries. On the contrary, what we may conclude from the above is that the touting of creative movement and mobility online, the trumpeting of the new age of all things mobile and net-free, is in fact a dangerous guise that effaces the growth of *motion capital* in online forms of data accumulation and exploitation. And this is not a system that can go on without exhausting itself. Data mining exhausts those areas of data analysis that are intensely explored and exploited, leading BI analysts to the endless need to recover new sites and to continue exploring and continue mining, which in turn provokes the endless desire to accumulate more data—more intelligence. What we have here is a Big Data machine, a Moloch that produces endless electronic information to satisfy data money-making: an enterprise that in this author's opinion bluntly ignores that human movement ought to anchor us to our most essential human experience of connection, and not only between ourselves but with our own interior selves.

CONCLUSION

Terminations

> All the terms in which I chose to think are for me TERMS in the literal sense of the word, that is, true terminations, borders of my mental [ ] of all the states to which I have subjected my thinking. I was truly LOCALIZED by my terms, and if I say that I was LOCALIZED by my terms, I mean that I did not recognize them as valid in my thought. I was truly paralyzed by my terms, by a series of terminations. And however ELSEWHERE my thought may have been at those moments, I had no choice but to bring it out through those terms, however contradictory to itself, however parallel, however ambiguous it may have been, or else I would have had to pay the penalty of no longer being able to think. (Artaud 1988, 83)

A list of terms can be produced to sum up this book from a purely terminological point of view. Thus, various historical ways of describing movement have been addressed: kinesis, chronokinesis, telekinesis, autokinesis, heterokinesis, kinesics, chronemics, proxemics. Various ways of representing movement graphically have been mentioned: kinetography, chronography, chronophotography, cyclography, kymocyclography, computography, geometric animation, photogrammetry, motion capture. Various concrete and embodied languages of movement have been touched on: choreutics, balletic mathematics, ballet, tai chi. This book has also put together a list of terminological concepts: kinesphere, dynamosphere, kineme, dyneme, kinesymbolism, kinesception, kinestruct, traceforms, traces, clickstream. Finally, a number of new terms have been coined to address concepts that these histories formulate, but for which they do not provide a terminological definition: stereomotion, liaison forms, tracewriting, innermotion, pensement, kinetopoiesis, kinectic, e-motion (hypermovement), e-trace, glocomotion. All these terms are, in the literal sense, in the sense evoked by Artaud in the passage quoted above, "terminations." Terminology is a basic form of capture, of seizing movement within the confines of (linguistic) language. These terms stem, as I pointed out in the introduction, from an analytical view. From analysis, the continuum gets broken down into its component parts, and terms are by necessity invented to nominate each of the parts of a seamless whole. Hence an important frame for the acquisition of the knowledge of movement, and from which a system of representation (including a system of linguistic formalization) can emerge, was the analytical vision of motion.

And so this book has addressed different histories of human movement analysis from a *stand*point, from the point of view of an academic *state*ment: literally, I have written all this with the intention of stating and thus bringing the knowledge of movement to rest. In the process, I have identified how, in striving for knowledge of movement via an analytical frame, movement furnishes the mover with terms that supposedly objectify representation. Because of this paradoxical connection between infinite motion and finite languages, *Motion and Representation* illustrates a never-ending cultural enterprise of naming, of numbering, of coding, of diagrammatizing, of treeing, of drawing the forms of movement, and in the process, of finding new means of representing movement language through mathematical and computational means, or indeed through different formal languages of movement that are realized at the concrete level of an embodied discipline.

This book has shown that this enterprise of ongoing representation is never free from the materiality of inscription, and from the material means of writing and inscribing the terms with which movement is captured. Thus, represented movement is objectified so that it can be mediated, and so that this knowledge can be exchanged, distributed, circulated, and processed in some mediological and culturally determined way. Within this process, movement is liable to the material conditions laid down by many specific technologies of representation and mediation, none more so than digital technology. Thus, our understanding of movement, and our means of representing movement, are also liable to the technologies of mobility and the tracking technologies available to us.

But movement does not terminate here; of course not. No single epistemology and no single technology can find the terms that truly terminate, given the interminable repertoire of movement available to the three intelligences of movement I have discussed: physical, mental, and systemic. Thus, these epistemologies mix, merge, modulate, evolve and coevolve, creating a never-ending cultural stream of languages and of language machines, of media and technology that help further terminate and determine the way human beings communicate movement. And because the enterprise of movement capture cannot be fully exhausted, in seeking to bring human movement to rest in this book, and in seeking to write down a cultural theory of human movement and representation, my intention was not to terminate movement, actually, but on the contrary to trigger more movement among thinkers and practitioners, to stimulate, from the rather static and disembodied medium that is the book, further mobilization of kinetic knowledge. Thus, my intention with *Motion and Representation* was not to provide any definitive terminology, or any definitive terms from which knowledge of movement can be obtained, but simply to show that movement does not terminate here, or anywhere else, but that the search for representation and description is, in fact, interminable. Knowledge of movement comes to rest in my writing only so that it can awaken an interpretation in others, and so that this knowledge can be endlessly requestioned, critiqued, probed, challenged, delocalized, and thus remobilized.

Determinations

> Spontaneity of life is manifested by a continual creation of new forms succeeding others. But this indetermination cannot be complete; it must leave a certain part to determination. (Bergson 1983, 91)

Motion is an odd thing because it moves both ways: it settles and unsettles, it brings together and scatters, it attracts and repels, it starts and stops, it integrates and disintegrates, it converges and diverges, it moves toward both conformation and deformation. Part of this book has been devoted to a study of how movement settles, how it becomes inert in the domain of representation and capture. As the quotation from Bergson shows, indetermination must leave a part to determination. And so the terms I have used in this book—some of which I have listed in this conclusion—bring about a basic insight, an idea. Thus we come to the other key frame of this book: eidesis. Not only does movement generate knowledge via analytical frameworks, but also via eidetic frameworks. One can ideate—one can create mental concepts out of movement, or physical concepts (kinestruction), as part of our human experience of kinetic eidesis. One can think through movement, and thus reveal an innermotion, a thought, a logic, a reasoning, a mental motive underlying the physical issuance of bodily movement. Movement is a carrier of thought, not only at the philosophical level or the choreosophical level but also at the neurophysical level. Movement is the result of programming brains and complex systems of neurological motor control.

Over the course of writing *Motion and Representation* I have remained determined to consolidate a cultural and media theory of human movement that is unsystematic and broad enough to integrate different historical perspectives and different histories. My determination has been underpinned by a desire to show that the quest for representable movement and technologically recorded movement is an ancient one as well as a contemporary historical one. My determination was to stay close to a more creative way of approaching this representation, which is why I have focused on a transdisciplinary integration of mathematical-computational disciplines and artistic creative disciplines of movement. Thus, this book has created a disciplinary bridge through what I have called "kinetopoiesis," a making of new structures of thought through movement. This applies to the making of new mathematics as much as to the making of new dance, of new animation, and so on. What this book has shown, or what it has determined, is that kinetopoiesis is not confined to a certain type of creative discipline, but belongs to a relationship between mathematical/computational and artistic creativity. There are, however, many other domains of movement creativity that could have been explored to further determine the way human movement is represented and performed through this creative or kinetopoietic expression of movement.

Thus, although I have limited myself to the interaction between branches of mathematics and the arts, movement is also culturally and creatively expressed in sports, in gymnastics, in athletics, in therapy, in biomedical sciences, in transport—and in physical culture generally. As such, further studies can determine how people move differently and creatively, how they represent and interpret movement across different domains of everyday physicalization. Movement is determined not only by the movement languages or by the kinetic formalisms I have discussed in this book. Human movement is also influenced by a great many environmental and internal factors: by weather, by food and diet, by social context, by gender, by race, by age, by physical ability and disability, by geographic conditions, and so on. My determination is not only to provide a conclusion but also to open up those many other avenues of exploration, those many other cultural theories of movement and mediation that could have been written instead of this one.

One determination in particular remains a critical concern, regarding the reification of movement and its technologization within a digital economy. Among all the many ways in which movement can be determined, there is a need for further scholarship that can address and critique the growth of motion technologization. For the most part, I have spoken of technology in favorable terms, considering the way in which technologies support the effort of kinetopoiesis. However, it is important to determine how movement has also been monetized, sessionized, sampled, commoditized, commercialized, industrialized, and how, in the context of motion capitalism, creativity and innovation are driven by the very narrow criteria of quantification, circulation, accumulation, and other terms that define human movement as capital (or kinetic capital).

Indeterminations

> There is an in-between. ... It surges in the center of indetermination. It is a coincidence
> of subject and object ... relating movement to a quality as lived state. (Deleuze 1997, 65)

For the ancient Greeks, the kinesis and stasis problem was addressed from a dialectical position. Thus, the question was how to determine whether true terminations exist, and whether reality is static or kinetic. Zeno's paradox thus begins a Western history of movement theory. In a current history, movement is better explained in a nondialectical way, as the essence of being neither one thing nor the other. The third frame of this book was introduced in terms of "movement synthesis." This refers to the mixing, the fusing, the enveloping of different forms of analysis and of eidesis. Movement is a crucible in which different ways of knowing can mix: it is a vast container that can be filled with various cultures of embodiment, various languages of embodiment, various styles of moving. The more movement systems mix, and the more our systems of representation become liable to fusion and to cross-disciplinary integration, the more complex and elusive this knowledge of movement becomes. In the end, our synthetic knowledge can bring together and condense old and new traditions, but we are still not able to make the perfect blend, and thus we continue to provoke further mixings of kinetic knowledge. Like movement itself, the knowledge of movement is neither objective nor subjective but in-between, as this passage from Deleuze indicates. Movement is, indeed, a coincidence of subject and object. As such, in order to study movement I have had to move along various "centers of indetermination." By contrast, dialectics is a center of determination—a one true way of determining what is true, what is not, what is real, what fails reality. But in splitting the body from the mind, real from unreal, we find that movement is somehow divorced from its naturally indeterminate behavior.

This book has addressed four key centers of indetermination. First, I asked whether integrated human movement (or total movement) is something that occurs in space or in time. In part I, I addressed this question by noting that the representation of movement is often caught up in this artificial and divorced understanding of movement either in terms of proxemic or of chronemic determinations. Second: is movement an expression of an outer form or an inner effort? Does movement occur in bodily activity or mental activity? In part II, I offered insights into an enveloping of inner and outer relations. From here I moved to a discussion of pure interiority of movement as thought, or what I called pensement: the thinking of movement. Third: does movement refer to its performance, or to its record—its notation? The technology of writing movement down must grapple with the problem of symbolic representation, and the slowness of the written symbol to transmit the communicational content of live movement, which led me naturally to my fourth center of indetermination. Current technologies have superseded alphabetic and word-based notation in creating truly mobile and versatile systems of kinetic information capture and transfer. But in doing so they have opened up an indeterminate behavior caught between local and global determinations.

In moving along these centers of indetermination, my intention was not to finally solve the problem of the ancients, nor to locate the center of human movement in any way. I have not subscribed to anthropocentric theories of movement, whether the Vitruvian model or Laban's idea of the center of the kinesphere, nor indeed in terms of locating the center of the Internet, which programs like the Internet Mapping Project have tried to do. These centers of indetermination avail themselves of a special way of understanding while moving, of thinking while being in two places at once, and thus of knowing-as-you-go. It is only by being in between that the knowledge of both subject and object, of both here and there, of self and other, of myself and that which is not myself can be integrated. Thus, knowledge moves us and is moving. Thus, movement might start to coincide also with growth, with a kind of creative evolution or transformation. We move in order to know our inner selves from the outside. Then we can return to ourselves again as though for the first time, changed. Thus we are transformed, and thus we creatively move on. Here is a knowledge that has existed always: it is as "old as the hills," in Laban's words (1966, vii). Indeed, knowledge *through* movement ought to be written again on hills, on our environmental spaces, so as to reconnect bodies with the landscapes we walk, with journeys we make, with the physical and virtual processes we undergo, and thus to fashion more embodied ways of learning and knowing, more visceral ways of critiquing a knowledge *of* movement.

NOTES

1 IN SOLID MOTION

1. iWeave was an interdisciplinary collaborative research project within the field of digital archiving and dance reconstruction. The project made use of 3D data capture and interactive technology and applied it to the digitalization of two kinds of objects: material objects (i.e., four original costumes from the Madge Atkinson dance collection dating back to the 1920s), and immaterial objects (i.e., four reconstructions of Atkinson's original dances based on photographic footage). Computer-animated versions of the dresses and dances were developed as part of a Kinect interface, enabling users to try on the historical costumes and to interact with the choreographic reconstructions. The project was led by Rachel Fensham, and the research team included John Collomosse, Quizi Yu, Nicolás Salazar Sutil, Melina Scialom, and Bernardette Limon. Available at http://www.moveresearch.net/iweave/.

2. Borges's essay, written in 1951, speaks of a universal history of a spherical God that shifted in the sixteenth century—"the inanimate century"—toward a less exultant belief in the infinite sphere. According to Borges (1981), people started to become lost in a relative sense of time and space, and so by the time Pascal got to write about it, the sphere had become a labyrinth and an abysm. God *ad ovo* then became a "dreadful" sphere. Jacques Lacan echoed this sentiment when he said in his introduction to topological psychoanalysis (Seminar XII): "throughout the centuries, the significance of the sphere, with all the exclusiveness that it involves, is what dominated a whole way of thinking." See Lacan (1964–1965), 13.

3. Marcus Vitruvius Pollio, sometimes loosely referred to as the first architect, described in his book *De architectura* a model for the construction of well-shaped buildings in relation to a standardized, geometric notion of the body. Belying a tendency for universalism and political integration, Vitruvius's work can be read as an expression of a historical striving toward the ordering of the known world in relation to a single geographic point and universal standard: Rome. Well-shaped man, Vitruvius reasoned, possessed a perfect architectural design, whose ideal physique hinted at the natural correlation between human proportion and ideal geometric form. In Book III of *De architectura*, which is dedicated specifically to the sacred architecture of temples, Vitruvius explained that the ideal design depended on two things: symmetry (*symmetria*) and proportion (*proportio*), and that the beauty of these principles was applicable as much to temples as to the human body. Although the iconic imagery of the Vitruvian Man was of course made famous by da Vinci, Vitruvius himself lives on as an iconic figure of popular imagination and fiction, resurfacing most recently in the character of Vitruvius, the great architect of the fabulous postmodern universe of Lego in Phil Lord and Christopher Miller's *The Lego Movie* (Warner Bros., 2014).

4. Bubbleman is an early computographic model using spherical primitives developed by Norman Badler and Stephen Smoliar at the University of Pennsylvania. Badler and Smoliar overlapped spheres to approximate a curved surface, which solved basic problems involving joint deformation. Model generation, which was particularly difficult for many object representations in the 1970s, was simplified by Badler and Smoliar's software

program. In 1983, NASA bought Bubbleman in order to test the responses of the human body to certain procedures and workstation arrangements on the space shuttle. Badler developed the model and subsequently created Jack™, a more advanced program capable of responding more specifically and precisely to various stimuli; he used this new program in the early 1990s to see how human bodies responded to different car cockpit setups. See Badler and Smoliar (1979).

5. The Sensory Ego-Sphere (SES) is a short-term memory structure for a robot developed by Richard Alan Peters II, Kimberly E. Hambuchen, Kazuhiko Kawamura, and D. Mitchell Wilkes at the Center for Intelligent Systems, Vanderbilt University School of Engineering, Nashville. There have been few applications of the SES, but they include the design of humanoids at Vanderbilt University and Robonauts at NASA's Johnson Space Center.

6. Named after British mineralogist William Hallowes Miller (1801–1880), Miller indices are used to specify directions and planes within crystal lattices. Crystallography notation, according to this system, is also concerned with the understanding and notation of crystals in a twofold manner, as I have been discussing in this chapter. The three coordinate axes of a crystal lattice that make up a point in the crystal can be represented as h,k,l. The system uses differentiation in the bracket systems to define key features of a crystal's growth, or its movement, if you like. For instance, [hkl] represents direction; <hkl> represents a family of directions, (hkl) represents a plane, and {hkl} represents a family of planes.

7. The five Platonic solids are the tetrahedron (four faces), cube (six faces), octahedron (eight faces), dodecahedron (twelve faces), and icosahedron (twenty faces), the faces of which are made up of the same regular two-dimensional shape (triangle, square, or pentagon). When connected in a three-dimensional configuration, the polygon makes up a regular three-dimensional solid. For a discussion of how Laban applied each of these five solids to the modeling of harmonic movement and to a theory of dynamic crystallography, see Salazar Sutil (2013).

8. Leonardo da Vinci produced a design for the first mechanical automaton known in the Western canon in 1495. An outgrowth of Leonardo's extensive work in the field of anatomy and kinesiology, this robot is a mechanical plan based on the Vitruvian Man model. Leonardo's robot marks the beginning of a robotic epistemology of human movement that is hugely influential in modern conceptions of human automatons. In a diary entry dated spring 1925, Schlemmer wrote of constructivist approaches in terms of new forms of engineering coupled with an added spiritual dimension. He continued: "According to Leonardo, the work of art consists half of fantasy, half of reality, united in him in equal portions." This statement can be read as a definition of Schlemmer's own approach to the design of human automatons. See Schlemmer (1990, 165).

9. Rudolf Laban wrote in his posthumous book *Choreutics* (1966) that the nearest term to describe the essential ideas of his research was "choreosophia," a coinage from the Greek *choros* (meaning "circle," according to Laban—by which he probably meant a circular dance) and *sophia* (meaning "knowledge" or "wisdom"). Laban had proposed the term as early as 1920, to some extent inspired by the esoteric thinking he had picked up from fellow members of the Monte Verità movement. Monte Verità was an alternative community based in Switzerland that was to become a model for new age and hippie ideology, and which advocated theological, Rosicrucian, and hermetic beliefs. From his early esoteric experimentations, Laban continued to refine and

develop the notion until his death in 1958. In his book *Die Welt der Tänzers*, Laban wrote that choreosophy is grounded on a comparative study of myth, ritual, and philosophy, particularly the Pythagorean cosmogony described in Plato's *Timaeus*, the beliefs of Jalal ad-Din Rumi and his followers of the Sufi order (and the dancing dervishes), Taoism and the educational rituals of Confucius (particularly insofar as they have a marked leaning toward tai chi), and Nietzsche's view of the dancer as a complete being in his *Zarathustra*. Choreosophy is an evolving idea in Laban's thinking which looks at the traditions and even the magic of dance. Choreosophy, accordingly, is all things to do with what Laban sees as the participation of the soul in dance over the ages. See Salazar Sutil (2012).

10. Schlemmer (1961) wrote that his work found great delight in mathematics, but not the kind one learns in school. Rather than being a language acquired through purely intellectual learning, mathematics in motion is a language one produces naturally and by necessity, especially in formal motor languages within the movement arts and sports. Schlemmer believed that mathematics in motion corresponds to the inherent mathematics of the human body, which creates its balance by means of movements. He spoke of two creative paths—emotion and mathematics in motion; the latter involves the mechanics of joints and swivels and the exactitude of eurhythmics and gymnastics. See Salazar Sutil (2014).

3 MOVEMENT FORMS

1. C8's *Flatland* is a digital dance theater production loosely based on Edwin A. Abbott's novella *Flatland: A Romance in Many Dimensions*. The piece was performed at the Ivy Arts Centre, University of Surrey, in June to July 2012. It was directed by Nicolás Salazar Sutil, with multimedia art direction by Sebastián Melo, Kinect design and music by Max Worgan, and choreography and dance by Sarah Rogers and Angelina Jandolo. See Salazar Sutil and Melo (2013). Video footage of the piece is available at http://www.moveresearch.net/flatland/

2. Nora Zuniga Shaw, "Introduction: The Dance," *Synchronous Objects for One Flat Thing, reproduced* website, March 2009, http://synchronousobjects.osu.edu/blog/introductory-essays-for-synchronous-objects (accessed March 19, 2014).

4 TOPOLOGIES

1. Deutsch's short story has also been adapted to the big screen. *Moebius* is a 1996 Argentinian science fiction film directed by Gustavo Mosquera that deals with the mysterious disappearance of a train in the Buenos Aires subway. A topologist is called in by local investigators to solve the puzzle of a cross-dimensional twist in the railway's infinitely complex network topology.

2. Bernstein's research locates the motor thought, or motor image that triggers the motor activity, in terms of a complex neurophysical process. Motor activity, according to Bernstein, involved coordinating activity in the sense that the brain organizes a complex array of connections and structures in the acentered and nonlinear arrangement of a motor plan. His clinical, physiological, neurological, and mathematical investigations led him to a so-called synthetic grasp of complex motor activity. Key to Bernstein's thesis is the notion that

the brain utilizes a programmatic plot, a plan of movement (otherwise referred to as the motor image), constructed ahead of its issuance as an external motor activity. For Bernstein, the totality of spatial properties that make up a living movement could be generalized under the term "motor field," which he meant to be analogous to the term "visual field," and which includes both metric and topological characteristics. It is worth noting that his use of the term "topology" did not coincide exactly with the strict mathematical term; instead, Bernstein adopted this term to refer to "the whole of the qualitative characteristics of space configurations and of the form of movement, in contrast to the quantitative, metric one." So, according to Bernstein's definition, a motor topology is any geometrical representation that is not metric. More specifically, the geometric topology of living movement might refer to qualitative peculiarities regardless of size, magnitude, or deformation. Bernstein thus considered calligraphy and the drawing of formal signs as topological activity, in the sense that the topological character of the motor field is transferred onto the graphic record of movement. He wrote: "As proof of this I suggest the experiment of drawing ten [five-pointed] stars in succession and comparing them. I doubt if it is at all possible to make a metrically perfect copy of a similar object without the help of a compass and a ruler, that is, the human motor system cannot attain a high degree of metric proficiency, but it can be said that our motor system is very sensitive to topological distinctions." See Bernstein (1984a).

3. The seven-link mobile chain is effectively a Moebius strip made up of seven linked tetrahedrons. Based on the seven-part series of the diatonic musical scale (five whole intervals and two half intervals), which Laban called the "diaformic scale," the chain was a continuous band made up of seven angles, five wide and two narrow. Though it is relatively unknown, Laban's theory of seven-ring movement is key to understanding his theory of topological motion as an appreciation of universal forms, where inner and outer are related in a continuous and ongoing way. J. S. Longstaff quotes an unpublished letter by Laban in which he explains how in movement analysis, the simplest unequal proportion between inner and outer is two movements + three movements, and how observations always reveal one movement transition inner-to-outer, and one movement transition outer-to-inner, totaling seven motions in entirety. This sequence of inner-to-outer and outer-to-inner creates a continuous circuit in the form of the seven-part Moebius band. See Salazar Sutil (2013).

4. In his manifesto on "Futurist Photodynamism," first published in 1913, futurist photographer Anton Giulio Bragaglia wrote that the recent experiments in long-exposure photography conducted by the futurist avant-garde could not be interpreted as an innovation applicable to photography in the way that chronophotography was. Instead, photodynamism was a scientific-artistic experiment intended to convey a nonrepresentational expression of futurism's concern with change, speed, and mechanization. Photodynamism was not interested in the precise reconstruction of broken-up and analytical movement, but was concerned only with the area of movement that produces *sensation*. Thus, futurist photographers achieved a blurred and subjective perception characterized by intensive volumes of movement. Responding to critics of photodynamism, who allegedly argued that the photodynamic image was unsure and difficult to distinguish, Bragaglia responded that the desired effect in photodynamism is to record the image deliberately in a distorted state, since images themselves are inevitably transformed in movement. See Salazar Sutil and Melo (2014).

5. Copies of the three Laban drawings and footage of the videos are available at the *Labanimations* project website: http://www.moveresearch.net/labanimation. The original drawings are housed at the Laban Archive, National Resource Centre for Dance, University of Surrey.

5 NUMERICAL PROGRESSIONS

1. Named after the Italian mathematician who was also known as Leonardo da Pisa, the Fibonacci sequence is a mathematical progression in which each new number in the progression is the sum of the preceding two (0, 1, 1, 2, 3, 5, 8, 13, 21, 34, 55, 89, 144, …). Besides the work of Mario Merz, Fibonacci numbers are seen in many different places, from the logarithmic spirals found in nautilus shells and sunflowers to classical music, architecture, dance, and even furniture making.

2. *Musica,* or the music of the spheres, is a Pythagorean concept that became hugely popular in the Middle Ages and continued to inspire artists into the neoclassical era—for instance in baroque counterpoint and J. S. Bach's *Art of the Fugue.* In the Pythagorean tradition, numbers and music could be said to be related representations of a preexisting cosmic order and universal language. Hence, the notion of *musica universalis,* as well as the dance of the spheres, does not relate to sonic music or choreographic dance but to the harmonic rhythms of universal cosmic order, which are, in this Pythagorean philosophical sense, a numerical music and a disembodied dance.

3. Brian Rotman, email to the author, January 26, 2010.

4. *Blame Not Our Author* (anonymous, 1613) is a science-fictional play whose learned protagonists are figures of Euclidean geometry: Square, Rectangle, Compass, Line, Circle, Triangle, Semicircle, Rhombus, and Ruler. The theatrical action involves much physical cavorting and capering, centering on Square's repeatedly foiled attempts to become a circle. See Mazzio (2004). For other examples of Renaissance geometric mime, see Turner (2006).

5. *Binary Flesh* was first shown at DRHA 2010, "Sensual Technologies: Collaborative Practices of Interdisciplinarity," Brunel, West London, September 5–8, 2010. The piece is a looped, durational installation/dance conceived and choreographed by the author, with artwork and sculpture by Juley Hudson, and performed by Elizabeth Restrepo. See Salazar Sutil (2011a).

6 THE LOGIC OF MOVEMENT

1. "Paradance" is an idea I came up with while devising the piece *I Am Not I* (2010), which I developed with Juley Hudson (C8) as part of the event "Performing Topologies" presented at Goldsmiths College, University of London. The piece explored the idea of a movement paradox—that is, a movement that does not link two different positions, but where the mover returns to the same position after moving. An example of this is the stereotypy, a movement that can be considered to lie somewhere between voluntary and involuntary. When a caged animal performs a stereotypy, it moves in figure eights. The animal is moving, and yet it is going nowhere—hence the paradox (or paradance). See Salazar Sutil (2011b).

7 NO NOTATION

1. See Guest (1998).

2. Chatwin's book makes an interesting analogy between Jesus' saying "I am the way" and the Central Australian idea of *tjurna djugurba* ("the footprints of the ancestors"). Chatwin wrote that each ancestor, while singing his way across country, was believed to have left a trail of life cells or spirit children along the line of his or her footprints. Of course, the reading of footprints as an ancestral form of foot-writing and landscape writing is not unique to Australian Aborigines. See also Ingold (2010).

3. And so LabanWriter was developed in 1987 at the Ohio State University under the leadership of Lucy Venable. LabanWriter took advantage of the graphics capabilities of the Mac computer to develop a system capable of creating and editing Labanotation scores following the word processor paradigm. Parallel efforts were carried out by Rhonda Ryman and her colleagues at the University of Waterloo. In 1990, Ryman and her team developed MacBenesh, a Mac computer application developed to assist notators in the production of Benesh scores. Similarly, Kozaburo Hachimura, Minako Nakamura, and colleagues developed LabanEditor in 2001, followed in 2004 by LabanXML, a system that enables the text representation and transfer of Labanotation online using extensible markup language (XML). The problem with these technologies is that while they offer working prototypes, they all provide restricted application.

4. The project was intended as a Mac and Windows prototype tool that would enable computer-generated animation from Labanotation. The prototype was essentially a synthesis of Venable's LabanWriter and Calvert's DanceForms.

8 ALPHABET AND POSTALPHABET

1. English philosopher, politician, and scientist Francis Bacon wrote in his book *Of the Proficience and Advancement of Learning, Divine and Human* (1808, first published 1605): "The lineaments of the body disclose the disposition and inclination of the mind in general; but the motions of the countenance and parts do not only so, but do further disclose the present humour and state of the mind and will." The tradition of writing in the air with one's hand, and of gestural communication in general, is hugely significant for Bulwer's interest and for the emergence of a chironomic science in the late eighteenth century; these early studies in human gesture also foreshadow more contemporary attempts to develop a scientific study of gesture, language, and cognition, for instance in the writings of George Lakoff, Danielle Bouvet, Armstrong, Stokoe and Wilcox, Giles Châtelet, or Brian Rotman.

2. Originally used by hacker group Dead Cow Cult to access Windows 95, leet or 1337 speak evolved into a subcultural language of elite or leet hackers ("1337 h4x0rz"), from where it made its way to text messaging and even cultural theory, for instance in the work of performance and cultural theorist Jon McKenzie. McKenzie has proposed a model of performance theory as a lemniscate or figure 8—a feedback loop—based on the Schechner-Turner model of social dramas/aesthetic drama first put forward in the late sixties within the field of theater anthropology. The loop model is also applied to the trajectory of McKenzie's book *Perform*

or Else: From Discipline to Performance (2001). It serves as a graphic and performative device, almost to the extent that it manifests itself as the book's logo/logic. The book takes a remarkable turn in its concluding pages, written largely in leet speak. The image of the feedback loop appears graphically illustrated as text—in fact, at this stage the text is more like text art. The passage from presence to mediation is emblematized in the constitution of a new infinity loop, which serves according to this author as a metamodel of a theory of technoperformance. The conceptual model helps pave the way for a consideration of technological as well as human aspects of cultural performance, and the resulting transformation of alphabetic writing into alphanumeric writing.

3. Stick figures are also icons of popular culture, featured in a number of memorable items including the sixties cult series *The Saint* (1962–1969), the graffiti character of Kilroy, or the popular game Hangman. Besides these iconic appearances in popular media, stick figuralism is also significant as a comprehensive system to convey information without words. An example of this is the DOT pictogram system, developed by the US Department of Transportation in 1974 and based on a previous prototype used in the Tokyo and Munich summer Olympic games. DOT pictograms are 50 public-domain stick figure symbols for use at transportation hubs, large events, and other contexts defined by universally understood kinetic situations (i.e., sporting and transport). Beyond the immediate utility of stick figure drawing, however, the need to supersede worded communication to explain a situation in kinetic terms is also becoming more widespread, given the now-established tendency to make electronic text more graphic and more animational.

9 INTERLINGUA

1. Unmoved mover or uncaused cause: God. The unmoved mover is a philosophical and theological concept, described by Aristotle as a primary cause of all the motion in the universe. The concept has its roots in cosmological speculations of the earliest Greek pre-Socratic thinkers, especially Parmenides. The idea became highly influential and widespread in Scholastic literature. It has been debunked and defended through the centuries, entering popular cultural imagination as a definition of pop gods (celebrities or stars), i.e., famous people who appear unmoving in the face of crowds of fans and adorers who throng around them.

10 DIGITAL MOVEMENT

1. Using Western names for these classic positions, the tai chi position known as Beginning is derived from hexagram 35, Grasp Sparrow's Tail is derived from hexagram 1, Single Whip is derived from hexagram 49, Play Guitar is derived from hexagram 17, Retreat Shoulder is derived from hexagram 34, and so on.

2. Another source of inspiration for Leibniz's calculating machine was an instrument designed by French philosopher and mathematician Blaise Pascal. But whereas Pascal's calculator—the Pascaline—could only add and subtract, Leibniz set himself the task of creating a machine that could calculate any arithmetic operation (addition, subtraction, multiplication, and division).

3. In fact, the oldest known computer is the Antikythera mechanism, an ancient analog computer designed to predict astronomical positions and eclipses. Its construction has been attributed to the ancient Greeks and

dated to the early first century BCE. Georges Ifrah notes that the ancient computer emerged from odometric machines, which are the direct ancestor of the mileage recorders in modern automobiles, "themselves analogue devices even though their display is digital." See Ifrah (2001), 155–156.

4. Elsenaar has the character of Perfect Paul, the agent controlling the artist's face, argue: "When humans persons [sic] are not afraid to wire themselves up with digital computers, the human face will become a site for unprecedented digital dance and computational expression." An algorithmic and computer-controlled face liberates the human face, affording it a relative kind of freedom, "the feeling you may have when you are bounded by a box." See Elsenaar (2013).

11 THE LANGUAGE OF MOTION CAPTURE

1. Ralph Cudworth was an English philosopher and personal friend of John Locke (as well as an acquaintance of Leibniz). Writing on the subject of the soul in his *Treatise Concerning Eternal and Immutable Morality* (1731), Cudworth argued that when the soul (by which he also means the nerve conjunctions) moves the body, "natural instinct takes notice of some corporeal things existing without bodies" (Cudworth 1996, 83). This suggestion that physicality can exist without bodies is interesting, and certainly worth bearing in mind when I come to discuss motion capture in similar terms. In a more contemporary sense, movement can be explored as a physical language that may or may not be written on anatomical bodies, but that demands some body, some material element, upon which to be written.

2. E. S. Forster's translation (1961) offers a very different interpretation from A. S. L. Farquarson's 1912 translation (quoted above). In Forster's text we read: "If a man were to walk on the ground alongside a wall [with a reed dipped in ink attached to his head], the line traced [by the reed] would not be straight but zigzag, because it goes lower when he bends and higher when he stands upright and raises himself" (Aristotle 1961, 501). It is worth adding that Aristotle also described an apparatus that resembles the pinhole camera, thus preempting the conception of the camera obscura. In Book XV of his *Problems*, Aristotle recorded basic photographic techniques to demonstrate his understanding of optics, for example the crescent shape of a partially eclipsed sun projected on the ground through the holes in a sieve and through the gaps between the leaves of a plane tree.

3. In 1971, Gunnar Johansson joined James B. Maas, professor of psychology at Cornell University, to produce two short films, *Two-Dimensional Motion Perception* and *Three-Dimensional Motion Perception*, in which optical motion capture is shown to reveal properties of two- and three-dimensional motion perception. To demonstrate that rapid spontaneous organization is a basic fact in motion perception, the films showed complex patterns such as folk dancing, shooting the dancers in a darkened surround, with twelve LED point sources attached to key joints. The films depict the complex self-organizing dynamics involved in the perception of complex movement such as dancing: in seeing the dance, the mind is capturing changing patterns and data, which the mind then organizes in an attempt to resolve the complexity into patterns, or structures that generate an understanding through kinetic perception. Johansson and Maas managed to produce a system that processes the data not only observationally but computationally, as the data is fed directly into a computer which

can read the twelve points as alphanumerical variables. This experiment constitutes not only a landmark in the development of optical motion capture, but also a major contribution to an understanding of human movement that is mediated by technologically aided observation and a computational approach to data analysis.

4. Soruce: Microsoft Kinect. Kinect for Xbox also boasts the Guinness World Record for being the fastest-selling gaming peripheral, as it sold an average of 133,333 units per day in its first 60 days on sale from 4 November 2010 to 3 January 2011. Source: Guinness World Records, http://www.guinnessworldrecords.com/records-9000/fastest-selling-gaming-peripheral/ (accessed September 15, 2014).

5. Extra Credits (EC) is a Canada-based collaborative devoted to the creation of "edutainment" video lesson series that discuss issues pertaining to video games and game studies. EC was created by animator/narrator Daniel Floyd and game designer James Portnow in 2010 from a series of lecture videos. Between September 7, 2011, and December 31, 2013, the eponymous show aired on PATV, a distribution channel hosted by Penny Arcade TV (PATV). A hugely popular webcomic focused on video games and video game culture written by Jerry Holkins and illustrated by Mike Krahulik, *Penny Arcade* launched in 1998. Now firmly established in its own site, *Penny Arcade* is among the most popular and longest-running gaming webcomics currently online, listed in 2010 as having 3.5 million readers. *Extra Credits*'s episode "Kinect Disconnect" is available via YouTube at https://www.youtube.com/watch?v=ijcezUy3ZzY (accessed March 27, 2014).

6. In a highly influential 1970 article, Mori described the phenomenon whereby the appeal of animated beings decreases as they become increasingly similar to humans. Mori argued that as robots become more humanlike, the sense of familiarity produces a dip in the levels of familiarity, at the end of which lie totally unhuman paradigms like "corpse" and "zombie." Mori's notion, subsequently labeled the "Uncanny Valley" with reference to Sigmund Freud's 1916 essay on the uncanny, is one of the most frequently revisited concepts in the fields of robotics, design, gaming, computer animation, art, and plastic surgery. Mori wrote that movement is especially telling in the pronunciation of this dip in familiarity levels: "For creatures, including robots, movement is generally a sign of life. ... Adding movement changes the shape of the uncanny valley by exaggerating the peaks and valley. For the industrial robot, the impact of movement is relatively slight because we see it as just a machine. If it stops moving, it just stops working. But if programmed properly to generate humanlike movements, we can enjoy some sense of familiarity. Humanlike movement requires similarity of velocity and acceleration. Conversely, if we add movement to a prosthetic hand, which is at the bottom of the uncanny valley, our sensation of strangeness grows quite large. ... This hand can move in a way that causes some healthy people to feel uneasy. If you shook a woman's hand with this hand in a dark place, the woman must be shocked!" See Mori (1970).

7. Source: Microsoft. See also GamePolitics.com, http://www.gamepolitics.com/2013/02/12/kinect-surpasses-gamecube-lifetime-sales-figures#.U2od5hGJI8E (accessed August 31, 2014).

8. The community website is available at http://www.kinecthacks.com. The website also features interviews with Kinect hackers who have contributed to the development of this technology.

9. BBC, "Apple Buys Motion Sensor Maker PrimeSense," November 25, 2013 (accessed August 31, 2014).

1. This project was carried out as a collaboration between the Digital Library Research and Prototyping Team, Research Library, Los Alamos National Laboratory (Johan Bollen, Herbert Van de Sompel, Ryan Chute, Lyudmila Balakireva), the Theoretical Division, Mathematical Modeling and Analysis Group and Center for Nonlinear Studies, Los Alamos National Laboratory (Aric Hagberg, Luis Bettencourt, Marko A. Rodriguez), and the Santa Fe Institute, Santa Fe, New Mexico (Luis Bettencourt).

REFERENCES

Agamben, Giorgio. 1993. *Infancy and History: Essays on the Destruction of Experience*. Trans. Liz Heron. London: Verso.

Aristotle. 1912. *On the Gait of Animals*. Trans. A. S. L. Farquharson. In *The Internet Classics Archive*. Available at http://classics.mit.edu/Aristotle/gait_anim.html.

Aristotle. 1961. *Parts of Animals / Movement of Animals / Progression of Animals*. Trans. A. L. Peck and E. S. Forster. Cambridge, MA: Harvard University Press.

Artaud, Antonin. 1988. *Selected Writings*. Ed. Susan Sontag and Helen Weaver. Berkeley: University of California Press.

Austin, Gilbert. 1966 [1806]. *Chironomia: or a Treatise on Rhetorical Delivery*. Ed. Mary Margaret Robb and Lester Thonssen. Carbondale: Southern Illinois University Press.

Bacon, Albert M. 1875. *A Manual of Gesture: Embracing a Complete System of Notation Together with the Principles of Interpretation and Selections for Practice*. Chicago: J. C. Buckbee.

Bacon, Francis. 1808 [1605]. *Of the Proficience and Advancement of Learning, Divine and Human*. London: T. Payne.

Badler, Norman, and Stephen W. Smoliar. 1979. "Digital Representations of Human Movement." *ACM Computing Surveys* 11 (1): 19–38.

Beckett, Samuel. 1959a [1953]. *Watt*. New York: Grove Press.

Beckett, Samuel. 1959b. *Molloy, Malone Dies, The Unnamable*. London: John Calder.

Beckett, Samuel. 1990. *The Complete Dramatic Works*. London: Faber and Faber.

Bergson, Henri. 1983 [1907]. *Creative Evolution*. Trans. Arthur Mitchell. New York: University Press of America.

Bernstein, Nikolai. 1984a. "The Problem of the Interrelation of Co-ordination and Localization." In H. T. A. Whiting, ed., *Human Motor Actions: Bernstein Reassessed*, 77–120. Amsterdam: Elsevier.

Bernstein, Nikolai. 1984b. "Trends in Physiology and Their Relation to Cybernetics." In H. T. A. Whiting, ed., *Human Motor Actions: Bernstein Reassessed*, 531–544. Amsterdam: Elsevier.

Birdwhistell, Ray L. 1970. *Kinesics and Context: Essays on Body Motion Communication*. Philadelphia: University of Pennsylvania Press.

Blum, Andrew. 2012. *Tubes: Behind the Scenes at the Internet*. Harmondsworth, UK: Penguin.

Bochner, Mel. 2013. "Thoughts Reinstalling a Theory of Sculpture." Press release, Peter Freeman, Inc., New York. Available at http://www.peterfreemaninc.com/exhibitions/mel-bochner_4/pressrelease/ (accessed September 10, 2014).

Bök, Christian. 2011. *Crystallography*. Toronto: Coach House Books.

Bollen, J., H. Van de Sompel, A. Hagberg, L. Bettencourt, R. Chute, M. A. Rodriguez, and L. Balakireva. 2009. "Clickstream Data Yields High-Resolution Maps of Science." *PLoS ONE* 4 (3): e4803.

Borelli, Giovanni Alfonso. 1989 [1680]. *On the Movement of Animals*. Berlin: Springer-Verlag.

Borges, Jorge Luis. 1981. *Borges, a Reader. A Selection from the Writings of Jorge Luis Borges*. New York: Dutton.

Bragaglia, Anton Giulio. 1973. "Futurist Photodynamism." In Umbro Apollonio, ed., *Futurist Manifestos*. London: Thames and Hudson.

Braune, Wilhelm, and Otto Fischer. 1987. *The Human Gait*. Berlin: Springer-Verlag.

Cage, John. 2010. *Silence: Lectures and Writings*. Middletown, CT: Wesleyan University Press.

Calvert, Tom. n.d. "Representing and Animating Human Movement for Dance." Available at http://www.catgames.ca/files/KyotoSlides3.pdf.

Camurri, Antonio, P. Morasso, V. Tagliasco, and R. Zaccaria. 1986. "Dance and Movement Notation." In P. Morasso and V. Tagliasco, eds., *Human Movement Understanding: From Computational Geometry to Artificial Intelligence*, 83–124. Amsterdam: Elsevier.

Certeau, Michel de. 1984. *The Practice of Everyday Life*. Trans. Steven Rendall. Berkeley: University of California Press.

Chambers, Ian. 2002. "Citizenship, Language and Modernity." *PMLA* 117 (1): 24–31.

Châtelet, Gilles. 2000. *Figuring Space: Philosophy, Mathematics and Physics*. Trans. Robert Shaw and Muriel Zagha. Dordrecht: Kluwer.

Chatwin, Bruce. 1987. *Songlines*. London: Jonathan Cape.

Cherry, Colin. 1957. *On Human Communication: A Review, a Survey, and a Criticism*. New York: John Wiley.

Cheswick, Bill, Hal Burch, and Steve Branigan. 2000. "Mapping and Visualizing the Internet." Usenix 2000 general conference, San Diego. Available at https://www.usenix.org/legacy/event/usenix2000/general/full_papers/cheswick/cheswick.pdf.

Chomsky, Noam. 1957. *Syntactic Structures*. The Hague: Mouton.

Chtcheglov, Ivan. 1981. "Formulary for a New Urbanism." In Ken Knabb, ed., *Situationist International Anthology*, 168–171. Berkeley, CA: Bureau of Public Secrets.

Connor, Steven. 2000. "Shifting Ground." In *Samuel Beckett, Bruce Nauman*, exh. cat., 80–87. Vienna: Kunsthalle Wien. Available at http://www.stevenconnor.com/beckettnauman/.

Cresswell, Tim. 2006. *On the Move: Mobility in the Modern Western World*. London: Routledge.

Cudworth, Ralph. 1996. *A Treatise Concerning Eternal and Immutable Morality, with A Treatise of Freewill*. Ed. Sarah Hutton. Cambridge: Cambridge University Press.

Cunningham, Merce. 1968. *Changes: Notes on Choreography*. Ed. Frances Starr. New York: Something Else Press.

Debord, Guy. 1981. "Theory of the Dérive." In Ken Knabb, ed., *Situationist International Anthology*, 50–54. Berkeley, CA: Bureau of Public Secrets.

deGraf, Brad, and Emre Yilmaz. 1999. "Puppetology: Science or Cult?" *Animation World Magazine* 3.11. Available at http://www.awn.com/mag/issue3.11/3.11pages/degrafmotion.php3.

Deleuze, Gilles. 1992. "Postscript on Societies of Control." *October* 59:2–7.

Deleuze, Gilles. 1995. "The Exhausted." Trans. Anthony Uhlman. *SubStance* 24 (78): 3–28.

Deleuze, Gilles. 1997. *Cinema 1: The Movement-Image*. Minneapolis: University of Minnesota Press.

Deleuze, Gilles. 2001. *Cinema 2: The Time-Image*. Trans. Hugh Tomlinson and Robert Galeta. Minneapolis: University of Minnesota Press.

Deleuze, Gilles, and Félix Guattari. 2011. *A Thousand Plateaus: Capitalism and Schizophrenia*. London: Continuum.

Delsarte, François, and Genevieve Stebbins. 1887. *Delsarte System of Expression*. New York: Werner.

Dempster, Wilfred Taylor. 1955. "The Anthropometry of Body Action." *Annals of the New York Academy of Sciences* 63:559–585.

Derrida, Jacques. 1998. *The Derrida Reader: Writing Performances*. Lincoln: University of Nebraska Press.

Deutsch, A. J. 1958 [1950]. "A Subway Named Moebius." In Clifton Fadiman, ed., *Fantasia Matematica*. New York: Simon and Schuster.

Downie, Marc. 2005. "How Long Does the Subject Linger on the Edge of the Volume? An Interview with Marc Downie." In *artificial.dk*. Available at http://www.artificial.dk/articles/downie.htm.

Elsenaar, Arthur. 2013. *Perfect Paul: On Freedom of Facial Expression*. Lecture-performance delivered at "Corporeal Computing" conference, University of Surrey, September 3, 2013. Available at http://vimeo.com/77526863.

Elsenaar, Arthur, and Remko Scha. 2002. "Electric Body Manipulation: A Historical Perspective." *Leonardo* 12 (December): 17–28.

Époque, Martine, and Denis Poulin, dirs. 2006–2014. *CODA, the finale of No-Body Dance: The Rite of Spring*. Color. Canada.

Eshkol, Noa. 1978. "Principles of Movement Notation." In *Diminishing Series, Dance Suite*, 1–22. Tel Aviv: Movement Notation Society.

Feynman, Richard. 2005. *The Pleasure of Finding Things Out: The Best Short Works of Richard P. Feynman*. New York: Basic Books.

Forsythe, William. 1999. *Improvisation Technologies: A Tool for the Analytical Dance Eye*. CD-ROM. ZKM Digital Arts Edition.

Forsythe, William, and Paul Kaiser. 1999. "Dance Geometry: William Forsythe in Dialogue with Paul Kaiser." *Performance Research* 4 (2) (Summer): 64–71.

Foucault, Michel. 1988. "Technologies of the Self." In L. H. Martin, H. Gutman, and P. Hutton, eds., *Technologies of the Self: A Seminar with Michel Foucault*, 16–49. Amherst: University of Massachusetts Press.

Fülöp-Miller, René. 1927. *The Mind and Face of Bolshevism*. London: Putnam.

Furniss, Maureen. 1999. "Motion Capture." *MIT Communications Forum*. Available at http://www.sfu.ca/~gcorness/Research/Articals/motion%20tracking/movment%20anal/Motion%20Capture,%20M%20Furniss.pdf (accessed September 10, 2014).

Ghostcatching. 1999. Motion capture animation by Paul Kaiser and Shelley Eshkar. Choreography by Bill T. Jones.

Gondry, Michel, dir. 2013. *Is the Man Who Is Tall Happy? An Animated Conversation with Noam Chomsky*. 88 min. France.

Gould, Stephen Jay. 2011. *Leonardo's Mountain of Clams and the Diet of Worms*. Cambridge, MA: Harvard University Press.

Grau, Oliver. 2003. *Virtual Art, from Illusion to Immersion*. Cambridge, MA: MIT Press.

Green, Richard. 2008. "Spatially and Temporally Segmenting Movement to Recognize Actions." In Bodo Rosenhan, Reinhard Klette, and Dimitris Metaxas, eds., *Human Motion: Understanding, Modelling, Capture and Animation*, 213–242. Dordrecht, Netherlands: Springer.

Greenaway, Peter. 1989. *Fear of Drowning by Numbers*. Paris: Dus Voir.

Gregory, Derek. 1985. "Suspended Animation: The Stasis of Diffusion Theory." In Derek Gregory and John Urry, eds., *Social Relations and Spatial Structures*, 296–336. Basingstoke: Macmillan.

Guest, Ann Hutchinson. 1998. *Choreo-graphics: A Comparison of Dance Notation Systems from the Fifteenth Century to the Present*. Amsterdam: Gordon and Breach.

Haeckel, Ernst. 1999. "Foreword of Crystal Souls: Studies of Inorganic Life." *Forma* 14 (1): 31–34.

Hägerstrand, Torsten. 1970. "What about People in Regional Science?" *Papers of the Regional Association* 24 (1): 6–21.

Hall, E. T. 1966. *The Hidden Dimension*. New York: Anchor Books.

Hattrick, A. 2012. "The White Review—Interview with Manfred Mohr." Available at http://www.thewhitere view.org/interviews/interview-with-manfred-mohr.

Hegedüs, Agnes. 2003. "My Autobiographical Media History: Metaphors of Interaction, Communication, and Body Using Electronic Media." In Judy Malloy, ed., *Women, Art and Technology*, 260–275. Cambridge, MA: MIT Press.

Hou Je Bek, Wilfried. n.d. "Algorithmic Psychogeography." *Space Hijackers*. Available at http://www .spacehijackers.org/html/ideas/writing/socialfiction.html (accessed August 19, 2014).

Hutchinson [Guest], Ann. 1977. *Labanotation: The System of Analyzing and Recording Movement*. New York: Routledge.

Ifrah, Georges. 2001. *The Universal History of Computing: From the Abacus to the Quantum Computer*. Trans. Sophie Wood and Elizabeth Clegg. New York: John Wiley.

Ingold, Tim. 2010. "Footprints through the Weather World: Walking, Breathing, Knowing." *Journal of the Royal Anthropological Institute* 16 (1): 121–139.

Ingold, Tim. 2011. *Being Alive: Essays on Movement, Knowledge and Description*. London: Routledge.

Ingold, Tim, and Jo Lee Vergunst, eds. 2008. *Ways of Walking: Ethnography and Practice on Foot*. Aldershot, UK: Ashgate Publishing.

Kaiser, Paul. 2013. "On the Particularity of Minds and Bodies (Real and Virtual)." Keynote paper presented at "Corporeal Computing" conference, University of Surrey, September 2, 2013. Available at http://vimeo .com/77527722.

Kipman, Alex. 2010. "Interview with Alex Kipman, Director of Incubation for Xbox." *Popular Mechanics. com*, November 24, 2010. http://www.popularmechanics.com/technology/gadgets/video-games/how-microsoft kinect-was-made.

Kirstein, Lincoln, and Muriel Stuart. 1952. *The Classic Ballet: Basic Technique and Terminology*. New York: Knopf.

Kittler, Friedrich. 1999. *Gramophone, Film, Typewriter*. Trans. Geoffrey Winthrop-Young and Michael Wutz. Stanford: Stanford University Press.

Kozel, Susan. 2007. *Closer: Performance, Technologies, Phenomenology*. Cambridge, MA: MIT Press.

Kroker, Arthur and Marilouise. 2005. "Eye-Through Images." In Gary Genosko, ed., *Marshall McLuhan: Fashion and Fortune*, 326–333. New York: Routledge.

Laban, Rudolf. 1953. "Topological Explanations, Qualitative Aspects." Unpublished manuscript, Laban Archive, National Resource Centre for Dance, University of Surrey.

Laban, Rudolf. 1956. "How to Make Your Movement Training Rational and Efficient: Use the Chromatic Movement Dial." Unpublished manuscript, Laban Archive, National Resource Centre for Dance, University of Surrey.

Laban, Rudolf. 1966. *Choreutics*. London: MacDonalds and Evans.

Laban, Rudolf. 1977. Foreword. In Ann Hutchinson [Guest], *Labanotation: The System of Analyzing and Recording Movement*. New York: Routledge.

Laban, Rudolf. 1984. *"Film about the Harmonious Movement of the Human Body."* Unpublished film script. Trans. Vera Maletic. Laban Archive. National Resource Centre for Dance, University of Surrey.

Lacan, Jacques. 1964–1965. "Crucial Problems for Psychoanalysis—Seminar XII." Trans. Cormac Gallagher. In *Jacques Lacan in Ireland*. Available at http://www.lacaninireland.com/web/wp-content/uploads/2010/06/12-Crucial-problems-for-psychoanalysis.pdf.

Lacan, Jacques. 2006. *Écrits*. Trans. Bruce Fink, in collaboration with Héloïse Fink and Russell Grigg. New York: Norton, 2006.

Lautman, Albert. 2011. *Mathematics, Ideas and the Physical Real*. Trans. Simon Duffy. London: Bloomsbury.

Leibniz, Gottfried Wilhelm. 1863. "Explication de l'arithmétique binaire." In Leibniz, *Die mathematische Schriften*, ed. C. I. Gerhardt, 7: 223–227. Halle: Druck und Verlag H. W. Schmidt. English translation available at http://www.leibniz-translations.com/binary.htm.

Leroi-Gourhan, André. 1993. *Gesture and Speech*. Cambridge, MA: MIT Press.

Lewin, Kurt. 1936. *Principles of Topological Psychology*. Trans. Fritz and Grace Heider. New York: McGraw-Hill.

Llinás, Rodolfo. 2002. *I, of the Vortex: From Neurons to Self*. Cambridge, MA: MIT Press.

Lury, Celia, Luciana Parisi, and Tiziana Terranova. 2012. "Introduction: The Becoming Topological of Culture." *Theory, Culture and Society* 29 (July-September): 3–35.

Maffesoli, Michel. 1996. *Time of the Tribes: The Decline of Individualism in Mass Society*. London: Sage.

Manning, Erin. 2009. "Propositions for the Verge: William Forsythe's Choreographic Objects." In *INFLeXions*, 2. Available at http://www.senselab.ca/inflexions/volume_2/nodes/manning_1.html.

Marey, Étienne-Jules. 1895. *Movement*. Trans. Eric Pritchard. London: William Heinemann.

Marino, G., P. Morasso, E. Troiano, and R. Zaccaria. 1986. "NEM: A Language for the Representation of Motor Knowledge." In P. Morasso and V. Tagliasco, eds., *Human Movement Understanding: From Computational Geometry to Artificial Intelligence*, 127–167. Amsterdam: Elsevier.

Maxwell, Delle Rae. 1983. "Graphical Marionette: A Modern-Day Pinocchio." Master of Science in Visual Studies thesis, Massachusetts Institute of Technology, Cambridge, MA. Available at http://dspace.mit.edu/bitstream/handle/1721.1/76176/11521682.pdf?sequence=1.

Mazzio, Carla. 2004. "The Three-Dimensional Self: Geometry, Melancholy, Drama." In David Glimp and Michelle R. Warren, eds., *Arts of Calculation: Quantifying Thought in Early Modern Europe*. New York: Palgrave.

McKenzie, Jon. 2001. *Perform or Else: From Discipline to Performance*. London: Routledge.

Menache, Alberto. 2000. *Understanding Motion Capture for Computer Animation and Video Games*. San Francisco: Morgan Kaufmann.

Merleau-Ponty, Maurice. 2010 [1945]. *Phenomenology of Perception*. Trans. Colin Smith. London: Routledge.

Merz, Mario. 1989. "Interview with Mario Merz." In Germano Celant, ed., *Mario Merz*, exh. cat. New York: Guggenheim Museum.

Metheny, Eleanor. 1968. *Meaning and Movement*. New York: McGraw-Hill.

Metheny, Eleanor. 1975. *Moving and Knowing in Sport, Dance, Physical Education: A Collection of Speeches*. Mountain View, CA: Peek Publications.

Mori, Masahiro. 1970. "The Uncanny Valley." Trans. Karl F. MacDorman and Takashi Minato. *Energy* 7 (2): 33–35.

Nauman, Bruce. 2005. *Please Pay Attention Please: Bruce Nauman's Words, Writings, and Interviews*. Ed. Janet Kraynak. Cambridge, MA: MIT Press.

Newton, Isaac. 2003. *Sir Isaac Newton's Mathematical Principles of Natural Philosophy and His System of the World*. Trans. Andrew Motte. Whitefish, MT: Kessinger Publishing.

Noland, Carrie. 2009. *Agency and Embodiment: Performing Gestures / Producing Culture*. Cambridge, MA: Harvard University Press.

Noll, Michael A. 1965. "Computer-Generated Three-Dimensional Movies." *Computers and Automation* 14 (11): 20–23.

Noll, Michael A. 1967. "Choreography and Computers." *Dance Magazine* 41 (1): 43–45.

O'Rourke, Joseph, Norman Badler, and Hasida Toltzis. 1979. "A Spherical Representation of a Human Body for Visualizing Movement." *IEEE Proceedings* 67 (10): 1397–1403.

O'Rourke, Karen. 2013. *Walking and Mapping: Artists as Cartographers*. Cambridge, MA: MIT Press.

Palazzi, Maria, N. Z. Shaw, W. Forsythe, M. Lewis, B. Albright, M. Andereck, et al. 2009. "Synchronous Objects for One Flat Thing, Reproduced." Paper presented at the ACM SIGGRAPH 2009 Art Gallery, New Orleans, Louisiana.

Parks, Lisa. 2004. "Kinetic Screens: Epistemologies of Movement at the Interface." In Nick Couldry and Anna McCarthy, eds., *Media/Space: Place, Scale and Culture in a Media Age*, 37–57. London: Routledge.

Pchelkina, Liubov. 2013. "The Biomechanics of Voice and Movement in Solomon Nikritin's Projection Theatre (1920s)." In *Electrified Voices: Medial, Socio-Historical and Cultural Aspects of Voice Transfer*, 149–163. Göttingen: V&R unipress.

Plato. 2012. *Gorgias and Timaeus*. New York: Dover.

Portanova, Stamatia. 2013. *Moving without a Body: Digital Philosophy and Choreographic Thoughts*. Cambridge, MA: MIT Press.

Portnow, James. 2012. *Kinect Disconnect*. Ed. Daniel Floyd, art Allison Theus. Extra Credits, Season 4, Episode 9. Aired date: April 11, 2012. https://www.youtube.com/watch?v=ijcezUy3ZzY.

Rotman, Brian. 1993. *Ad Infinitum—The Ghost in Turing's Machine: Taking God out of Mathematics and Putting the Body Back In: An Essay in Corporeal Semiotics*. Stanford: Stanford University Press.

Rotman, Brian. 2000. *Mathematics as Sign: Writing, Imagining, Counting*. Stanford: Stanford University Press.

Rotman, Brian. 2008. *Becoming Beside Ourselves: The Alphabet, Ghosts, and Distributed Human Being*. Durham: Duke University Press.

Rotman, Brian. 2011. "Embodied Performance and Mathematics." Plenary paper presented at Performance Studies International 17, "Camillo 2.0: Technology, Memory, Experience," May 16, 2011.

Salazar Sutil, Nicolás. 2010. "Theatres of the Surd: A Study of Mathematical Influences in European Avant-garde Theatre." Doctoral thesis, Goldsmiths, University of London.

Sutil, Salazar. Nicolás. 2011a. "Binary Coded Performance." *Body, Space and Technology* 10 (2) (June). Available at http://people.brunel.ac.uk/bst/vol1002/nicolassalazarsutil/home.html.

Salazar Sutil, Nicolás. 2011b. "Paradox and Paradance: A Study of Configur8's *I Am Not I*." In Johannes Birringer and Josephine Fenger, eds., *Tanz und WahnSinn / Dance and ChoreoMania*, Yearbook of the German Dance Association, 223–236. Leipzig: Henschel.

Salazar Sutil, Nicolás. 2012. "Laban's Choreosophical Model: Movement Visualisation Analysis and the Use of Graphic Media in Dance Studies." *Dance Research* 30 (November): 147–168.

Salazar Sutil, Nicolás. 2013. "Rudolf Laban and Topology: A Videographic Analysis." *Space and Culture* 16 (2): 173–193.

Salazar Sutil, Nicolás. 2014. "Mathematics in Motion: A Comparative Analysis of the Stage Works of Schlemmer and Kandinsky at the Bauhaus." *Dance Research* 32 (1): 23–42.

Salazar Sutil, Nicolás. Forthcoming. "Intelligence behind Movement: Laboratories of Biomechanical Movement and the Engineering of a Kinetic Utopia." In Nicolás Salazar Sutil and Sita Popat, eds., *Digital Movement: Essays in Motion Technology and Performance*. London: Palgrave.

Salazar Sutil, Nicolás, and Sebastián Melo. 2013. "Digital Dance Theatre as a Multidimensional Romance: Notes on the Production of C8's *Flatland*." *Performance Research* 18 (5): 38–47.

Salazar Sutil, Nicolás, and Sebastián Melo. 2014. "Exposed to Time: Cross-Histories of Human Motion Visualisation from Chrono- to Dynamophotography." In Douglas Rosenberg, ed., *Oxford Handbook of Screendance Studies*, 23–42. Oxford: Oxford University Press.

Schlemmer, Oskar. 1961. "Man and Art Figure." In Walter Gropius and Arthur S. Wensinger, eds., *The Theater of the Bauhaus*. Middletown, CT: Wesleyan University Press.

Schlemmer, Oskar. 1971. *Man: Teaching Notes from the Bauhaus*. Ed. H. Kuchling, trans. J. Seligman. London: Lund Humphries.

Schlemmer, Oskar. 1990. *The Letters and Diaries of Oskar Schlemmer*. Ed. Tut Schlemmer, trans. Krishna Winston. Evanston: Northwestern University Press.

Shanken, E. A. 2009. *Art and Electronic Media*. London: Phaidon Press.

Simanowski, Roberto. 2011. *Digital Art and Meaning Reading Kinetic Poetry, Text Machines, Mapping Art, and Interactive Installations*. Minneapolis: University of Minnesota Press.

Sloterdijk, Peter. 1998–2004. *Sphären*. 3 vols. Frankfurt: Suhrkamp. Vol. 1 has been translated into English as *Bubbles: Microspherology* (Cambridge, MA: Semiotext(e), 2011).

Sloterdijk, Peter. 2005. "Foreword to the Theory of Spheres." In Melik Ohanian and Jean-Cristoph Royoux, eds., *Cosmograms*. Berlin: Lukas and Sternberg.

Smirnov, Andrey. 2013. *Sound in Z: Experiments in Sound and Electronic Music in Early 20th Century Russia*. London: Koenig Books.

Stepanov, Vladimir Ivanovich. 1892. *Alphabet des mouvements du corps humain: essai d'enregistrement des mouvements du corps humain au moyen des signes musicaux*. Paris: Imprimerie M Zouckermann.

Theusinger, Christiane, and Klaus-Peter Huber. 2000. "Analysing the Footsteps of Your Customers: A Case Study by ASK|net and SAS Institute GmbH." Available at http://robotics.stanford.edu/people/ronnyk/WEBKDD2000/WEBKDD2000_ARCHIVE/ii_2.pdf.

Turner, Henry S. 2006. *The English Renaissance Stage: Geometry, Poetics, and the Practical Spatial Arts 1580–1630*. Oxford: Oxford University Press.

Virilio, Paul. 1997. *Open Sky*. Trans. Julie Rose. London: Verso.

Vitruvius. 2005. *The Ten Books of Architecture*. Trans. Morris Hicky Morgan. Whitefish, MT: Kessinger Publishing.

Von Neumann, John. 1958. *The Computer and the Brain*. New Haven: Yale University Press.

Weibel, Peter. 1996. "The World as Interface." In Timothy Druckrey, ed., *Electronic Culture*, 343–351. New York: Aperture.

Wilke, Lars, Tom Calvert, Rhonda Ryman, and Irene Fox. 2005. "From Dance Notation to Human Animation: The LabanDancer Project: Motion Capture and Retrieval." *Computer Animation and Virtual Worlds* 16 (3–4): 201–211.

Wilson, Catherine. 1989. *Leibniz's Metaphysics: A Historical and Comparative Study*. Manchester: Manchester University Press.

Zalamea, Fernando. 2012. *Synthetic Philosophy of Contemporary Mathematics*. Trans. Zachary Luke Fraser. New York: Sequence Press.

Zorn, Friedrich Albert. 1905 [1887]. *Grammar of the Art of Dancing, Theoretical and Practical; Lessons in the Arts of Dancing and Dance Writing (Choreography) with Drawings, Musical Examples, Choreographic Symbols, and Special Music Scores*. Trans. Alfonso Josephs Sheafe. Boston: Heintzmann Press.

Zukav, Gary. 1979. *The Dancing Wu Li Masters: An Overview of the New Physics*. New York: Bantam Books.

Zuniga Shaw, Nora. 2009. "Introduction: The Dance." *Synchronous Objects for One Flat Thing, reproduced*, March 2009, http://synchronousobjects.osu.edu/blog/introductory-essays-for-synchronous-objects (accessed March 19, 2014).

265

269

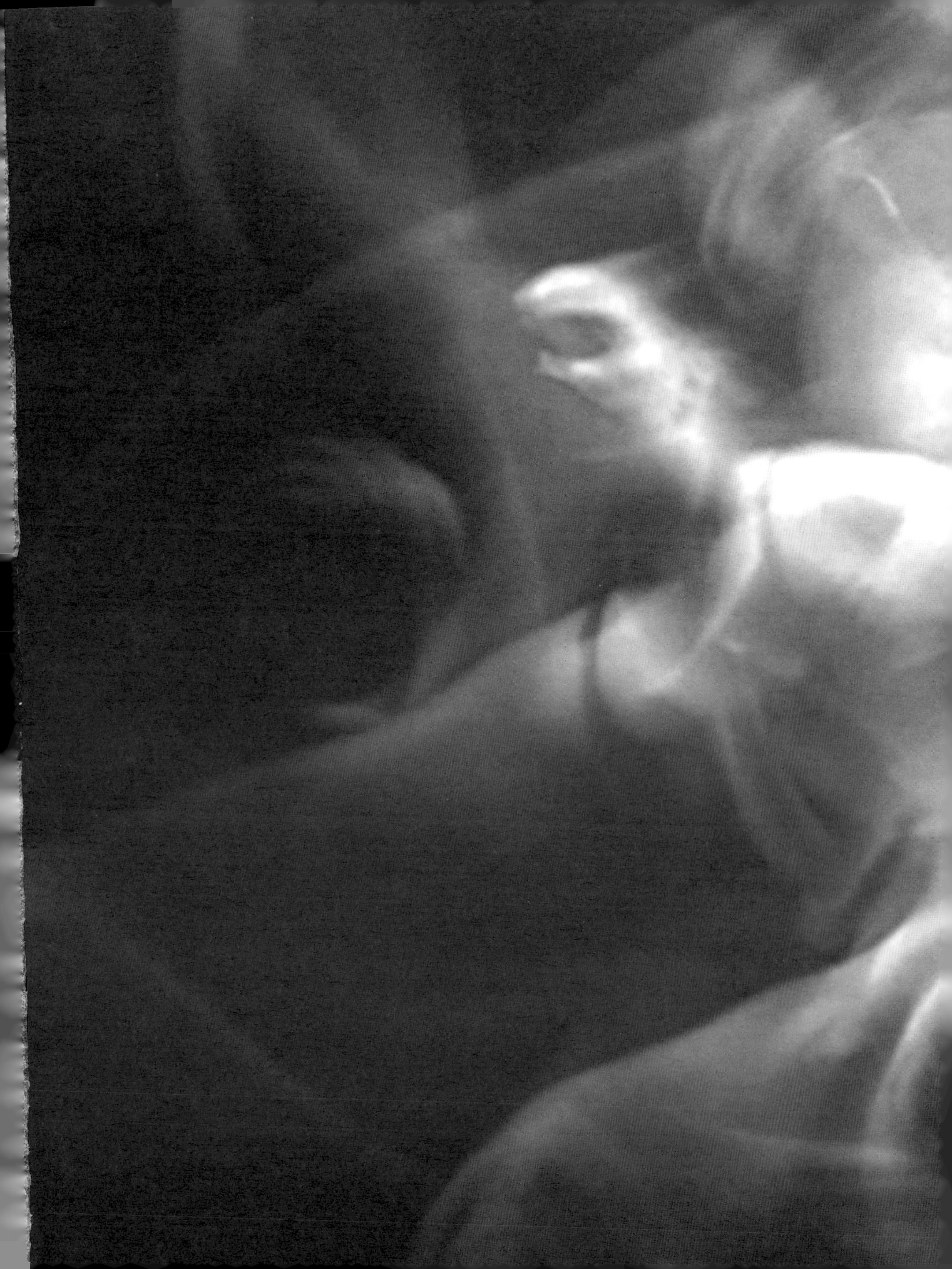

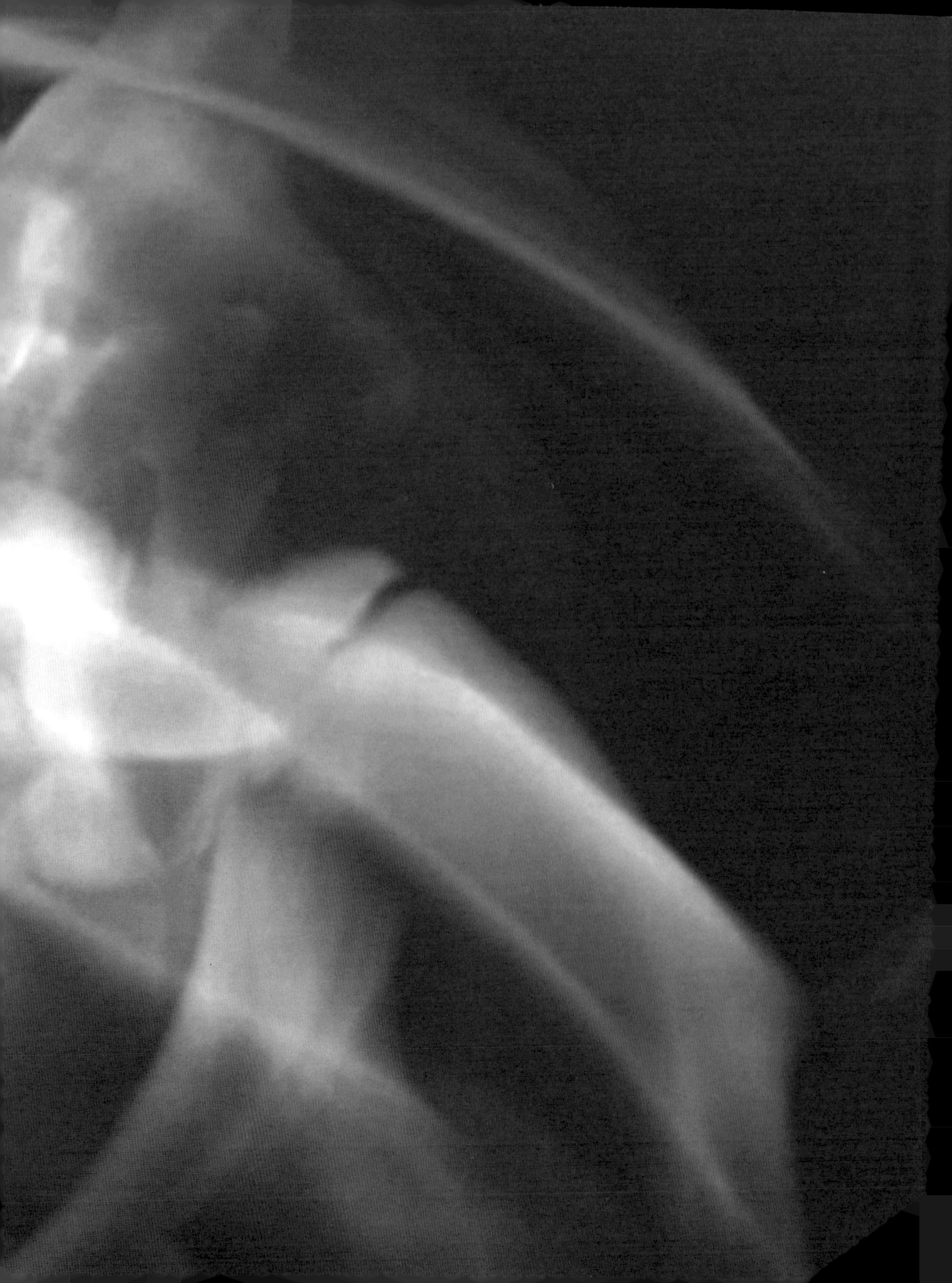